By Receiving This Ticket You Have Just Been Given The Opportunity Of A Lifetime... This ticket entitles you to join us for FREE at...

Property Entrepreneurs Conference

Promo Code:
116298

Make sure you activate this ticket today at:
www.TGRProperty.com.au or Free Call **1800 899 058**

By Receiving This Ticket You Have Just Been Given The Opportunity Of A Lifetime... This ticket entitles you to join us for FREE at...

The Ultimate

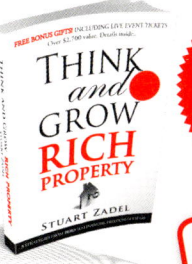

PAID

Property Entrepreneurs Conference

Promo Code:
116298

Make sure you activate this ticket today at:
www.TGRProperty.com.au or Free Call **1800 899 058**

By Receiving This Ticket You Have Just Been Given The Opportunity Of A Lifetime... This ticket entitles you to join us for FREE at...

The Ultimate

think & Grow Rich®

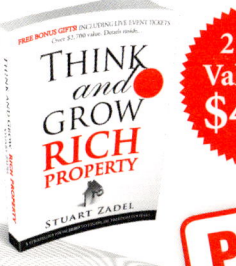

Property Entrepreneurs Conference

Promo Code:
116298

Make sure you activate this ticket today at:
www.TGRProperty.com.au or Free Call **1800 899 058**

HIGH PRAISE FOR
THINK AND GROW RICH® LIVE EVENTS

"I'm seeing life for the first time"
"You beautiful people are massive! Words do not express the life-changing thinking this weekend has made to my wife-to-be and myself. Unbelievable! You have really woken me up, to my life importance. It's like I'm seeing life for the first time. Thank you, Thank you, Thank you! Or as we say in Maori - Kia Ora, Kia Ora, Kia Ora."

David, South Australia

"Now I've seen it in action!"
"Thank you for a stunning FREE weekend program in Adelaide, so crammed with information, opportunities, even gifts! I learned a lot and I now have a lot of clues as to how I can learn more. You (and those of your Mastermind group who were there too) are truly proving that the THINK AND GROW RICH principles really work. I've never doubted it, but now I've seen it in action. With gratitude..."

Annie, Adelaide

"The best book"
Hi Stuart, loved your real estate book. Probably the best I have read from a list of about fifty."

Lindsay Meares, Melbourne

"My eyes are now open"
"I love your work mate. I had a ball. My eyes are now open to the abundance and unlimited possibilities out there. Thank you for the roller coaster ride. Now I am going to release my inner millionaire so as to help my family, friends and whoever I want. Trust me when I say this...I will be sending you an email of thanks when I am a millionaire and helping people. Your friend for life!"

LC, South Australia

"Words cannot express my gratitude"
"Words cannot express my gratitude towards your enormous effort in bringing the most life changing event I have ever attended. It's only two days after the conference and I'm already well on my way to "Think and Grow RICH". Your friendly "kick up the butt" was something that I desperately needed, and I will never be able to thank you enough for it!

Kaden, Adelaide

HOW TO CLAIM YOUR FREE BONUS GIFTS*

As a "thank you" for purchasing this book, Stuart and the members of his Rich Property Entrepreneurs Mastermind Group would like to give you some valuable **free gifts...**

FREE GIFT # 1 ($1,491 value): **Stuart Zadel** offers you three (3) FREE tickets (worth $497 each) to **The Ultimate Think and Grow Rich® Property Entrepreneurs Conference.**

FREE GIFT # 2 ($59.90 value): **Stephen Tolle and Cherie Barber** offer you a FREE **How to do a Renovation Financial Feasibility Tips Sheet** plus a FREE **Trades Register Template** - Keep the contact details of all your tradies in one handy place for when you're in the thick of it on-site!

FREE GIFT # 3 ($495 value): **Sam Saggers** offers you a FREE **Property Analyser Report** - This valuable tool enables you to accurately analyse any property in relation to its income and expenses by producing a cashflow projection.

FREE GIFT # 4 ($147 value): **Carly Crutchfield** offers you a FREE Audio Download – **"Property Secrets of the Wealthy"**.

FREE GIFT # 5 ($147 value): **Rick Otton** offers you a FREE Audio Download - **"Why You Can't Use Old Systems to Solve New Problems!"** Listen as Rick and his mentoring students challenge conventional wisdom in this closed-door training.

FREE GIFT # 6 ($29 value): **Aussie Rob** offers you a FREE eBook – **"Death of the Managed Fund"** by Aussie Rob and Scott Goold. Learn why exchange traded funds are taking over from managed funds and how to profit from them.

FREE GIFT #7 ($354 value): **Adrian Hill** offers you a FREE **Yearly Budget Template** to facilitate a review of all personal income and expenses, plus a FREE Rental Property **Purchasing Checklist.**

TOTAL VALUE OF YOUR BONUS GIFTS: $2,722.90

Visit the website below to receive these free gifts
www.TGRProperty.com.au/Gifts

* The FREE bonus gifts offered are current at the time of printing. We reserve the right to change, substitute or remove these gifts without notice.

FREE BONUS GIFTS! INCLUDING LIVE EVENT TICKETS
Over $2,700 value. Details inside...

THINK *and* GROW RICH PROPERTY

SECOND EDITION

STUART ZADEL

5 STRATEGIES FROM **ZERO** TO FINANCIAL FREEDOM IN **5** YEARS

© Copyright 2010 TGR Seminars Pty Ltd
This work is copyright. All rights reserved by the publisher. Apart from any use as permitted under the *Copyright Act 1968*, no part of this publication may be reproduced, stored in a retrieval system, or transmitted in any form or by any means, electronic, digital, mechanical, photocopying, recorded or otherwise, without the prior written permission of the copyright owner. Requests and inquiries concerning reproduction and rights should be addressed to: The Publisher, Think and Grow Rich® Pty Ltd, *Think and Grow Rich® Property*, P.O. Box 1232, Sutherland NSW 1499.

DISCLAIMER
The information, strategies, comments, concepts, techniques and suggestions within this book are of a general nature only and do not constitute professional or individual advice in any way. You must seek your own independent professional advice relating to your particular circumstances, goals and risk profile if you intend to take any action as a result of reading this publication. The publisher, authors and experts who participated in this project do not accept any responsibility for any action taken as a result of reading this publication. Every care has been taken to ensure the accuracy of the material contained in the book.

National Library of Australia Cataloguing-in-Publication entry:
Think and Grow Rich® Property / Stuart Zadel

First published 2009 (Reprinted with corrections 2009)
Second Edition 2010
ISBN: 9780975601471 (pbk)

1. Real estate investment.
2. Tax deductions.
3. Finance, Personal.

332.6324

Email: info@thinkandgrowrich.com.au
Website: www.TGRProperty.com.au
Website: www.ThinkAndGrowRich.com.au

THINK AND GROW RICH® is the registered trademark and property in Australia of Think and Grow Rich® Pty Ltd ATF TGR Holdings.

This book/websites/products etc. were not prepared, approved, licensed or endorsed by the Napoleon Hill Foundation, Napoleon Hill Associates or Napoleon Hill Australia or any associated entity. These materials make many references to the 1937 book *Think and Grow Rich* by Napoleon Hill. The references to the book title *Think and Grow Rich* are for illustrative purposes only and are not authorised by, associated with, endorsed by, or sponsored by the Napoleon Hill Foundation.

CONTENTS

Preface — 1

Introduction — 5

Chapter 1
Stuart Zadel
Mind-Money Connection — 9

Chapter 2
Stephen Tolle and Cherie Barber
Renovating For Profit — 29

Chapter 3
Sam Saggers
Positive Cashflow Property — 101

Chapter 4
Carly Crutchfield
Profitable Property Development — 161

Chapter 5
Rick Otton
Creative Cashflow — 207

Chapter 6
Aussie Rob Wilson
Renting Shares — 261

Chapter 7
Adrian Hill
Minimise Tax, Maximise Protection — 323

The Next Step… — 397

PREFACE

"Some books are to be tasted, others to be swallowed, and some few to be chewed and digested: that is, some books are to be read only in parts, others to be read, but not curiously, and some few to be read wholly, and with diligence and attention."

Sir Francis Bacon, 1561-1626

In my late teens, I discovered a book called *Think and Grow Rich* by Napoleon Hill. Since then, it's fair to say I've nibbled, gnawed, snacked on, picked at, tasted, chewed, munched, gorged and completely devoured what has now become the world's highest selling wealth creation and personal achievement text!

When I read this book at the age of 19, it was the very first of its kind I'd ever come across and it had a MASSIVE impact upon my life. I've personally used the principles in this book to build and run a successful health and fitness club for 11 years, to travel the world several times, to compete at elite level sports, to achieve a 2nd Dan black belt in martial arts, to win major speech competitions, to become a professional speaker and to reach many personal goals, including generating a massive passive cashflow. So I think I can confidently say they work.

So life-changing was *Think and Grow Rich*, so powerful its philosophy, that I embarked on an intense period studying the mind and its power, discovering even more advanced knowledge. I also established my own seminar company to teach others the mind-money connection and its role in financial freedom.

BONUS! FREE gifts at www.TGRProperty.com.au/Gifts

PREFACE

Based on practical research into the secrets of the world's wealthiest people at the turn of the 20th century, this book has been responsible for creating more millionaires than any other. Now, we're about to create some more...

You see, one of the 13 key principles of the original book is that of acquiring "Specialised Knowledge". Although this chapter gave specific instructions on where and how to acquire such knowledge, it didn't provide the exact specialised knowledge one needed, and quite frankly, most people are simply too busy to dedicate the time necessary to gather this information... until now.

Enter *Think and Grow Rich® Property* – the most significant development since *Think and Grow Rich*. *Think and Grow Rich® Property* brings together seven property millionaires and five unique strategies to show anyone how to generate massive profits and passive cashflows, often with very little exposure or risk.

These proven, step-by-step strategies will work for anyone, anywhere, in most countries where people are allowed to own and trade property. My hand-picked **mastermind** group of rich property entrepreneurs has made sure of it.

That's because they're all what I call prosperity millionaires. That means, they each have a prosperity mindset that has not only created enough wealth for themselves and their families, they now want to give something back by helping others achieve financial freedom. Good news for you right?

BONUS! FREE gifts at www.TGRProperty.com.au/Gifts

One of our goals at Think and Grow Rich® Seminars is to **inspire 1,000 new prosperity millionaires in the next 10 years** that do good with their new-found wealth. We've already helped create several prosperity millionaires and to create even more, we need the biggest opportunities and the absolute best strategies we can find to make it a reality... and I'm certain we've found them in this latest project.

I encourage you to read this book from cover to cover. In fact, taste it, chew it, completely devour it! Now, before you even turn the page to get started, I welcome you to register for your FREE bonuses which you'll find at www.TGRProperty.com.au/Gifts. Each member of my mastermind team of rich property entrepreneurs has offered you a unique special bonus to accelerate your journey.

My personal gift to you is to warmly invite you to attend a Think and Grow Rich® event, to see me live and learn even more from my mastermind group of experts. Recently, at an event in Brisbane, Queensland, I met a middle-aged gentleman who'd bought and read the original *Think and Grow Rich* in the 1970s. Ever since, he'd wondered about the real meaning of a particular line; in less than 30 seconds I was able to explain what had puzzled him for more than 30 years! The moral to this story is don't leave it another three decades before you get the full potential from *Think and Grow Rich* or *Think and Grow Rich® Property!*

Finally, in order to transform your intention to create wealth and develop a prosperity mindset into something tangible, download our "Prosperity Millionaire Commitment" from www.TGRProperty.com.au/Gifts. Print it out, sign it and place it wherever you'll see it regularly; beside your bed, on the bathroom mirror or on the fridge door – anywhere that will remind you that you really can think and grow rich!

In the meantime, I trust you will enjoy *Think and Grow Rich® Property*.

Bon appetit!

Stuart Zadel

Stuart Zadel

INTRODUCTION

Did you know that more millionaires make their fortunes through property than by any other means?

Would you believe me if I told you there were people making six-figure profits in months, weeks and even days, by simply spotting opportunities for others?

What about making enough money from just one renovation project to fund the purchase of an entire new home? Or how about buying a house for only $1?

You know you can rent out a house for three to five per cent return but did you know you can rent out shares for 10 times that?

Does it surprise you to know that the Tax Office can give *you* a refund for creating wealth through property? Or that less than one per cent of accountants are even aware of how to maximise the laws?

Most importantly, did you know that there is a mind-money connection that is so powerful that once you discover it, you'll agree with Napoleon Hill's suggestion in the original *Think and Grow Rich*: "When riches begin to come, they come so quickly, in such great abundance, that one wonders where they have been hiding all those lean years"?

If any of the above sounds too good to be true, the stuff of fantasy, reserved for only the rich and the privileged, then you must read on.

BONUS! FREE gifts at www.TGRProperty.com.au/Gifts

INTRODUCTION

In *Think and Grow Rich® Property*, you'll meet seven property entrepreneurs who make massive profits in their chosen niche. What's more, we'll reveal to you five unique property strategies to go from zero to financial freedom in five years or less.

You, too, can become a millionaire through property if you simply learn the closely guarded secrets of these masters! It's easier than you think once you "crack-the-code" of their strategies. This is what you have been waiting for...

In the first chapter, I'll reveal to you, possibly for the first time ever, your mind-money connection, the critical role it plays in manifesting your results as well as why you're not already where you want to be financially. I'll also share with you what to do about it plus a couple of extremely powerful processes proven by millions to create precisely the experiences in life you wish to live out.

Next, Australia's "Renovation King and Queen", Cherie Barber and Stephen Tolle, will let you in on how they regularly make more than $400,000 *per* renovation. They'll show you how to add value in either a rising or falling market – all without throwing a tool at a wall in frustration! Turn to chapter two for their eight-step, high-value, low-risk strategy.

It's so simple yet so profound that you'll wonder why you never thought up Sam Sagger's philosophy: "Profits are better than wages." In chapter three, Sam shares his fundamentals checklist including where and when to invest to buy and trade real estate for massive positive cashflow.

Then, you'll be amazed by Carly Crutchfield's journey from 12-year-old school drop-out to self-made millionaire, philanthropist, author, property developer and business owner.

BONUS! FREE gifts at www.TGRProperty.com.au/Gifts

Chapter four reveals her seven-step property development strategy, already used to generate more than $200 million worth of development projects.

Rick Otton is famous for buying houses for just $1! He introduced creative financing techniques and super cashflow concepts to the Australian market in 1990. If you don't believe this is possible, just wait until you get to chapter five.

Trading expert and educator, Aussie Rob Wilson, shares a little known strategy in chapter six. You know you can rent out a house, but what about renting out another form of property - shares - for 10 times the financial return? As Aussie Rob says, everything's easy when you know how!

Finally, what's the point of creating wealth if you can't keep and use most of it? Adrian Hill will uncover what more than 99 per cent of accountants don't know – how you can minimise tax, maximise asset protection and make the taxman work up a sweat! Chapter seven is not to be missed - it'll make and save you thousands.

So, there you have it. An introduction to my hand-picked mastermind group of rich property entrepreneurs. Learn from these masters and become one of our **1,000 new Prosperity Millionaires.**

To your success!

Stuart Zadel

Stuart Zadel

BONUS! FREE gifts at www.TGRProperty.com.au/Gifts

Chapter 1
MIND-MONEY CONNECTION

"Decide...believe...begin."

STUART ZADEL

STUART ZADEL

Stuart Zadel is the Director of Think and Grow Rich® Seminars.

His purpose is to inspire Australians to raise their awareness, find their purpose, and achieve financial freedom.

He's on a mission to inspire 1,000 new Prosperity Millionaires in 10 years who are dedicated to giving back and doing good.

After finishing high school, Stuart entered a physiotherapy degree while simultaneously working towards a professional soccer career. Unlike a good fairytale, Stuart failed in his sports dream but gained something far more powerful – an insight into the all-powerful subconscious mind.

At 19, Stuart travelled to the United States to study leading edge fitness training techniques, returning to revolutionise the personal training industry in Australia. At 21, he opened and ran his own fitness club for 11 years, training more than 10,000 people. Here he observed first-hand the only game in town – the mind-body connection.

Combining entrepreneurship, skill, drive and his specialised knowledge in the subconscious mind, Stuart now teaches more than 10,000 people each year about the mind-money connection and financial prosperity, personal leadership, sales success and peak performance.

He is the co-author of three best-selling books on leadership, sales and public speaking. In addition to *Think and Grow Rich® Property*, he has released *Think and Grow Rich® Cashflow* and *Think and Grow Rich® Internet*.

His company also publishes the highest selling wealth-creation book of all time, *Think and Grow Rich* by Napoleon Hill, as well as other classics including *As a Man Thinketh*, *Acres of Diamonds* and *The Common Denominator of Success*.

MIND-MONEY CONNECTION

DISCOVER THE TWO KEY CONCEPTS THAT WILL PROPEL YOU TOWARDS FINANCIAL PROSPERITY FASTER THAN ANY OTHER

> *"Whatever the mind can conceive and believe, the mind can achieve."*
> **Napoleon Hill**

The personal story of *Think and Grow Rich* author Napoleon Hill is a fascinating one.

Born into poverty in 1883, in a one-room log cabin in Virginia's Blue Ridge Mountains, Hill became a newspaper reporter while still in his teens and began writing stories for more than a dozen publications throughout the U.S. state. His original style soon caught the attention of former Tennessee governor Robert Taylor – owner of *Bob Taylor's Magazine* – who hired Hill to write success stories about famous men.

Hill's plan was to use the magazine money to pay his way through Georgetown University Law School. However, he was sent to interview billionaire industrialist Andrew Carnegie – then the world's richest man – and his whole life changed. At the end of their three-day interview, Carnegie had convinced Hill to create the world's first philosophy of individual achievement, based on the principles of success he had used to accumulate his vast fortune.

BONUS! FREE gifts at www.TGRProperty.com.au/Gifts

As a final test, Carnegie put a question to Hill and insisted he answer it immediately. He said, "If I commission you to become the author of this philosophy, and give you letters of introduction to people whose help you will need, are you willing to devote 20 years to research - because that's about how long it will take - earning your own way as you go along, without any subsidy from me? Yes or no?" Hill could think of many reasons why he couldn't do it: he didn't have the education, the time, the money or the influence – not to mention that he didn't even know what the word "philosophy" meant! There was something inside of him, though, that just wanted to go for it so he answered, "Yes, Mr Carnegie. I'll accept the commission and you can depend upon it, sir, that I will complete it".

And he did. The subsequent and ongoing success of *Think and Grow Rich*, the outcome of that irrevocable decision, demonstrates just how one's life can be created with new thinking. Carnegie may have produced as many as two dozen millionaires but the number of people Napoleon Hill continues to help become wealthy is too many to be counted. "Truly, 'thoughts are things'," was how Hill started *Think and Grow Rich*. He should have told us "thoughts are **everything**!" because that's where it all starts.

In this chapter, I'll reveal to you the mind-money connection, the critical role it plays in manifesting your results as well as why you're not already where you want to be financially. I'll show you two powerful and proven processes to create precisely the experiences in life you wish to live out. And I'll introduce you to the second key principle of success: that of the mastermind team.

But first, we need to understand that just about everything we were taught to think about money was wrong…

MIND-MONEY CONNECTION

MONEY

"Money is a good servant but a poor master."
Dominique Bouhours

Money is an idea. Understand it's not the paper or plastic in your wallet, the coins in your pocket or the numbers in your bank account. These are all just representations of money, not money itself. Why? Because money is an idea!

Money is neutral, neither good nor bad, just neutral. It has no characteristics except those we project onto it. It has no life, no language…it's neither dirty, evil, nor good nor… ?

Money is a tool. As such, like a hammer, it can be used to build or destroy based on the intent of the user. The effectiveness of its expression is totally dependent on the skill and belief of the person using it.

MORE MONEY

"There is no such thing as something for nothing."
Napoleon Hill

Always remember, money is a reward received for service rendered. If you want more money you are going to have to render more and better service. Presumably your purpose in reading this book is to create a financial surplus for yourself and your family, and the fact that we are using property to do this, is incidental. If you want a million dollars, you need to render a million dollars worth of service. That could mean one deal for a one million dollar profit, or 100 deals at ten thousand dollars profit. Your income and reward will be in direct proportion to the quality, quantity and spirit in which you render service to the market. An entrepreneur understands this. They simply take something of a lower value and turn it into something of a higher value according to the needs of the marketplace.

BONUS! FREE gifts at www.TGRProperty.com.au/Gifts

MORE PROSPERITY MILLIONAIRES

"I've been rich and I've been poor, rich is better."
Sophie Tucker

Prosperity Millionaires have a prosperous mindset and so attract wealth and opportunity. They are entrepreneurial and come from a space of abundance, good stewardship and common sense. They are good money managers as they value, protect, multiply and share a portion of every dollar that passes through their hands. They always seek to add massive value and engage only in transactions that benefit all (win/win). They continually grow, learn and seek out specialised knowledge of how to make more surplus to leave a legacy and increase the pie for all.

In contrast, Poverty Millionaires have a poverty mindset and they come from a space of lack and limitation, believing the supply of money to be restricted. This scarcity mentality causes them to hold on tightly to every dollar they have for fear of loss and lack of confidence in replacing it. Poverty millionaires always seek to drive hard bargains, while advancing only their own interests at the expense of others (win/lose).

So now that you can see that not all millionaires are created equal, you will understand why the world is better off for the presence of more Prosperity Millionaires. For me, inspiring 1,000 new Prosperity Millionaires in 10 years who are dedicated to contributing their wealth and energies to worthwhile projects is a goal worth striving for. By doing so, we will achieve our vision of raising the conscious and financial awareness of Australians.

MIND-MONEY CONNECTION

DECIDE... BELIEVE... BEGIN...

"Tell the world what you intend to do, but first show it."
Napoleon Hill

Just about everything we were taught about money is wrong.

It doesn't take money to make money.
It doesn't take a university degree to make money.
It doesn't take high intelligence to make money.
It doesn't take good grades, good looks or even good ideas.
You don't need a good job. In fact, you don't need a job at all.
You don't need friends of influence and to be "connected".
You don't need to come from a wealthy family.

None of these things matter. But you know what does? A decision. Yes, that's right. The only thing that matters is that you make an irrevocable decision to commit and see it through, no matter what. That's it.

So right now, before we even start, just as Carnegie did with Hill, I'm asking you to commit. I'm asking you to become one of our 1,000 new Prosperity Millionaires. Yes or No? The moment you make your decision and commit it to writing you will have made it tangible. Now make that commitment by signing here:

Think and Grow Rich® Prosperity Millionaire Commitment

I _____ (name) hereby make

an irrevocable commitment to becoming a Think and Grow Rich® Prosperity Millionaire, so that I can attain total financial freedom, serve, inspire and share my success with others and live a full life.

_____
Signed:

_____/_____/ 20_____
Date:

BONUS! FREE gifts at www.TGRProperty.com.au/Gifts

Next I want you to go to www.TGRProperty.com.au/Gifts and download your free Think and Grow Rich® Prosperity Millionaire Certificate. Print out several copies, fill them in and place them where you'll see them around your home or workplace many times a day.

As Napoleon Hill wrote, "Somewhere in your make up (perhaps in the cells of your brain) there lies sleeping, the seed of achievement, which if aroused and put into action, would carry you to heights, such as you may never have hoped to attain".

That seed has now been planted. It has begun…

CLARITY IS POWER

"The highest reward for a person's toil is not what they get for it, but what they become by it."
John Ruskin

Congratulations! I'm so glad you've decided to join us. Let's get started…

For some inexplicable reason, I have always wanted to be a Prosperity Millionaire. Ever since I can remember, I wanted to have influence so that I could make a difference and inspire others. The ideal and only way I thought to achieve that when I was young was to become a professional soccer player. I figured the fame would give me influence so people would listen and the money would give me the means to do good. So I trained hard, played hard and showed enormous potential in my early teens. I even earned the nickname there for a while of "Franz", after the legendary German soccer player, Franz Beckenbauer.

As the years went by, I trained harder and harder yet didn't seem to progress; if anything, I may have gone backwards. So…I

MIND-MONEY CONNECTION

trained harder. I even went to the lengths of getting my own Olympic running coach, working in a gym part-time to get stronger, and dropping out of university to spend more time training and, so I thought, following my dream.

Against the odds and in record time, I overcame what surgeons thought was a career-ending knee injury. Again, I did it by working hard and letting my obsession push my body, all the while missing the messages life was sending me. Despite playing a few more seasons, my dream to be a professional soccer player never came true. What annoyed me most when it was all over was that I didn't know why I didn't make it, especially when I was prepared to give everything for the chance.

Years later, I finally discovered the answer to my question: willpower, no matter how strong, will never overcome conditioning.

Let's start to understand why.

There are only three things you need to be successful in any sport.

1. Skill
2. Fitness
3. The right mindset/psychology.

As a soccer player, my skill level was average; I was neither the best, nor the worst. My fitness, however, was definitely superior. I was one of the fittest athletes in the league, if not the country at the time. The third and final element came down to my personal mindset and psychology. And that's where I let myself down. Outwardly you couldn't pick it, but inside something wasn't right. Later I would learn that in any field of achievement, experts unanimously agree that 80 per cent or more of a person's success comes down to their mental attitude, mindset and thoughts. This became evident to me when I opened my first business…

OBSERVATION IS POWER

> *"No problem can stand the assault of sustained thinking."*
> **Voltaire**

Shortly after my departure from the soccer field, I redirected that drive, energy and my desire to help people into establishing my own fitness club. Through my part time-work as a fitness instructor, I found I really enjoyed helping people improve their lives. I noticed when they started to get their act together physically, many other areas of their lives improved as well.

But the results were inconsistent. Why was it that some excelled while others were mediocre at best? How is it that two people start out with the same information, the same equipment, the same experience level, similar circumstances and environment, yet one achieves and the other doesn't? What makes the difference between success and failure?

Again, I found that success in the gym came down to just three things.

1. Exercise
2. Nutrition
3. The right mindset/psychology.

Are you starting to see a pattern here? I did. At best, most people only focus on the physical components of any success equation, such as skill plus fitness or exercise plus nutrition

MIND-MONEY CONNECTION

or intelligence plus application. What they lack is the most important component of all – the understanding that success and achievement in any field of endeavour starts and ends with the mind.

BE CONGRUENT

> *"There's a big difference between wishing for a thing and being ready to receive it. No one is ready for something until they believe they can acquire it. The state of mind must be belief and not mere hope or wish."*
>
> **Napoleon Hill**

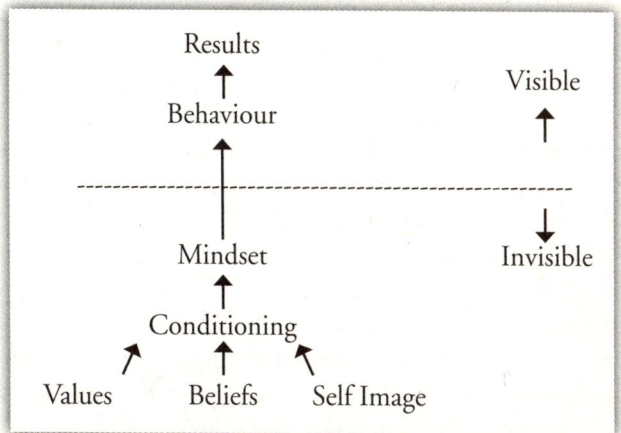

Take a look at the diagram above. You'll notice the word **results** is at the top of the hierarchy. Results are the name of the game and this applies to any area of your life, be that wealth, health, relationships or happiness. It's both normal and natural for every human being to seek more in life and to grow.

Now notice that results are created by **behaviour.** For example, Arnold Schwarzenegger pushes weights. Clearly that behaviour produces a certain result.

BONUS! FREE gifts at www.TGRProperty.com.au/Gifts

Beyond your behaviour however is where all the magic happens. Here is where we now cross over from the visible world into the invisible world, from the tangible world into the intangible world, from the physical world into the metaphysical world. You see, it's your underlying and prevailing **mindset** that motivates your behaviour on a moment by moment basis.

Your mindset is like the weather in that it can change at any moment and frequently does. For example, how often have you told yourself you should go for a run in the morning, but when morning comes your mindset has changed? Hmmm…Isn't that interesting?

Now for the really tricky part. What creates your mindset? Refer to the previous diagram once more and you'll discover it. The ultimate influence on your mindset, and therefore your behaviour and results, is your **conditioning**. Conditioning refers broadly to what you have been brought up to think and believe about the world you live in and yourself. It consists of three key elements: **values, beliefs** and **self image**.

According to psychologists, an estimated 90 per cent of your conditioning and indeed, your personality, is formed by the age of seven. This could be good or bad depending on your experiences in those first seven years. Secondly, most of this conditioning is below your level of awareness, or what we call subconscious, much like the majority of an iceberg is hidden below the surface of the water. It is invisible and intangible.

So if this was all formed so long ago, and it's invisible, and you're not aware of it - yet it controls **all** your behaviour and is responsible for **all** your results - the million dollar questions have got to be: How do you know what you have been conditioned with and how do you change it?

MIND-MONEY CONNECTION

"By their fruits ye shall know them."
Matthew 7:15

The answer to the first question is simple – just look at your results. Your results broadcast loud and clear to the world your conditioning. It can be no other way. Just like a river that has been dammed momentarily can, and will, find a way around it to the sea, so too your values, beliefs, and self image will always find their natural expression.

So if you want to see what you have been conditioned to believe about money, just check your bank statement. The amount of money you earn each year is, in fact, what you feel you are worth, and not a cent more or a cent less. Take a look at your health and your relationships while you're at it. The state of each will tell you exactly what you have been conditioned to believe.

Since you're presumably reading this book to make financial improvements, let's drill down to see how values, beliefs and self image relate to money.

Values - Everyone has a hierarchy of values. When it comes to finances, you will recognise your values by how you earn your money, how much of it you have and what you do with it. Make sense?

Beliefs - Recognise that your beliefs are not necessarily fact or even true. They are simply what they are, and can broadly be split into two categories: limiting beliefs and empowering beliefs.

Some limiting beliefs might be:

- the money supply is limited. For me to get more, others have to go without;

BONUS! FREE gifts at www.TGRProperty.com.au/Gifts

- money is the root of all evil;
- if this really worked, somebody would have already done it.

Some empowering beliefs might be:

- money is abundant. The more I create the more there is to share;
- the *lack* of money is the root of all evil;
- if it's working for them, it'll work for me.

Self Image - Scientists have determined the overriding cause of success or failure in life to be our invisible self image. This invisible force works much the same as a thermostat on a heater. Let's say the thermostat is set at 20 degrees. When the temperature of the surrounding air drops below this set point, the thermostat reacts to the drop and sends a message to the heater to heat the room; if the temperature of the surrounding air rises above the set point, the thermostat reacts to the increase and sends a message to the heater to switch off. Your self image works in the same way.

Anyone who has ever struggled with a weight problem will be familiar with this process. Dieting may shed pounds for a while but eventually the set point mechanism reacts to the dropping weight, causing the dieter to change the way they feel, change the way they behave and, ultimately, return to their pre-diet weight, or more.

How about financially? Do you think you have a set point there as well? You'd better believe it! The amount of money you earn is a direct reflection of what you feel you are worth. This is why somewhere between 70 and 95 per cent of major lottery winners squander their sudden fortunes in two years or less. The unexpected windfall is far in excess of their conditioned financial set point, causing them to subconsciously repel it.

MIND-MONEY CONNECTION

To raise your financial and other set points you not only have to take the right actions in the physical world, but you also need to adjust your in-built thermostat. Both need to be congruent: the visible and the invisible, the tangible and the intangible. You must repeatedly now see yourself as a highly prosperous person. You must create a new set point. Here's a powerful process and exercise that will help you…

THE MIND MOVIE PROCESS

"Any idea that is held in mind, that is emphasized, that is Feared of Revered will begin at once to clothe itself in the most convenient and appropriate form that is available."
Andrew Carnegie

First, put yourself in a completely relaxed state. Next, choose a goal that you would like to achieve, such as becoming a property entrepreneur. Then, create a short mental movie of yourself enjoying your goal NOW. Be sure you are fully in the picture, the star of the show! Allow yourself to feel the feelings you would expect if you were living out this goal for real. Imagine what this would be like in exact detail. Repeat this mind movie several times a day.

THE GOAL CARD EXERCISE

On a 3cm x 5cm card write an abbreviated version of your mental movie, commencing with the words: "I am so happy and grateful now that…" An example might be: "I am so happy and grateful now that I earn a passive income of $10,000 per month as a property entrepreneur." This is your Think and Grow Rich® Goal Card. Carry your goal card in your pocket or purse so that whenever you touch it from now on, the image of your mental movie will flash onto the screen of your mind.

BONUS! FREE gifts at www.TGRProperty.com.au/Gifts

Think and Grow Rich® Goal Card

I am so happy and grateful now that….
_____
_____
_____
_____
_____
_____

The Mind Movie process and the Goal Card exercise really work. Just as a seed is planted into the soil and begins to attract all things necessary for the fulfillment of its growth and potential, so too your goal has now been planted into the deep resources of your subconscious mind where it has begun to germinate and attract to you all that is required for the accomplishment of your goal.

THE MASTERMIND TEAM

The next big idea I'd like to share with you is that of the **mastermind team**. Although generous in content, *Think and Grow Rich* can actually be distilled to just three key principles:

1. A Dream
2. A Theme
3. A Team.

I'm going to assume that you have a **dream** in mind, perhaps to become one of our 1,000 new Prosperity Millionaires? And, given you are reading this book, your **theme** is likely to be that of property. So, the one thing we need to discuss now is your **team**.

MIND-MONEY CONNECTION

The business of property and wealth-creation are team sports. In the following chapters, you'll hear time and time again the experts talk about assembling a team. This has been the secret of my success and the key principle behind this very book. Carnegie himself put his entire success down to just two key principles in *Think and Grow Rich*, one being that of the mastermind team. He even wrote an epitaph for his grave that read, "Here lies one who knew how to get around him men cleverer than himself". Carnegie was renowned for working with the very best people. Here's how he picked them, as passed on to Napoleon Hill.

The six characteristics of top mastermind team members

1. **Honesty and loyalty**
   Hill placed both honesty and loyalty at the very top of his list for a good reason. Honesty and loyalty breed trust, and trust is the foundation upon which people do their best work. Specifically, Hill said, "If a person doesn't show loyalty to those that are entitled to it, I want no part of them". Of course, loyalty is not an automatic right and is not something you should ever take for granted. You have to earn the loyalty of your team members by proving to them that you're somebody who is worthy of it.

2. **Dependability**
   This comes in at number two, although dependability, honesty and loyalty are pretty much equal. After all, what good is a loyal person if you can't depend on them? The whole point of developing a team is so you can step back into more of a management role and allow those with the specialised skills you've chosen to do the hands-on work. It's a system that can only function correctly if you are able to assign a task and know that it's going to be done to a standard that will meet your requirements. If somebody comes back

to you with a half-finished job and a list of excuses, they're the wrong person for your team.

3. **Ability to do the job**
   This is probably the easiest one to detect but that doesn't make it any less important. It's absolutely essential that you surround yourself with people who actually know how to do what it is that you need them to do. It might seem reasonable to assume that a real estate agent would know everything necessary to successfully complete a property transaction or that a qualified tax accountant will be able to pick up all the deductions you're entitled to but experience has shown these things can't be taken for granted. Still, it's interesting that Hill placed this quality in third place behind honesty, loyalty and dependability.

4. **Positive mental attitude**
   Speaking very broadly, there are just two types of people in life: optimists and pessimists. It's been my experience that optimists have, by far, the better end of the deal. They are positive, encourage others and always look for the opportunity in adversity. Attempting anything in life above mediocrity is going to attract both adversity and criticism, often from those who are close to you. Therefore, it's important to surround yourself with positive people who will be able to encourage and support you. I find the "can do" attitude of optimistic people means they're far more motivated and are always keener to get going, which is good for business and excellent for customer service.

5. **Willingness to go the extra mile**
   You'll know you've got a truly excellent team member

MIND-MONEY CONNECTION

when you find somebody who not only does the job that is required of them but goes that extra distance to make sure it's done to the absolute highest standard possible. This type of person is incredibly hard to find and well worth holding onto once you have them. I'm talking about the kind of person who will do extra jobs for you, whether or not they are stipulated in their contract, and who will spend their weekend feverishly working on a project they've been given at short notice without any complaint. It's very hard to find such people but by no means impossible. I know this because I have a number of them in my own team.

6. Applied faith

Let me start by saying this has nothing at all to do with religion. It's about individual minds discovering themselves and establishing a working relationship with the lawful power of the universe, known in this case as infinite intelligence. There's a very important distinction that needs to be made here, between applied faith and mere belief. Simply believing in something is far too passive and no more potent than daydreaming when it comes to achieving your goals. Applied faith is all about action. The more action, the better, not only on your part but that of your mastermind allies as well.

When you've found someone with all six Carnegie characteristics, you're in the presence of royalty. And if they are lacking in just one, you'll need to be careful. Your job from here is to maintain perfect harmony between your team members and discover how to utilise them for maximum effect. Learn the strengths and weaknesses of each member in your team so you can help them reach their potential and, in doing so, achieve your own.

BONUS! FREE gifts at www.TGRProperty.com.au/Gifts

KEEP THEM IN MIND

"If a person advances confidently in the direction of their dream, and endeavours to live the life they have imagined, they will meet with success unexpected in common hours."

Thoreau

We've now covered two of the most important keys to financial prosperity: the mind-money connection and the mastermind team. This chapter has been deliberately placed at the beginning of the book because understanding both concepts will propel you towards your goals faster than any other.

So, with that firmly in mind, let's discover the five unique property strategies to go from zero to financial freedom in five years or less...

FREE BONUS GIFT

Stuart Zadel has generously offered a FREE BONUS GIFT valued at $1,491

Three (3) FREE tickets (worth $497 each) to **The Ultimate Think and Grow Rich® Property Entrepreneurs Conference.**

Visit the website below to receive these free gifts
www.TGRProperty.com.au/Gifts

BONUS! FREE gifts at www.TGRProperty.com.au/Gifts

Chapter 2
RENOVATING FOR PROFIT

"We can't afford to have a job."

STEPHEN TOLLE & CHERIE BARBER

STEPHEN TOLLE & CHERIE BARBER

Stephen Tolle and Cherie Barber are full-time professional renovators. Both threw in their full-time jobs when they realised they were making more money from their weekend renovation projects than they did during the week.

In the first 12 months of their renovating career, Cherie and Stephen bought, renovated and sold six houses with a combined value of $6.3 million – despite having no stable income and very little money behind them. In their first year, they made a net profit of $1.15 million, which well and truly launched their renovation and property investment career.

The couple attributes their success to very specific disciplines and strategies used for all renovation projects. Having developed their own unique due diligence system, they are masters at knowing property values and are willing to tackle those renovations that others put in the "too hard" basket. They're skilled at adding maximum value for the least possible cost.

Dubbed "Australia's Renovation King and Queen", Cherie and Stephen have been regularly featured in local and national media, including countless property investment and renovation magazines, numerous newspapers and web sites. They've made regular television appearances including Channel Seven's *Today Tonight*.

Unrivalled in what they do, Cherie and Stephen are Australia's top renovators, continuously averaging a staggering $300,000 to $400,000 profit - or more - per renovation. With each project taking just three to five months to complete, they prove that lucrative profits can easily be made if you know how to do it right. In the last eight years they've completed 35 renovation projects and transacted over $48 million in property.

RENOVATING FOR PROFIT

HOW TO EARN A SIX-FIGURE SALARY FROM PROPERTY RENOVATIONS – ANYONE CAN DO IT!

Are you keen to turn old properties into gold? Are you searching for that diamond in the rough that will send you on your way to financial freedom? Do you start frothing at the mouth when agents knock up those "Renovate or Detonate" signs? If this sounds like you, welcome to the wonderful world of renovating!

We've all seen the TV renovating shows that make it look so easy. Properties are transformed in the blink of an eyelid with no apparent fuss or effort. Now for the reality. The truth is that to renovate and do it successfully, you'll need expert property knowledge and a systematic approach to ensure you bring home a lucrative profit at the end of it all. After all, profit is the name in the renovating game.

Anyone can renovate but not everyone knows how to make amazing profits from it. Inexperienced renovators underestimate their costs and overestimate their selling price. Time blows out and costs spiral out of control, leaving nothing more than a battered ego and huge loss at the end of it all. So why is it that so many renovations are doomed before they even begin? Quite simply, it's nothing more than a lack of knowledge on all of the critical steps involved in the renovation process. Like anything, renovating is a business. Your aim is to get the renovation done as quickly and efficiently as possible and with insight into what buyers or renters want. This can be the difference between a profit or loss on your project.

BONUS! FREE gifts at www.TGRProperty.com.au/Gifts

This chapter explains the different types of renovation projects you can undertake, the systematic approach you need to follow in the renovation process, along with key strategies that will put you a step ahead of others who don't take the time to educate themselves with such powerful knowledge. The strategies we've listed are just a small sample of the hundreds we have. They are tried, tested and used on a daily basis in all our projects to find, buy and renovate properties for huge profits. As such, this chapter focuses on unrenovated properties with the intention of reselling them for a profit, a great strategy for people with no cash or minimal equity behind them.

Our first renovation was 95 per cent cosmetic with a touch of structural work. From there we moved rapidly into full blown major renovations with increasing amounts of structural work, often involving partial demolition of the property. If you're seriously considering renovating as your wealth-creation vehicle, determine where your comfort level lies in respect to the type of renovation you do and the amount of work you'll undertake in each project. Typically, the more work to be done to a property, the larger the profit up for grabs. And if the thought of alterations and additions causes you to lose anything more than 10 minutes sleep, start with cosmetic renovations and slowly move into more challenging projects as your skill, experience and confidence develop.

So what sort of person does a professional renovator need to be? Definitely someone who is not happy to sit back and "wait" for things to happen. Renovators want results now, not in 2, 5 or 10 years time waiting for capital growth or their development deals to pay off. Renovators take action, many of them rolling up their sleeves to do large portions of the work themselves. Often coined "Sweat Equity", renovation is the fastest way to get quick cashflow. And once your equity starts to build after every successful renovation, you can step back a little, project manage and let other people do the sweating for you.

RENOVATING FOR PROFIT

Renovation is and always will be one of the safest, most reliable and least volatile property strategies you can use. It offers investors the ability to add value, regardless of whether the property market is rising or falling. More importantly, renovation is extremely low risk. For starters, you only need to sell one property as opposed to selling 30 units in your development deals. Renovation also offers shorter lead times that allow you to sell your property in a predicted market. Unlike other property vehicles, it is far easier to estimate your selling price in two months' time as opposed to two years' time. What we like best is the fact that we have total control over our property. The outcome we achieve is a result of our direct actions and input, no one else's. And lastly, property renovation gives you the choice to keep costs down by simply electing to do more or less of the work yourself. This is something you don't often get with other property vehicles. What better way for you to get started in property? You'll soon discover it's not as hard as you first thought. Anyone can do it, you just need to be shown how.

For us, renovating is in our veins. We're two of the few people that can truly say we love what we do and it doesn't feel like work. Achieving huge profits is real; we are living proof of that. You can also achieve this simply by having the skills, faith and motivation to get out there and make it happen. Throw any procrastination you may have in the mini skip bin!

So what are you waiting for? Hold on and fasten your seatbelts for you're about to take the renovation rollercoaster ride. No doubt you'll have many ups and downs, as well as a few curly twists along the way. You'll feel so exhilarated at the end that you'll want to do it all over again. So jump in, let's go for a ride. It's going to be fun!

BONUS! FREE gifts at www.TGRProperty.com.au/Gifts

WHAT EXACTLY IS "RENOVATION"?

People love to talk about renovation but its meaning can differ greatly from one person to the next. So before we go into any further detail, let's clarify the two most common definitions of renovation used today. They are:

1. Cosmetic renovations
2. Structural renovations.

Cosmetic renovations are improvements made to a structurally sound property to give it a makeover or facelift. Just like humans, properties become old and tired-looking with age, so work needs to be done to give them new-found appeal. This is done through simple cosmetic enhancements that, ideally, add more in perceived value than actual cost. The most common methods of cosmetic improvements are painting, replacing carpets, tiling, polishing floorboards, fixing or replacing blinds, updating kitchens and bathrooms, landscaping and any other general repair designed to fix a property and portray a clean, modern appearance. Cosmetic renovations do not involve any change to a structural element of a property – adding rooms, removing load-bearing beams etc. – and therefore require a much lower skill level. As a general rule, cosmetic renovations should account for no more than 15 per cent of the property's purchase price.

Structural renovations are improvements aimed at either preserving the integrity of a property or reconfiguring it to add space and maximise its overall use and efficiency. Many structural renovations include part-demolition of the property with approval for new alterations and additions. Rarely is an old house so derelict that it has to be completely demolished. Unlike cosmetic makeovers, structural renovations need council approval and permits to carry out the work and generally require

RENOVATING FOR PROFIT

licensed tradespeople. As structural renovations can be major changes to a property, there is no industry average as to what you should and shouldn't spend. It's simply a case of analysing each property on an individual basis and assessing your return on investment against the amount of work to be performed.

COSMETIC RENOVATIONS vs	STRUCTURAL RENOVATIONS
Don't require council approval	Does require council approval
Low level skill required	Medium to high level of skill required
Minimal expense	Minimal to major expense
Short timeframes (<2 months)	Longer timeframes (2-12 months)
Active or passive role (your choice)	Project management role
Small trade teams required	Larger project teams required
Smaller profits	Larger profits

Any property that is completely demolished or starting from scratch is defined as "new construction" and does not fit within the realm of renovation.

THERE ARE TWO TYPES OF RENOVATORS:

1. Owner/occupier renovators
2. Professional renovators.

Owner/occupier renovators focus purely on improving the home they currently live in. Undeterred by the thought of having no shower, kitchen or dust-free clothes for a period of time, owner/occupier renovators focus on one thing – what they want. They create a wish list of things that will increase their comfort, then set about transforming their property. They commonly take a long-term view of the property and make decisions based on emotion and what personally appeals to them. While they're likely to have a renovation budget, it's not

BONUS! FREE gifts at www.TGRProperty.com.au/Gifts

uncommon for their budgets to blow out simply because they splurge on items they desperately want. They have to juggle their full-time job, can easily take 10 months to finish the three-month renovation, usually come close to getting divorced and often end up with something entirely different to what they first planned. It's not their fault, they're simply inexperienced and approaching the renovation with a different mindset. While not all owner/occupier renovators are totally tragic, it's members of this group that are most likely to amuse us all with their tales of being traumatised by tradespeople and inexplicably going from mild-mannered people to uncontrollable maniacs within a short space of time.

Professional renovators, on the other hand, are concerned with just one thing. Make no mistake, it's all about profit. Professional renovators are business savvy people who analyse the implications and merits of every decision they make in the renovating process. They have intimate knowledge of their market and know what buyers want, sometimes when buyers don't know themselves. They are well-organised, thorough and don't change their mind 30 times when deciding what colour tiles to put on the floor. Professional renovators have the "buy and add value" mentality etched firmly in their brains. For them, lost time is lost money. As each deal is done, they increase their renovation knowledge to make their next project even better. Most importantly, professional renovators never get emotional about their projects. As the last ones to be paid in the deal, their greatest love is the thrill of seeing their bank balance rise a few levels on settlement day.

WHY RENOVATE?

The thought of getting dirty and living in mayhem is enough to turn most people off renovating. I wonder if the opinions of those people would change, though, if they knew it was possible

RENOVATING FOR PROFIT

to make six-figure profits in relatively short periods of time. Renovation is unarguably one of the easiest ways to make your start in property. What's more fantastic is the fact that it's within the skill level of the average person.

So if you're seriously considering property renovations, congratulations! Our first tip is to make sure you know what you're going to do with a property before you buy it. The path you adopt is likely to be determined by the kind of cashflow you have. The three options below have differing attributes and will require a different renovation approach. The key is to have a clear vision right from the start.

OPTION 1: Buy, renovate, reside.
OPTION 2: Buy, renovate, rent.
OPTION 3: Buy, renovate, sell.

The **buy, renovate, reside** strategy deals with the owner/occupier renovators we've described above, who renovate their primary place of residence. They make up a huge proportion of the renovation real estate market. Owner/occupier renovators are entitled to one owner/builder permit every five years through the Department of Fair Trading. It's a great way to get a start in property if you're short on dollars and don't mind putting in some sweat equity. The key advantage is that your costs are kept to a minimum and whatever profit you make is totally tax free, provided the home is used as your primary place of residence. While that all sounds great, you need to face the reality. Unless you have a relationship more solid than the CaesarStone® bench top you've been dreaming of, you should be careful about facing the challenges of living together with your family in a construction zone. Like it or not, renovating can be the quickest path to divorce. We struggled with it as much as anybody and it took us years of flying off the handle, numerous break-ups

BONUS! FREE gifts at www.TGRProperty.com.au/Gifts

and a few narrowly-missed shots to the head with the closest tool to finally develop a strategy that allows us to diligently and peacefully renovate together.

The **buy, renovate, rent** strategy targets investors who renovate their properties for the purposes of attracting a rental tenant. This type of renovation does add value but normally doesn't maximise the full potential of the property. More so, properties are held to increase equity through longer term capital growth. The ultimate goal of the property owner is to emotionally attract tenants, get the highest rental revenue and have the least possible maintenance issues to detract from their rental return. Cosmetic renovations are fantastic in this scenario. Renovations focus on tenant needs, practicality, long-term durability of fixtures and fittings, and an appropriate level of style and quality to match the rental income of the property. Leave the "wow" factor for properties you intend to buy, renovate and sell. Renovators in this category need to be diligent in keeping costs low to avoid overcapitalising on the property beyond the rental return they'll receive.

The **buy, renovate, sell** strategy deals with professional renovators who buy property, add value to it and sell with the intention of generating a profit within short timeframes. Sometimes referred to as "property traders", the buy, renovate and sell strategy is all about demand and supply. You want to identify a gap in the market and buy a property that can be transformed to satisfy that demand. These properties also need to strike an emotional chord with buyers, so its important renovators in this category understand the buyer psychology. The buy, renovate and sell strategy is our specific area of expertise and the remainder of this chapter largely focuses on this. Saying that, many of the strategies we share with you could easily apply to the other two strategies mentioned.

RENOVATING FOR PROFIT

THE BASICS OF RENOVATING

We all know that one of the quickest ways to make money in real estate is to buy a property that no one wants (i.e. the dump), magically transform it, put it back on the market and hopefully have buyers competing for it. Although the plan sounds extremely simple, it's a lot easier said than done. In essence, the three basic elements in the buy, renovate, sell strategy are:

STEP 1: BUY — Know the true value of the property when buying. → **STEP 2: RENOVATE** — For the least cost possible to achieve the desired result. → **STEP 3: SELL** — At the highest price possible. → **PROFIT**

Know the true value of a property when buying doesn't always mean buying the property for less than it's worth or below the vendor's asking price. In some instances, you can afford to pay more for the property than its current market value if the property can turn an increased profit from a different or better use. The key here is not to have tunnel vision when assessing properties. Confidently know what can be done with the property and how you are able to fully maximise its potential without being detrimental to others. Once you know this, you can determine what the property is worth. Property developers commonly assess property values in this way.

Renovate for the least cost possible to achieve the desired result. Renovations do not always have to be done on the cheap. What is important is that the quality of the renovation reflects the value of the property being re-sold. A luxury home in a wealthy suburb will fail to sell if you paint the kitchen cupboard doors or install cheap fixtures and fittings. Recognise that different properties, at different price points, require different renovation strategies.

BONUS! FREE gifts at www.TGRProperty.com.au/Gifts

Sell at the highest price possible in order to maximise your profits. Give consideration to the time of year you go to market. For example, December and January are great months to buy property but never to sell. Ensure you have a great selling agent working for you and always present your property professionally. Doing this creates a mood that emotional buyers are lured into.

THE SECRET TO OUR SUCCESS

This is it, the nuts and bolts of what it takes to be a professional renovator. Our process is designed to guide you through the three basic renovation elements listed above. Though it's somewhat time consuming initially, you should aim to follow each and every step in our process. These steps are in the correct sequential order that you would follow in real life. Miss one step and you will expose yourself to risk.

Many other property experts reduce the number of steps in their renovation theory. We take the opposite approach. We pride ourselves on being thorough. The more detail we have, the less chance of an oversight that could potentially cost us thousands.

We're honest people, so we'll happily admit that for the first few years we winged our way through renovations, getting ripped off by many, paying way too much for goods and materials, accepting poor behaviour and workmanship from tradies, and undertaking tasks that added no value. Did I forget to mention we also came close to killing each other every single day? We made great profits up to that point but we knew they could be far better, so we decided to get serious about our renovation processes and set out to consciously document and refine them to perfection. We feel that anyone who possesses this knowledge, gained through our hard learning curve of experience, will have a serious advantage over others who don't learn how to renovate right. Like it, hate it, debate over it if you want to. The reality is that our process

RENOVATING FOR PROFIT

is tried, tested and proven. It's no fluke we make hundreds of thousands of dollars profit on all our renovation projects in relatively short timeframes. Use our process religiously, it will be what safeguards your profits regardless of whether you're in a boom or gloom real estate market.

You will notice that the first five steps of our renovation process focus on the "buying" phase of the renovation. Considering this, it's fair to say that 63 per cent of the renovators work is done (five out of eight steps) before you even pick up a hammer. Many people get so caught up in the actual renovation work they lose sight of where their skills are best utilised. There's an old saying: "Work on your business, not in it." For structural renovations this is especially relevant and incredibly important. Learn to be a good project manager and let tradespeople do what they do best. Focus your efforts on where it will make a difference.

OUR EIGHT-STEP RENOVATION PROCESS

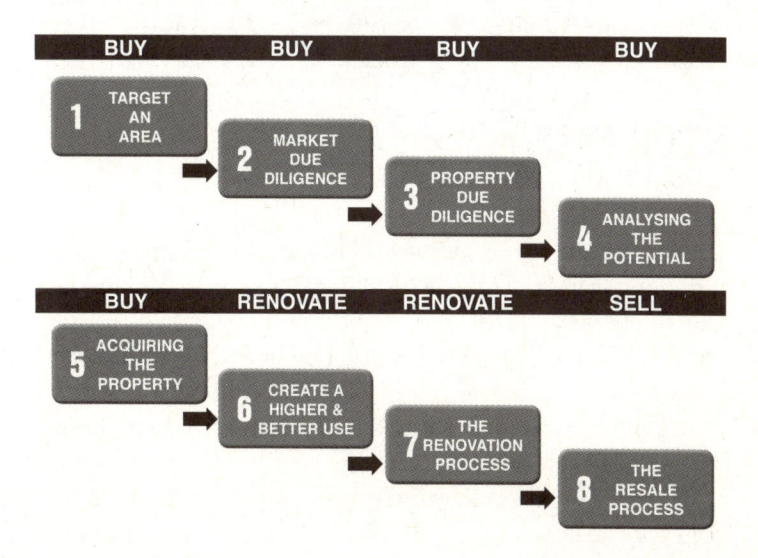

BUY	BUY	BUY	BUY
1. TARGET AN AREA	2. MARKET DUE DILIGENCE	3. PROPERTY DUE DILIGENCE	4. ANALYSING THE POTENTIAL

BUY	RENOVATE	RENOVATE	SELL
5. ACQUIRING THE PROPERTY	6. CREATE A HIGHER & BETTER USE	7. THE RENOVATION PROCESS	8. THE RESALE PROCESS

BONUS! FREE gifts at www.TGRProperty.com.au/Gifts

There are hundreds of strategies, methods and tricks of the trade within our eight-step renovation process – far too many to detail at length in just one chapter. With this in mind, we've handpicked and will share with you some of the more important points, including workable strategies for some of the steps. Take comfort in knowing these strategies are what we use each and every day to make unbelievable profits. They are realistic, achievable strategies you can successfully implement today.

If you're starting to feel exhausted just looking at our model and are thinking it's all too much hard work, let us share a little secret with you. Steps one to six, as well as step eight, are the ones you need to carry out regardless of whether you're a professional renovator, developer, property options trader or anyone else who dabbles in property. Our model is a universal system that can be applied to literally any type of property deal. It's purely the use of these steps that distinguishes the people who are successful in property from those who aren't. Those who skip steps increase their chances of failure. We have never lost money on any of our properties because we are thorough. It's as simple as that.

STEP ONE:
TARGET AN AREA

Let's start at the very beginning. The Australian property market is not one market. It's made up of literally thousands of markets and submarkets. Think macro and micro marketing theories. Some suburbs in Australia are currently in despair while others are still achieving record prices. Why? Because every suburb in Australia is unique and characterised by its own environment and set of circumstances. Therefore, your role as a professional renovator is to select the best suburbs you can possibly afford, then seize and capitalise on the renovation opportunities that lie within them.

RENOVATING FOR PROFIT

So where do you start? If you're smart, you'll realise it's better to be an expert in a few suburbs instead of stretching yourself too thin and not doing anything particularly well. Don't try to focus on 10 suburbs, less than three is a good number and even that will keep you busy. Specialising in a small number of suburbs will give you three things: education, knowledge and, ultimately, results.

The great news is that we became property experts in our area in just less than three months. That's all it takes. Every Saturday we got up early, made a list of all the properties that were open for inspection and trotted off to view them all. We inspected 20 to 40 properties every week, from budget priced to the most expensive, unrenovated to renovated, apartments to sprawling mansions. We went through them all. Yes, it was time consuming but it was also a fantastic way to learn quickly.

By doing this every weekend, and then attending the respective auctions, we quickly learned which properties were overpriced and which represented good value. We learned what types of properties sold quicker than others, which ones pulled higher prices, what property styles people paid higher money for and, most importantly, who the buyers were. The supply and demand became more and more apparent to us. I'm sorry to say that simply sitting at your computer clicking buttons will not give you this level of knowledge. If you truly want to be a property expert in your area, you have to get your bum off the seat and get yourself inside other people's homes. This is the quickest and easiest way to becoming an expert in property values.

Many property experts will advise you to start in suburbs you are already familiar with, one you are already living in or one close to the area where you grew up. That's good advice, though if you're confident enough there's nothing to stop you going

BONUS! FREE gifts at www.TGRProperty.com.au/Gifts

for a complete change, particularly if you have a hunch that a suburb has good prospects. Either way, the key is to get into the suburb and do your homework on it. It's not just about location, location, location; it's also about research, research, research.

Which suburbs you target as your new playground will depend on some key variables:

- **Affordability** – Where you can afford to buy, using your money or other people's money;

- **Supply versus demand** – The ratio of properties available for purchase weighed against the number of potential buyers in the marketplace;

- **Capital growth prospects** – Home buyers ultimately want to buy in suburbs with good capital growth potential;

- **Availability of unrenovated stock** – Some suburbs, like new housing estates, don't have any unrenovated properties so ensure you invest your time in suburbs where genuine opportunities lie.

The beauty of property renovation is that there are plenty of fixer-upper opportunities everywhere, regardless of whether you're in a prime inner city suburb or even in a remote outback area. It will be a relief for many to know that opportunities exist in affordable outer suburbs just as much as in the more affluent areas. You just have to be certain that demand exists for a particular type of property within those areas, then meet that demand.

The following list is just a small list of the areas where property renovations can work.

RENOVATING FOR PROFIT

INNER CITY AREAS
- Suburbs located within 15 kilometres of the main CBD.
- Suburbs with lifestyle zones that include cafés, restaurants, bars, shops etc. Buyers are prepared to pay extra to be closer to these amenities.
- Desirable suburbs with limited stock.

HERITAGE CONTROLLED AREAS
- Areas under conservation or heritage controlled zones.
- Suburbs with difficult, strict councils. Most people put these areas in the "too hard" basket, allowing renovators to capitalise on opportunities that others leave on the table.
- The calculation is simple:
    - difficult councils = shortage in housing stock
    - shortage in housing stock = high demand
    - high demand = rising/premium property prices (the renovation jackpot).

ESTABLISHED SUBURBS
- Established suburbs provide restricted opportunity for new development.
- Close to private schools.
- No new development (such as high-rise apartments) creates a housing scarcity, driving demand up.

SPILL-OVER SUBURBS
- Choose spill-over suburbs close to established blue chip suburbs.
- These suburbs rise in value when their blue chip neighbour becomes too expensive.

OUTER AREA ENTERTAINMENT SUBURBS
- Target properties in outer areas where established entertainment and lifestyle facilities exist.

BONUS! FREE gifts at www.TGRProperty.com.au/Gifts

- Must be close to shopping centres or shopping strips.
- Must be close to public transport facilities.

OUTER AREA ESTATES
- Choose suburbs which contain expensive, opulent housing where wealthier people live. Not all rich people live in waterfront mansions.
- Substandard properties may be able to be brought up to this level.

LOW COST HOUSING IN OUTER AREAS
- Target suburbs and estates where good standard housing exists.
- Choose suburbs where owners take pride in their homes and have pleasant streetscapes.
- Bring poor quality homes up to equal or better standard than current homes in these areas.
- Look for areas where land supply is exhausted.

> **TIP:** Your local council often sells suburb maps for a small fee. These maps are a great way to mark out pockets within suburbs and enable you to view the area in one easy glance. These maps often contain details about zoning, suburb boundary lines, infrastructure routes and, if you're lucky, even individual property boundaries. Buy a copy and hang it on your wall at home for constant reference or as a source of motivation for you to take action.

STEP TWO:
MARKET DUE DILIGENCE

"Due diligence" is the name professional renovators, developers and investors give to the research they carry out. You need to know everything about a particular area so you can become a property expert in it. Your aim is to have better knowledge than most real estate agents in your area. They don't go through other agents' properties but you can, which puts you in a great position to make a phenomenal profit with little risk. Why? Because if you know your market well there's a greater chance that you will buy wisely (because you know precisely what the unrenovated property is worth) and will accurately estimate your selling price (because you also know what renovated properties sell for).

By this time you have finished step one and should have a rough idea of some suburbs you may like to target. Now you need to drill down a level and explore those suburbs in intimate detail. There are some suburbs that look rosy on the outside but present a much bleaker picture once you scratch the surface and find out what's going on inside.

So how do you become an expert on your chosen suburb? Again, there are exhaustive lists on what things you can do to increase your knowledge of a suburb, as well as an abundance of books that focus purely on this topic. To save you the effort of trawling through all of them, though, we'll highlight the top five things you can do, starting today, to set you on the path to uncovering all the things you need to know about your suburb:

- If you can afford it, live in your chosen suburb. To know what the suburb is really like you need to wake up inside it every morning, walk around the local parks, eat breakfast in the local cafés and see the type of people who live there. You need to find out when it's at its busiest and quietest, which parts suffer traffic congestion, which parts are the noisiest and so on. Some of these factors can affect property values so it's better to personally experience them before you buy.

- Establish a due diligence research system, one that enables you to record information on the different properties you've inspected in your market. I'm proud to say we've developed our own unique due diligence system that we believe can't be rivalled. It is somewhat labour intensive but the information we have at our fingertips in terms of market pricing and property condition is phenomenal. We attribute a large part of our success to this system. As they say, knowledge is power. Aim to create your own research system so you too can accurately know property values in your area.

- Have a firm grasp of the resident demographics in your suburb. Normally, people looking to buy into the area will be a similar demographic to those people already living there. For instance, in our chosen area we have three identifiable demographics. The first is 28 to 35-year-old young professionals with high disposable incomes and no kids. The second demographic is 35 to 50-year-old professional families who moved into the suburb in their late 20s or early 30s and have stayed there ever since. The last demographic is aged 70 or over and are down-to-earth, Aussie battler types who've lived in the area their whole lives. You see, our area used to be poor man's territory, where blue collar workers lived in virtual slums. It definitely wasn't an area you would have wanted to live at the time. At some stage, though, the suburb began to transform until it finally became trendy and desirable, with a matching increase in property prices. Most of those 70-year-olds battlers are now sitting on properties that are worth anywhere between $1 million and $3 million,

RENOVATING FOR PROFIT

simply through capital growth alone. Our target is the second demographic, the young professional families who have money to spend and no time or patience to renovate themselves. It's how we make such large profits. The moral of this story is for you to get the detailed knowledge that will allow you to match your renovated property to active buyers.

- Visually inspect all properties within your target area, across all price ranges, property types and sizes. This will give you fantastic knowledge on the difference in price values between 1, 2, 3, 4 and 5 bedroom properties, which is particularly important for structural renovators. It will also help you tackle such questions as federation style versus contemporary, garage versus no parking, apartments versus houses and so on. Attend as many auctions as possible, too, and know what it is you're looking for. Unlike everybody else, when we go to auctions we don't watch the auctioneer; we watch the buyers. We want to know who they are, how old they are, whether they're a single buyer or there as a family unit. These visual inspections will give you a number of things, among which you will:

1) Start learning the value of properties in your area.

2) Be able to recognise good value properties and tell them apart from those that are over-priced.

3) Be able to recognise the reasons why some homes are in higher demand than others.

4) Know what price you should expect to pay for unrenovated properties and, more importantly, what you'll be able to sell them for when they're fully renovated.

BONUS! FREE gifts at www.TGRProperty.com.au/Gifts

5) Have the benefit of personally seeing the condition, style and features of the property with your own eyes rather than relying on glossy marketing material from agents.

6) Have an excellent way of collecting renovation ideas. If you walk through someone's house and a particular room or feature emotionally draws you to it, think about including something similar in your next renovation project.

- Develop good relationships with agents in your area, preferably the best agent and sales director of each local agency. Explain to them the specific type of unrenovated property you want to purchase and the price range you are looking at. If you say to them, "I'm serious, bring me the right deal and I'll buy immediately", it confirms that you're a qualified buyer, ready to act now. When an unrenovated property does become available you want the agent to bring it to you first. Our rule with agents is that if they bring us a deal, such as an unrenovated property, we will resell the property with them. Agents love this because they get to double dip by drawing two commissions out of the same property in a relatively short time. If the relationship you have with your agent is good, you'll be able to talk comfortably about the real estate market and how it's performing in your area. After all, you aren't talking to buyers directly, the real estate agents are.

Once you've established a good understanding of your suburb(s), it's time to look at the immediate area and street characteristics of the property. This is step three and it's called property due diligence.

STEP THREE:
PROPERTY DUE DILIGENCE

It's easy to buy a great house in a great suburb but it's a lot harder to avoid a great house in a poor performing street within that suburb. To put it another way, you should be aware that property values can be very high in one street but substantially lower the next street over. You'll often find pockets of streets within a suburb that hold higher values than others. As a professional renovator, you need to be aware of these price pockets. Otherwise you may grossly overestimate your selling price and put yourself at risk of a loss.

These are some basic pointers for you to consider when assessing unrenovated properties at the street and individual property level. In an ideal world, always aim to purchase unrenovated properties that:

- are in established residential streets that are fully built-out;

- are in close proximity to expensive brand new developments;

- have no adverse property (factories or industrial zones) in the surrounding area;

- preferably have a higher concentration of owner/occupiers instead of renters;

- are in proximity to public transport (but not too close);

- are not smaller in size than the suburb average;

- have a pleasant and consistent streetscape;

BONUS! FREE gifts at www.TGRProperty.com.au/Gifts

- offer good parking (particularly relevant for inner city properties where space is in short supply);

- are not in narrow streets (inner city people know the hassles this can cause);

- offer good quality neighbouring homes (if your renovated project is the only decent looking property in your street, it will struggle to sell);

- do not have any adverse property features, such as a steep driveway or a home that is below street level.

As a renovator, the perfect scenario is for your property to have as few buyer objections as possible. The fewer objections, the greater your likelihood of reeling in a buyer.

WORKABLE STRATEGY NUMBER 1: FOUR WAYS YOU CAN SECURE UNRENOVATED PROPERTIES

1) **Door knock** – Drive or walk around the streets in your area and you'll soon identify properties that have renovation potential. Don't be scared to knock on people's doors and ask if they're interested in selling. In our experience, people don't get offended or irate and will often take it as a compliment. It all depends on your approach. If you're friendly and humble it will be all right but if you go in there wearing your developer's hat you may get a personal introduction to the family dog. If property owners are not interested in selling, always leave your business card. People's circumstances do change over time. We bought one property, off market, from a man who we door knocked two years earlier.

RENOVATING FOR PROFIT

2) **Letter box drops** – If you don't feel entirely comfortable knocking on random doors you might like to try a letter drop. A personalised letter always goes down well, especially because you've taken the time to handwrite it. When we use this method we always receive a call back from property owners. We once received a call from an older gentleman who wasn't keen to sell us his property, but he made sure to mention he had another property that might be up our alley. For an example of the type of letter you should send, see the next page.

3) **Monitor council DAs** – If you're keen to do a structural renovation there's no better way to source your deals than by monitoring the development applications already in progress through your local council. Property owners sometimes have no intention of renovating, they simply want to sell their property as "DA approved". Get in contact with owners and ask if they're interested in selling, before these unrenovated properties are advertised publicly.

4) **RP Data search** – It pays to subscribe to RP Data, an Internet site that allows you to view individual property information. This facility allows you to view houses from above via aerial photograph mapping. It enables you to quickly and effortlessly identify which houses are on under-utilised blocks. It's perfect for structural renovators who want to add substantial value through alterations and additions. Once you've identified desirable properties you can go and knock on the door or, at the very least, send that letter.

> Dear Property Owner,
>
> We are local residents and noticed your house when walking by. We are currently looking to buy a property which we can renovate and were wondering if you had any interest in selling?
>
> If so, we would love the opportunity to meet up with you for an informal chat.
>
> Our contact number is below and we sincerely hope to hear from you.
>
> With Kind Regards,
>
> Cherie & Steve

An example of one of our personal handwritten letters, used to acquire unrenovated properties. The language is kept simple, while the tone is friendly and relaxed so the property owner feels comfortable calling us.

STEP FOUR:
ANALYSING THE POTENTIAL

So how do you find that "diamond in the rough"? Unfortunately, there's no magic formula to finding the perfect property. Buying any old rundown shack simply isn't enough these days; you need to be able to identify which fixer-uppers represent high profitability potential for you. That's what step four is all about.

RENOVATING FOR PROFIT

This step has two facets. The first is to understand how you can unlock potential and add value to the property to maximise its resale price. The second is to do your number crunching, also known as financial feasibility.

So how do you unlock potential? If you've done your homework on steps one, two and three you'll already know the types of property that are in demand in your area. The rest is therefore simple: buy a property that can be renovated to fulfil that demand. If you can't do this your property will languish on the market as it desperately awaits an offer from somebody, then eventually from anybody.

Our target area is dominated by two bedroom semis with a young, affluent 28 to 35-year-old demographic. Most residents join the suburb in their late 20s and buy one of these properties. They love the area and don't leave. Next comes marriage and kids, then suddenly they need a bigger family home of four or five bedrooms. Ever wondered why some properties sell immediately while others sit on the market for months? It's all about supply versus demand.

UNLOCKING POTENTIAL IN COSMETIC RENOVATIONS

Cosmetic renovations still need to address the issue of supply and demand in your area. There is no point buying and renovating a two-bedroom home if the other homes in your area typically have four bedrooms. The key to unlocking potential and adding value in cosmetic renovations is to lift the condition and quality of the property, raising it to at least equivalent of other high priced homes in your area in the shortest time possible.

With cosmetic renovations you need to think creatively about how you can create the perception of higher value for a low actual cost. There are hundreds of ways to do this. Whenever we do a cosmetic renovation we initially look for effective ways to enhance the property by studying the internal and external floor plan.

One of our early cosmetic renovations. Nothing more than a lick of paint inside and out, ripping up the carpets and sanding the floors. It brought us a $23,000 net profit for just three days' work.

What to look for when analysing the internal floor plan

- Can I significantly beautify the property internally?
- Can I make it look new internally?
- Can I give the property a boutique feel?
- Can I add any brand-name items to the property to increase perceived quality?
- Can I make the internal space unique in any way?
- Is the kitchen close to the family and dining rooms?
- Can non load-bearing walls be easily removed to create more open family areas?
- Can small family/living rooms be increased in size by removing unwanted rooms?

- Can I open up rooms to make them seem larger and more appealing?
- Can I get an extra bedroom in by reducing the size of another room?
- Can I add an extra room without compromising the quality of other rooms?
- Can I reduce a larger area into two smaller areas by adding a plasterboard wall?
- Can I get whatever the property is missing into the space somehow?
- Can I add a small home office in the unused corner of a larger room?
- Can I add features that help to better define rooms?
- Can I re-design and enhance existing features?
- Does the house have an entry/foyer/hallway of some form? If not, can this be added?
- Is there enough light in the house? If not, can this be rectified by skylights or other means?
- Does the property have adequate ventilation? If not, can this be rectified?
- Can I upgrade fixtures and fittings to improve perceived quality?
- Can I give the house strong owner/occupier appeal?
- Can I add any special features to the property that will emotionally draw people to it?
- What value adds, such as a home cinema system, can I include to maximise the price?

STEPHEN TOLLE & CHERIE BARBER

An extra bedroom is easily created in this cosmetic renovation simply by bricking in the existing wall arch.

An additional bedroom in our area can add between $100,000 and $200,000 in extra value to a property, especially in inner city suburbs where space is at a premium.

This is one of our current projects undergoing renovation. Unrenovated for over 60 years, this property has fantastic bones that make it ideal for cosmetic renovation. At the rear is an old warehouse building that was approved for business use over 40 years ago. Most buyers would not have realised this approval was still in place. We plan to cosmetically renovate this room to be a 10-person home-based office, adding significant value to the property at minimal cost. If you think outside the square, cosmetic renovations can pull huge profits by utilising rooms well.

RENOVATING FOR PROFIT

This photo shows that if you can be creative and imaginative with your cosmetic renovations, you can add perceived value at no extra cost. This example shows exterior weatherboards placed vertically instead of their normal horizontal position. It didn't cost any extra to do this and it made the property look more architectural, giving it a higher perceived value.

What to look for when analysing the external footprint

- Can I significantly beautify the property externally?
- Is there good access to the front of the property?
- Is there good access to the rear of the property?
- Can I easily install a carport to increase value?
- Can existing carports be cosmetically rejuvenated by becoming enclosed?
- Can outdoor entertaining areas be easily created?
- Can an outdoor kitchen/BBQ area be easily installed?
- Can fencing be installed to define boundaries and provide security?
- Can pathways be added in critical points where needed?
- Can planting be added to give a pleasing appearance?
- Can outdoor storage areas be included?
- Can anything be done with the roof to make it look new?
- Can any features be added that strike an emotional chord with buyers?

BONUS! FREE gifts at www.TGRProperty.com.au/Gifts

STEPHEN TOLLE & CHERIE BARBER

This renovation of ours shows how a property can have substantial value added to it through simple cosmetic enhancements, in this case, paint, render, new roof sheets, tiling, plants and a new picket fence.

The crucial thing to remember is that you want to add more in perceived value than the improvements actually cost. Don't spend $3,000 on new carpet that only adds $2,500 in value. Instead you're better off to spend $3,000 ripping up the carpet and polishing the floorboards, which may add as much as $5,000 in value to the property. Can you see how one decision results in a profit, while the other incurs a loss? By planning ahead, before you start your renovation, you'll eliminate costly errors of judgement during the actual process.

With cosmetic renovations, things that can't be seen tend not to add value. Of course, there are exceptions and you need to know when to spend money on hidden things that will contribute positively to the value of a property. For instance, installing new insulation batts in the roof cavity won't have the same perceived value as a house that's been completely rewired.

With cosmetic renovations, always aim to give the internal space a designer look at the least possible cost, regardless of the property's value. Use items that look expensive but don't actually cost very much. Today there are lots of fake clones of luxury items, all designed to give your cosmetic renovation the illusion of quality. Tiles are a great example. Real travertine tiles cost, on average, $150 m^2. Fake travertine tiles, on the other hand, that are virtually identical cost just $40 m^2$. It's a great example of how you can get a champagne look on a beer budget.

Cosmetically, it's best to invest your money in the two rooms of the property that add the biggest value: kitchens and bathrooms. Kitchens sell houses so make sure this room is always perfect from top to bottom. Doing so is the easiest way to lure in emotional buyers. The main aim with bathrooms is to make them look bigger, brighter and cleaner. Add features and inexpensive decorative elements into the property that notch up the "wow" factor.

As a cosmetic renovator, always keep your underlying focus on the numbers so you don't overcapitalise. Keep reminding yourself that profit is the sole reason you're spending your weekends painting and not sipping daiquiris by the pool with your friends.

UNLOCKING POTENTIAL IN STRUCTURAL RENOVATIONS

Make no mistake, structural renovations can be intense. Of course it depends on what degree you go to but, generally speaking, the more work that needs to be done, the more profit will be up for grabs. It goes both ways, though. Not knowing what you're doing with structural renovations can cause you to burn money faster than a socialite on a shopping spree.

Unlike cosmetic renovations, structural renovations give you the ability to substantially change, reconfigure and add new space to an existing property. Buying under-utilised dumps and maximising their value allows you to create phenomenal financial gains between the price you buy the property for and its resale price. The tricky part is being able to control your costs so you pull a profit at the end of it all.

BONUS! FREE gifts at www.TGRProperty.com.au/Gifts

STEPHEN TOLLE & CHERIE BARBER

One of our structural renovations. This small two bedroom workman's cottage was transformed into a four-bedroom family home with a study. It retained the original character of the cottage but now has a modern new rear wing.

With structural renovations, your ability to identify true potential is slightly more difficult. You may need to enlist some help for your first few projects (such as an architect or town planner) until you start to figure out how far you can go with alterations and additions to rundown dwellings in your area. Local councils control the extent of development in your area so a basic knowledge of controls – such as floor to space ratios, building setbacks and height limits – will help you quickly identify which properties have the potential for additional rooms and floor space.

With structural renovations, the best ways to add significant value are by:

- relocating rooms to improve functionality within the property;
- adding rooms to make the property larger in size;
- adding rooms that meet a need, such as a garage;
- opening up areas to create open plan living;
- making rooms larger to better accommodate the occupants of the home.

Always design with the end buyer in mind, not to your own taste. Aim to appeal to the majority of the market, not the minority. Choose neutral colours with simple clean lines to make the most of the space and resist the urge to paint rooms in different colours. You want your renovated property to look like there's been thought put into it to give it an integrated look throughout. Select materials that are timeless and won't date, ones that will add positively to the value rather than detract from it.

YOUR FINANCIAL FEASIBILITY

So you've found a property that you think may have great renovation potential. But how do you really know, beyond your own gut instinct, if a great profit can be made? It all comes down to your financial feasibility.

A financial feasibility is your ability to estimate costs, as close to reality as possible, so you can determine whether a project is justified from an economic point of view. It's a process that gives renovators the ability to make clear business-based decisions as to whether they should commit funds, resources, time and effort to potential renovation projects. Using this, renovators are able to see the total cost of not only buying the property but also holding and renovating it as well.

Estimating costs is a fine art and, speaking frankly, your first financial feasibility may not be worth the paper it's written on. Rest assured, though, that as you do more projects your financial feasibilities will become increasingly accurate. If you're unsure of costs you should use sensible guestimates (a cross between a guess and an estimate) or, better still, get real quotes if time allows. In our early days, we'd often walk from room to room with a clipboard in hand to visually inspect the place and record everything that needed work done to it. We'd then make allowances for all those things in the financial feasibility. Remember, all of this has to happen before you buy.

You must always resist the urge to buy a property for which you haven't done a financial feasibility. It's the only true test to determine if you can turn a profit from the project. Don't be in a position where you renovate for months on end, only to find out you haven't made a profit or, worse still, have lost money. Constant number crunching is a habit that's shared by all successful renovators and property developers.

Renovators can easily produce their own financial feasibilities. Microsoft Excel is great for creating your own financial spreadsheets quickly and easily or you can buy property feasibility software. Smart renovators do a preliminary feasibility either in their head or on a piece of paper, using quick calculations. This is called a "back of the envelope" calculation. If the preliminary calculations look good a more detailed feasibility, generally using software, will follow.

When we look back on the financial feasibilities we did for our first few renovations it seems a miracle we made any profit at all. Our initial feasibilities were just 20 vague lines, with broad assumptions as to the costs. Oh, how we have evolved. The financial feasibility we use today is over 400 lines long. Why? Because each renovation we've completed has given us a new set of costs that we've added back into our base template. Now when we sit down to crunch numbers on any new deal it's a fairly easy task, without the risk of us forgetting to include anything.

The good news is that there is no right or wrong way of actually doing a financial feasibility. Generally speaking, renovators use a cost versus profit formula to calculate their anticipated selling price, or else they work back from that sales price and use what

RENOVATING FOR PROFIT

is called the Residual Land Value Method to determine what they can afford to pay for the property. Either way, the key pieces of information you need in your financial feasibility are revenue details (income you expect to receive from the sale of the property) less the expense details (acquisition, finance, holding, professional, construction, resale, miscellaneous and tax costs). The financial summary section of your feasibility will tell you if the project is considered financially viable, which will allow you to decide whether or not to buy the property.

Keep in mind, though, that the financial feasibility is only as good as the accuracy of the information contained within it. If you're unsure of costs, check the cost assumptions with appropriately qualified people such as a quantity surveyor, your suppliers or tradespeople. Also, don't forget to factor in any taxes that may be applicable to your renovation project (GST, Capital Gains Tax and so on). Taxes can be significant and can wipe out your renovation profit in one fell swoop, so be aware of these costs before you buy.

STEP FIVE:
ACQUIRE THE PROPERTY

All right, you've finally found the perfect fixer-upper. Hallelujah! There are now two things left to do before it officially becomes yours. The first is to organise your finance and the second is to negotiate the actual purchase of the property.

ORGANISING YOUR FINANCE
Is it better to organise your finance before you start looking or find your deal first and then figure out how to fund it? There's no one right or wrong answer to that question; it comes down to personal choice. We adopt the latter strategy, as we've discovered it's harder to find great renovation deals than it is to get finance.

BONUS! FREE gifts at www.TGRProperty.com.au/Gifts

Our most profitable deal ever was on a property that was way out of our price league. We were so excited by the profit potential the property offered that we secured it with a minimal deposit and financed it with the help of a wealthy but time-poor friend of ours. When we walked away with $750,000 in profit we had more than enough proof that you should never have tunnel vision when it comes to seeking finance. The reality is that if you're hungry to win the renovation race and you really want to do a deal, you'll always find a creative way to fund it. Quite often your finance broker can offer ideas in this regard.

The question we get asked most often is, where do you get all your money from? The answer is that smart renovators use other people's money. We've made all of our profits by using the bank's money. The key to getting finance is to think creatively and put as much effort into obtaining a mortgage as you put into looking for a property. Not all banks are created equal and you should never take the words of one bank as being representative of the entire industry. Some lenders are more flexible than others, so you may have trouble getting a loan from one bank and then walk across the street to get it easily from another.

Renovators today have a huge choice as to where they obtain money. There are traditional banks, non-traditional lenders, deposit bond companies, mezzanine funders, solicitor's funds, private funders – the list goes on and on. It's a good idea to make time to educate yourself on finance suppliers and learn about the product they're offering.

Loan applications are generally assessed on four merits:
1. **Income** – How much you earn and how stable your source of revenue is;

RENOVATING FOR PROFIT

2. **Serviceability** – Your ability to repay the debt as well as your living expenses;

3. **Loan to Value Ratio (LVR)** - The value of the property less the amount being financed, expressed as a percentage. The lower your LVR, the higher chance of a loan approval;

4. **Your credit history** – Your ability to manage your money and your financial performance to date.

If you fall short on one of the above criterion, put your creative hat on and think of an alternative solution. For example, your income may be too low to service the loan but you could have some equity behind you. In this situation, you could turn to a no/low documentation loan.

When organising finance, you mustn't forget the costs of doing the actual renovation. Here are some of the obvious lines of credit that people sometimes overlook:

- utilise credit cards with 55 day interest-free periods (great for cosmetic renovations);

- take out a personal loan;

- get a line of credit against the property by having the property revalued as you carry out the renovation;

- borrow from family and friends. You can entice them with the prospect of a higher interest rate than what they're currently getting or a small percentage of your renovation profit;

- find an investment partner. This would ideally be time-poor professionals who have no time to spend their cash or high income earners who have the money stream to service the loan. Motivate them with a percentage of your profit.

BONUS! FREE gifts at www.TGRProperty.com.au/Gifts

There are a few key things you can do to increase your chance of getting a renovation loan:

- **Develop good business relationships with personal or private banking managers** – These are senior bank staff who have the authority to comment and positively influence your application. You should work hard to develop a relationship with them. You want them to view you as a property expert, someone who knows what they are doing and is therefore of low risk to the bank;

- **Prepare a bank proposal** – Put time and effort into preparing a bank proposal that convinces your banker to give you a loan. Ninety-nine per cent of people who need a mortgage never consider doing this. Professional renovators spend time, prior to their bank meeting, preparing a finance presentation with critical information on the property and its financial viability;

- **Spread your loans amongst different banks** – Some banks restrict your borrowing capacity when you have too many properties. If you want to do multiple renovations at a time, spread your loans around a couple of banks. Don't put all your eggs in one basket;

- **Protect your credit reference file** – This is a list of the last seven years of your financial history, including any defaults, which banks view prior to giving you a loan. Your aim is to have a clean record and the fewer transactions, the better. Only proceed with loan applications that have a 99.9 per cent chance of being approved. Never purchase consumer goods on interest-free terms and always pay bills on time. Never let it get to default status. If you can't pay your $120 mobile phone bill on time, how can the bank trust you to pay a mortgage? The smallest things like this can make the difference between getting the loan and being declined;

- **Dress professionally** – Image counts. Never wear casual clothes, regardless of how well the banker knows you. Always wear a good suit and look your best from head to toe, even after your loan is approved. Like it or not, people judge others by their appearance. When borrowing money, look like you can afford to repay the loan.

WORKABLE STRATEGY NUMBER 2: HOW WE'VE MADE GREAT RENOVATION PROFITS WITH ABSOLUTELY NO MONEY

Let's face it, you may get knocked back by the banks. Does that mean you should give up and go home? No! Think outside the square and get creative. Here are a few ways we've made fantastic renovating profits with absolutely no money. Even if you have very little money behind you, no cash for a deposit and no money to buy a property yourself, you can still use these strategies to get started in property. Wherever there's a will, there's a way.

1. REAL EXAMPLE ONE

Ask your parents if you can borrow some of the equity on their house for a short period of time. Most parents have a lot of equity in their family home, without ever realising it. On one of our first renovations our parents allowed us to take out a no doc loan using the equity in their home. We used part of this loan for the property deposit and the remainder of it funded the renovation. When we sold the property we were able to repay the loan in full, only five months after taking it out. We also gave the parents $7,000 in cash, just to thank them for trusting us enough to take the risk. Everyone won in this deal. They got something for nothing and we made a great renovation profit. Smart property investors always use other people's money.

BONUS! FREE gifts at www.TGRProperty.com.au/Gifts

2. REAL EXAMPLE TWO

Another option is to find somebody who earns good money but has no time to renovate a property themselves. We are in the process of finishing a major renovation project with an Australian friend of ours who is currently working in China on a three-year contract. Being the time-poor professional that he is, he approached us to renovate one of his large rental properties for him. We struck a deal whereby he has funded the total renovation costs in return for a 50/50 profit share on the increased property value. Before starting we had it valued by agents at $1.4 million. Our costs throughout the process came to $630,000 (yes, it was a substantial property with a major overhaul) and it's since been estimated to be worth around $2.8 to $3 million. Our five month renovation has resulted in a net gain of at least $770,000, even in this real estate market of doom and gloom. When you do the sums you will see what an excellent deal it's been, particularly when we didn't put a cent of our own money into the project. We simply invested our time, which was worth something (a big something) to somebody else.

Over our renovating years there have been many who've asked us whether we worry about being so heavily in debt. Our answer is that in order to be successful in any aspect of property – be it renovation, property development, options or whatever – you need to change your thinking when it comes to money. There is good debt and there is bad debt. Racking up twenty thousand dollars on the latest designer dresses would be commonly viewed as bad debt, while acquiring assets that have the ability to generate an income is unquestionably good debt. We will always take as much money as we can possibly get from the banks, regardless of whether the market is rising or falling. Don't ever let fear get the better of you. If it does, you will always stay in your comfort zone and never move forward.

NEGOTIATING THE PURCHASE

Paying too much for a property is one of the most common mistakes buyers make. How you handle the negotiation process depends largely on how the property is being sold. If a great fixer-upper comes on the market and it's being sold via public auction, your ability to negotiate on the property may be limited.

Firstly, great dumps don't come along every day and can create a great deal of interest when they do. Vendors often know when they're sitting on a goldmine, so nine out of 10 times they won't negotiate prior to auction. Even when they do, they will usually have unrealistic price expectations. Here's something to be aware of at the auction: if you're a professional renovator bidding against emotional owner/occupier renovators, you should forget it. They'll always pay more than you, simply because they are full of emotion, will take a long-term view of the property and have probably underestimated their renovation costs. We've missed out on many opportunities because we've been forced to compete in an arena of people who have no idea what they're doing. We might as well have been at the circus. If you have to compete at a public auction for a property, there's a chance you may walk away with it but you'll probably have to pay full price or more for the property.

The best way to acquire good dumps is via off-market transactions or through properties that are for sale. Either of these methods will give you a chance to negotiate on your own terms.

Off-market transactions are properties that are available for purchase but haven't yet been publicly advertised. For instance, your neighbour might mention to you in conversation that she's thinking of selling. If she's living in a dump, you'll need to scale the fence quicker than an Olympic hurdler.

Off-market transactions are fantastic. Vendors normally have an idea what their property is worth but they don't get caught up in the hysteria that comes with the interest their unrenovated property generates. They are therefore realistic in their expectations. What they like best is the prospect of not having to pay agent's commission or marketing costs. In our area, agents and advertisers generally carve about $30,000 out of the money that ultimately goes into the pocket of the vendor.

When dumps are offered for sale, professional renovators find themselves with lots of leverage to negotiate. In real estate, the early bird gets the worm and we've bought great properties when we were the first and only people to inspect them. If you know potential when you see it, act with speed to secure the property before others have the chance to inspect it.

Now comes the fun part of actually negotiating on the property. As a professional renovator you have two main objectives:

1) source the property at the right price
2) have your terms of sale accepted.

Smart renovators don't negotiate just on price. There are other lucrative elements that can be negotiated as part of the deal. These are referred to as your terms of sale or your conditions. Make sure the conditions you ask for are going to work to your advantage, to a considerable extent.

Negotiation is an art form so it's important you make an offer that arouses the seller's attention. Making ridiculous offers will damage your credibility and is likely to insult the seller. Once they're off-side you'll struggle to win them back. That's why it's important to put a lot of thought and preparation into submitting your offer.

WORKABLE STRATEGY NUMBER 3: HOW TO IMPROVE YOUR RENOVATION PROFITS THROUGH CLEVER NEGOTIATION

Renovators who understand the importance of the time/money relationship structure their conditions to increase profit. Your offer should make both the agent and seller aware that a lot of time and effort is needed to bring the property up to its full potential. Your offer, therefore, should reflect the costs of doing this. Use the following conditions when negotiating your next property deal:

1. **Extended settlement** – 42 days is standard but longer settlement is achievable. Don't be afraid to ask for a settlement period that covers any waiting periods, such as a development approval, you may incur. Lost time costs you money so try to offset these costs through extended settlement. We once got eight months extended settlement in a growing market, which saved us 32 weeks worth of loan repayments and gave us two-thirds of a year worth of free capital growth;

2. **Early access** – Getting permission to move in and renovate the property before you actually own it is a favourite for cosmetic renovators. If you time it right, you can have the property renovated and back on the market by the time you need to settle. At that point the property can be revalued, thus eliminating the need for you to come up with money for a deposit;

3. **Subject to pre-DA or DA approval** – In some instances, offers can be subject to a favourable pre-DA or development approval from council. This is a great condition for structural renovators who want some certainty that their development plans will be approved. It eliminates risk for the structural renovator;

BONUS! FREE gifts at www.TGRProperty.com.au/Gifts

4. **Five per cent deposit** – Most vendors will happily accept a five per cent deposit instead of the normal 10 per cent. You simply need to ask for it. In tougher real estate times, even less than five per cent can be negotiated. I know a renovator who secured a $3.5 million unrenovated waterfront home on a $10,000 deposit with 12 months extended settlement. Just beautiful;

5. **Subject to finance** – It's likely that your finance is already approved but by requesting this condition you'll get some extra time to sign the contract, which is the starting date for your extended settlement stopwatch to start ticking;

6. **Subject to building and pest inspection** – This is another way to negotiate price away, especially if you know really expensive tradespeople.

Your aim is to get as many terms accepted as possible. Some of these will be eaten away during negotiation, which is fine as long as you arrive at a point where you are both happy to move to the contract of sale. If you can't get any of these conditions accepted you will have no option but to reduce your price or walk away from the deal. It's as simple as that. Never get emotional; there will always be another deal.

When negotiating real estate deals, do your homework and learn as much about the seller as you possibly can. It may put you in a better position to understand their motivations for selling and allow you to structure your offer so you can win them over.

STEP SIX:
CREATE A HIGHER AND BETTER USE

Step six largely applies to structural renovations that require local council development approval. There are different categories of development, some that give you approval in as little as 10 days. Each council is different but, as a general rule, three months or less is the normal lead time for development approval.

Intelligent renovators, when doing their homework, will research their local councils well. In areas where there are tight heritage controls and conservation zones it's not uncommon for structural renovators to be waiting up to a year for their development approval.

When doing your research, don't always take the council's word. When we first started doing renovations we were told by our council that the average lead time for approval was three months. Once we spoke to several local builders, we got a very different picture. All of them said the development lead time was actually about a year to 18 months. It turned out they were right, as our first DA took well over a year to be approved. When your property is costing you $4,000 a month in holding costs, that kind of delay can end up losing you as much as $50,000 out of your renovation profit. The key is to ask people in your area what experiences they've had with council, allowing you to know what kind of lead time you can expect.

Structural renovations provide the perfect opportunity to match properties to the needs of the market. The key to adding huge value is to get formal approval for a higher and better use of the property. Following is an example of one our projects, a two-bedroom unrenovated property (before) that we turned into a four-bedroom family home.

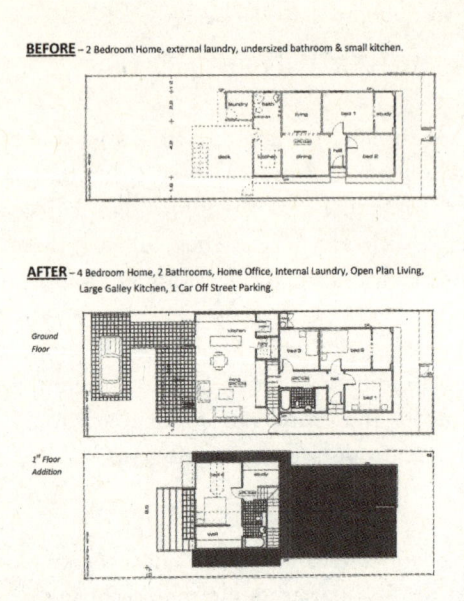

BEFORE – 2 Bedroom Home, external laundry, undersized bathroom & small kitchen.

AFTER – 4 Bedroom Home, 2 Bathrooms, Home Office, Internal Laundry, Open Plan Living, Large Galley Kitchen, 1 Car Off Street Parking.

Ground Floor

1st Floor Addition

We bought this property for $720,000, plus $30,000 in acquisition costs, then we obtained development approval for the higher and better use. Renovation costs were $390,000, after which the property was revalued by the bank at $1,750,000. An additional $600,000 in equity was gained through a four-month structural renovation, proving lucrative renovation profits can be made if you know how to do it right.

What about exempt and complying (E and C) development? This is a type of development approval you can get from council in as little as five to 10 days. It's fantastic for structural renovators because it allows you to demolish parts of a property, rebuild and add to it without needing to go through the whole development application process.

E and C applications are quick, virtually fuss-free development applications that allow structural renovators to get in and do the work without too much delay. However, there is a catch.

RENOVATING FOR PROFIT

You will be required to meet council's criteria on things such as building height, floor to space ratio and be limited on how much extra space you can add without going through the full development process. Each council differs so be sure to visit your local council chambers or download their exempt and complying development plan from their website. Most people don't even know this type of development application exists. It's this type of knowledge that can save you thousands upon thousands of dollars.

For structural renovators, the chart below details the typical process you can expect to go through to gain formal development approval for your unrenovated dump.

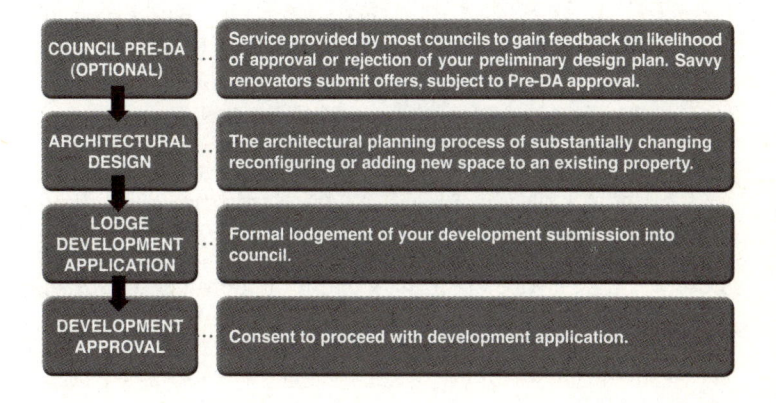

COUNCIL PRE-DA (OPTIONAL)	Service provided by most councils to gain feedback on likelihood of approval or rejection of your preliminary design plan. Savvy renovators submit offers, subject to Pre-DA approval.
ARCHITECTURAL DESIGN	The architectural planning process of substantially changing reconfiguring or adding new space to an existing property.
LODGE DEVELOPMENT APPLICATION	Formal lodgement of your development submission into council.
DEVELOPMENT APPROVAL	Consent to proceed with development application.

Yes, structural renovations do require more complex construction work than cosmetic renovations. All property owners are entitled to one owner/builder permit every five years through the Department of Fair Trading. If you go down this track, detailed construction knowledge won't be essential but, of course, it will certainly help.

BONUS! FREE gifts at www.TGRProperty.com.au/Gifts

More importantly, if you want to do structural renovations but don't want to do any of the construction work yourself, that's fine also. There are a lot of people making unbelievable profits by engaging a builder or experienced project manager to handle the renovation/construction side for them. If anything, these people end up making more money because they've got experienced people working on-site, saving them time and money.

Another alternative option for structural renovators is to get their builder or project manager to renovate their properties to lock-up stage, the point where all structural elements are completed. The renovator then comes in and takes over the cosmetic fit-out, an easy way to save costs and increase your experience at the same time.

CHERIE AND STEVE'S FORMULA TO CREATING A HIGHER AND BETTER USE FOR A PROPERTY

1. Buy a two or three-bedroom rundown property and turn it into a four or five-bedroom luxury family home.

2. Rework the layout to accommodate a large galley-style kitchen.

3. Rework the layout so the main bathroom becomes the size of a bedroom.

4. Use materials that look luxurious but don't cost the earth.

5. Renovate the property to a level where it makes a positive contribution to the streetscape.

6. Add "wow" features to lure in emotional buyers.

7. Get in and out of the deal as quickly as possible. Time is money.

8. Never get emotional about the property.

RENOVATING FOR PROFIT

Here's a small sample of some of the "wow" factors we include in our cosmetic and structural renovations. Large galley-style kitchens with 90cm appliances, long deep drawers, metallic polyurethane cabinetry and CaesarStone® bench tops. Our bathrooms have a luxury day spa feel about them and feature large solid stone baths with TVs recessed into the wall, double showers and designer taps and tiles. All these inclusions are designed to emotionally lure buyers to our properties.

STEP SEVEN:
THE RENOVATION PROCESS

Now that you've purchased your property, it's time to start the transformation. Got no clue where to start? Looking for some tricks of the trade? Take comfort that you're already a significant way through the renovation process, even though you haven't yet lifted a hammer. So many people get caught up in the physical renovation, they overlook the fact that most of the skill and hard work is really in the buying phase of steps one through to five.

The good news is that you don't need to be a builder or a tradesperson to successfully profit from renovations. As a professional renovator, either cosmetic or structural, your job is about effective project management. Whether you choose to do

BONUS! FREE gifts at www.TGRProperty.com.au/Gifts

all or some of the work yourself is entirely up to you. If you're starting out in your very first cosmetic renovation it's likely you'll be undertaking a large chunk of the work yourself, for no other reason than to earn sweat equity.

Many cosmetic renovators continue to do as much of the work themselves, project after project. Cosmetic renovations typically generate lower profits than major structural renovations but are done in a much quicker timeframe. In theory, doing all or some of the work yourself – especially in tasks that require very little skill – can put extra profit in the cosmetic renovator's back pocket. While that's very admirable and is a great way to build up small profit margins on a frequent basis, structural renovators need to take a different approach.

The reality is that we are on our renovation sites every day, working Monday to Friday from 7am to 3pm. Yes, we keep tradie hours. That makes us very hands-on, though not to the point where we are digging trenches or up to our arms in concrete. We are on-site for one reason: to effectively manage the project and co-ordinate our team so things happen when they should. Our most productive time on-site is spent on the phone, sourcing tradespeople we don't have, negotiating with suppliers and organising timely delivery of our materials. Being on-site also means you're there to deal with any problems that may pop up in the renovation process, allowing decisions to be made immediately so work can continue without any delays. This is your job as a structural renovator, to manage the entire project and not the actual work itself.

EFFECTIVE PROJECT MANAGEMENT
How well you go about transforming your derelict dump really comes down to your ability to be an effective project manager. Cosmetic and structural renovators who have their projects under control focus on three crucial elements:

1) Quality control
2) Time control
3) Cost control.

QUALITY CONTROL – Poor quality shows. Most buyers today undertake building and pest inspections so if poor quality doesn't get you now, it will get you later – and later is too late for you to fix it. Unfortunately, bad tradespeople exist and the really bad tradespeople are usually the ones available to do the job. Your project management role is to sort the good from the bad and ensure tasks are done to an acceptable level of quality. You don't need to bother yourself with all the complexities of how roof sheeting is attached to the batons or what size door jambs you may need. You're employing experts, your tradespeople, to do that for you. Give them some professional credit that they know what they're doing and won't screw it up. Quality control can be managed by having some understanding of the scope of the work you want performed. Be clear about what you want done, the quality level you expect and the end result you're looking for.

TIME CONTROL – When it comes to renovating, time is of the essence. This is where the professional renovator beats the amateurs hands down. Successful renovators get in and out of the deal as quickly as possible, as they know what the project is costing them on a daily basis. Our properties have an average holding cost of $230 a day. Every day that ticks by without substantial work on-site is another $230 in profit we don't get at the end of the project. If our renovation timeline blows out by as little as two weeks we lose $3,220 in profit, simply by not controlling the time factor. Time is money and once you lose that money there's no way to get it back. Poor time control can wipe out your entire profit. Furthermore, not controlling time can lead to more disastrous implications if you miss the ideal timing for your property to hit the market. The key is to get quotes in early, never at the last minute, and order materials that have long lead times early enough that your project is not delayed.

COST CONTROL - It's easy to lose track of costs, especially if unforeseen problems arise during the renovation. All too often, you're so focused on controlling the time factor that you resolve problems in the quickest manner possible, without considering the real cost implications. Therefore, it's important that you always start your renovation with your financial feasibility close at hand. If you plan and control where your renovation funds are spent you can protect the lump of gold waiting for you at the end of it all. Constantly remind yourself that every dollar saved is an extra dollar you've earned in profit.

Regardless of whether you're doing cosmetic or structural renovations you should always be thinking, "How can I create perceived value at the least possible cost?" There are exhaustive lists of ways you can keep your renovation costs low and countless tricks of the trade. Here's our top 10 ways to keep your renovation costs low:

1. Do some or all of the work yourself;

2. Negotiate and renegotiate everything, including supplies and labour;

3. Bulk orders mean bulk discounts – find suppliers who can give you everything you need;

4. Open trade accounts with key suppliers, which will give you further discounts on trade prices;
5. Simplify your design so you use more of one item, such as tiles, instead of multiple smaller items;

6. Get suppliers to compete against each other to keep prices low;

7. Buy materials and goods from auction sites;

8. Look for good quality second hand materials;

9. Buy cheaper imitations of more expensive items;

10. Enlist the help of family and friends to keep labour costs down.

THE ACTION PLAN
How can you effectively manage a project if you don't have a plan of attack? Good software programs are available to help in this regard, including Microsoft Project. It's important to get the renovating process right, with everything in the correct sequential order so that tradespeople can come in at the right time and complete the tasks that will keep your project moving forward. This is called your Renovation Project Plan.

A question you'll come across will be, is it better to renovate one room at a time or bring tradespeople in one step at a time? If you didn't have a renovation project plan you'd be hard pressed to answer this. Your project plan tells you what you need to do, when you need to do it and what materials you need to have on-site for those tasks to be completed. It gives you the ability to make good project management decisions and the ability to think in advance. It's this planning that will keep your costs on track, as you won't have to call tradespeople out at the last minute or do emergency rework.

What will give you more delight than the money in your bank account at the end is the fact that you only need to do a detailed

STEPHEN TOLLE & CHERIE BARBER

renovation project plan once. For every subsequent project you can simply modify your first plan as needed. Put one whole day aside to create your renovation project plan template. If you're overwhelmed by that thought you can purchase one or get someone knowledgeable in construction to do one for you. Either way, your renovation project plan is one of those things that are not negotiable. Don't fail to plan – plan to win.

We've attached a partial section of ours to give you an idea of what's involved:

PROJECT PLAN - 66 MORT ST

ID	Task Name	Duration	Start	Finish
1	DEMOLITION STAGE	5 days	Sat 4/03/06	Thu 9/03/06
2	Demolish Deck	1 day	Sat 4/03/06	Sat 4/03/06
3	Remove all internal fixtures & fittings	1 day	Tue 7/03/06	Tue 7/03/06
4	Demolish relevant sections of house	2 days	Tue 7/03/06	Wed 8/03/06
5	Remove waste from site	1 day	Thu 9/03/06	Thu 9/03/06
6				
7	EXCAVATION STAGE	30.5 days	Fri 10/03/06	Thu 20/04/06
8	Disconnect & relocate gas mains	5 days	Fri 10/03/06	Wed 15/03/06
9	Excavate backyard	2 days	Fri 10/03/06	Sat 11/03/06
10	Dig footings	1 day	Mon 13/03/06	Mon 13/03/06
11	Rough in Gas lines	0.5 days	Mon 13/03/06	Mon 13/03/06
12	Rough in plumbing	0.5 days	Mon 13/03/06	Mon 13/03/06
13	Install retaining walls	2 days	Mon 13/03/06	Wed 15/03/06
14	Install formwork	0.5 days	Thu 16/03/06	Thu 16/03/06
15	Arrange council inspection No. 1 & 2	30 mins	Thu 16/03/06	Thu 16/03/06
16	Council Inspection - Approval to Proceed	1 hr	Fri 17/03/06	Fri 17/03/06
17	Pour concrete slab	0.5 days	Fri 17/03/06	Fri 17/03/06
18	Slab Curing Time	24 days	Fri 17/03/06	Thu 20/04/06
19				
20	FRAMING STAGE	32.94 days	Thu 20/04/06	Tue 6/06/06
21	Arrange for timber to be delivered on site	1 day	Thu 20/04/06	Fri 21/04/06
22	Install structural frame to rear section	5 days	Fri 21/04/06	Fri 28/04/06
23	Arrange council inspection No. 3	30 mins	Fri 28/04/06	Fri 28/04/06
24	Council Inspection - Approval to Proceed	1 day	Fri 28/04/06	Mon 1/05/06
25	Check measure - glass skylights	0.5 days	Mon 1/05/06	Tue 2/05/06
26	Production Time - Glass Skylights	8 days	Tue 2/05/06	Fri 12/05/06
27	Install new frame to ground floor bathroom window	0.5 days	Mon 1/05/06	Tue 2/05/06
28	Check Measure - Aluminium Doors & Windows	3 hrs	Tue 2/05/06	Tue 2/05/06
29	Production Time - Aluminium Doors & Windows	20 days	Tue 2/05/06	Tue 30/05/06
30	Install new frame to Bedroom 2 window	0.5 days	Tue 2/05/06	Tue 2/05/06
31	Install new frame to Bedroom 3 window	0.5 days	Tue 2/05/06	Tue 2/05/06
32	Install new frame to Bedroom 3 door	0.5 days	Tue 2/05/06	Tue 2/05/06
33	Check measure - timber windows & doors	0.5 days	Tue 2/05/06	Wed 3/05/06
34	Production Time - Timber Windows	8 days	Wed 3/05/06	Mon 15/05/06
35	Install timber windows	2 days	Mon 15/05/06	Wed 17/05/06
36	Install aluminium windows & doors	5 days	Tue 30/05/06	Tue 6/06/06
37	Install glass skylights	1 day	Fri 12/05/06	Mon 15/05/06
38				
39	ROOF INSTALLATION	6 days	Wed 12/04/06	Wed 19/04/06
40	Delivery of roofing materials to site	1 day	Wed 12/04/06	Wed 12/04/06
41	Install new roofing	5 days	Thu 13/04/06	Wed 19/04/06
42				

BONUS! FREE gifts at www.TGRProperty.com.au/Gifts

RENOVATING FOR PROFIT

THE BEST WAY TO EFFECTIVELY MANAGE YOUR RENOVATION

- Have a Renovation Project Plan, listing key actions and timing.

- Decide whether to manage the project or do it yourself.

- Establish your chain of supply.

- Establish a good team of tradespeople.

- Negotiate hard with tradespeople.

- Understand that lost time means lost money.

DEALING WITH TRADIES

Tradespeople are an interesting bunch. Quite simply, you'll either love them or loath them. If you're going to lose the plot and blow a fuse at any time during your renovation, you can bet that one of your tradies has something to do with it. So how do you manage the relationship to meet the expectations of both parties? The big answer is to understand the needs of your tradies. Here are a few tips:

- Tradespeople want clear communication and direction so they know what you want done. They don't want to waste time listening to your stories of what you did on the weekend. Brief them clearly and with purpose, showing them photos or images that will help them visualise what you want. The more defined your communication, the less chance of errors.

- Be clear on your time constraints and what days you need them to work on your property. Ask for their agreement to this and make them aware of penalties caused by delays. If

BONUS! FREE gifts at www.TGRProperty.com.au/Gifts

tradespeople are clearly communicated to they will, in most circumstances, adhere to your requirements.

- Understand that tradies want to get in and get out as quickly as possible. Time is money to them too.

- Believe it or not, tradies like it when you ask for their opinion. If you're unsure of something, ask. It's free advice that can eliminate costly errors and save you money. Even today we still ask tradies for their help and opinions if we are unsure of something. Ninety-nine point nine per cent of the time they are only too happy to solve any problems for us.

- Tradies want to be treated with respect. Regardless of what some people may think, they have not had to resort to physical work because they don't have the intellectual means to do anything else. Tradespeople study at length to become skilled in their respective areas. It's not just physical work, it's often also mentally challenging. We always treat our tradespeople with respect and take extra care to let them know their skills are appreciated. Always tell them they've done a great job, as long as they truly have. They'll appreciate your comments and will want to work for you again.

- Pay on time. The constant bane of a tradesperson's existence is wondering when they will get paid. If your tradesperson turns up on time, does a good job and completes everything you ask without any hassle, then do the right thing and pay them immediately. Tradies love working for us simply because we pay them right at the end of the job. There's no chasing money or hearing excuses about how the cheque is in the mail.

RENOVATING FOR PROFIT

When dealing with tradespeople, ensure they are licensed and carry their own insurance policies. Don't be tempted to use anyone who doesn't have insurance. What may save you initially could cost you thousands later in law suits if an injury occurs. Don't ever risk it.

Negotiating labour costs with tradies can be fun. We drive hard bargains with our tradespeople in return for them being our preferred workers and getting all of our renovation work. The reality is that if they like you they'll want to work for you and will negotiate on price. If they don't like you, they'll be less willing to negotiate. Of course, your ability to negotiate will also depend on how much work the tradesperson has to keep themself, and any staff they may have, busy.

Sometimes little things can make a huge difference. We allocate a small portion of our renovation budget to keeping the trade workers on our renovation sites happy. Every day they're supplied with coffee, tea or cold drinks and, if they've picked a good day, sometimes cakes. It's a little gesture that goes a long way. We've often been told that people love working for us, simply because of the free food and coffee. Small but meaningful thank you gifts, such as a $20 Lotto ticket, are just some of the ways we express our appreciation for jobs well done. Of course, we always say there is a catch. If they do win Lotto, they don't have to work for anybody ever again – except us.

WORKABLE STRATEGY NUMBER 4: HOW YOU CAN FIND GOOD QUALITY TRADESPEOPLE

- Drive around to other people's renovation/building sites in your area and get details from tradies working there.

BONUS! FREE gifts at www.TGRProperty.com.au/Gifts

- Take a drive between 6-7am or 3-4pm. That's when the roads are full of tradies' utes and trucks, driving to and from work. Most tradies have their contact details on their vehicles. Look around, you'll have a smorgasbord of numbers to save in the memory of your mobile phone.

- Ask tradespeople if they know other good tradies. In the construction game, all the tradies have links to each other.

- Visit building industry websites, such as MBA and HIA, that have registered tradies listed.

There are thousands of tips we could share with you to handle the renovation process. Here are a few of the more pertinent points:

- Always make safety a top priority during your renovation. Insurance policies are available to safeguard you against accidents. Your tradespeople should always have their own insurance, so ensure you get a copy of their policy before they commence work on your property.

- If you're just starting out in renovation and want to tackle most of the work yourself, be careful not to undertake any work that breaches building code regulations or work that requires licensed tradespeople such as electricians and plumbers.

- Maintain a renovation site diary that you can use to record the details of tradespeople coming and going, contact details, prices quoted, the various stages of work, expenses incurred and any other key bits of information it might be helpful to record.

RENOVATING FOR PROFIT

- Get in the habit of updating your expense log (the actual column in your financial feasibility) every day. You'll be amazed at how fast money rolls out your door and how quickly you've forgotten what you've paid out. You want to be in a position at the end to work out what profit you actually made, right down to the last cent.

- If you want a free holiday to get over your intense two-month renovation, get in the habit of charging anything and everything to your credit card. Goods, materials and even some tradespeople can be paid with a credit card. Do your homework on which banks have the best credit card reward programs. We get two free international round-the-world airline tickets at the end of every renovation, simply by charging everything to our cards. It doesn't take long to rack up the points when renovating.

WORKABLE STRATEGY NUMBER 5: HOW YOU CAN GET 10 – 30 PER CENT OFF GOODS AND MATERIALS

One of your main aims as a professional renovator is to renovate your property for the least possible cost. Get into the mindset that if you're paying retail price for anything, you're paying too much. When you pay retail price you cut into your final profit. Tell your suppliers you're a professional renovator and don't be afraid to ask for trade price. Don't ever tell them you're renovating your own home. If you do, you'll pay retail price.

TIP 1 – BULK QUANTITIES MEAN BULK SAVINGS

If doing a single renovation, make a complete list of all the materials and goods you'll need to purchase for that property. Type up a Quotation Request, listing the items you need, and email it out to as many suppliers as you can. Suppliers love bulk orders and will give you a greater discount in order to win a large order. If you're doing multiple renovations at the same time it's even better.

BONUS! FREE gifts at www.TGRProperty.com.au/Gifts

TIP 2 – FORCE SUPPLIERS TO BE COMPETITIVE

Take your quotes to other suppliers. Avoid showing them, where possible, but ask if they can do a better price than what you already have. Nine out of 10 times, you can get the price even lower still. We filter our quotes in this manner. By the time we get to the fifth or sixth supplier we have hit the absolute rock-bottom price. When suppliers start saying no, you know you've got a good price on your goods and materials. In return for their reduced profit margins, we make them our preferred supplier and reward them with continuous business.

TIP 3 – SIMPLIFY YOUR DESIGN TO OBTAIN COST SAVINGS

By thinking carefully about the design of your renovation up front, you can save yourself substantial money. Ever heard of the phrases "less is more" and "keep it simple"? Think carefully about the materials you need. Do you really need different tiles in each bathroom? Do you need different tiles for the floor and wall or could you use one tile for both? The more you need of one material, the greater chance of getting a significant discount based on quantity. If you order small quantities of different tiles, you're likely to pay retail price.

TIP 4 – THINK OUTSIDE THE SQUARE WHEN ORDERING MATERIALS

If you need to buy a large quantity of materials for your project, it's worth taking a quick flight overseas to countries such as China and Thailand to pick materials up at a fraction of the cost. We once had two renovations on the go at a time and needed 1200 m^2 of tiles across all of them. A quick flight overseas enabled us to buy these tiles for a landed cost of $36 m^2, which compared well to the $140 m^2 it would have cost in Australia. Instead of paying $168,000 for these tiles we paid just $43,200, a whopping saving of $122,800 after taking out the $2,000 cost of the airfare. In doing this, you need to be savvy in which suppliers you deal with. You have to constantly ask yourself, how can I get this item cheaper?

TIP 5 – ALWAYS ASK FOR TRADE PRICE

Always, always ask for trade price. The fact that you're not a licensed tradesperson is totally irrelevant. You're a professional renovator in the construction industry. That gives you instant qualification to receive trade pricing. Expect to receive at least five to 10 per cent off the retail price in the blink of an eyelid.

Lastly, it's worth getting your hands dirty on your first couple of renovation projects. Not only will it give you a new found appreciation for tradespeople but it will give you a great understanding of the whole renovation process from start to finish. This knowledge will help you refine your own processes and perfect them accordingly. More effective processes lead to increased profits.

STEP EIGHT:
THE RESALE PROCESS

You're on the home stretch now and are keen to convert your trash into that big wad of cash. With your dump almost transformed, now is the time to find its new owner. So how do you go about finding the right buyer, the one who will give you the highest price possible?

In our experience, the key resale factors that a renovator needs to consider are:

1. Pre-sale opportunities
2. Selecting the right agent
3. Timing the market

BONUS! FREE gifts at www.TGRProperty.com.au/Gifts

4. Professionally present the property
5. The type of sale process
6. The legal exchange.

PRE-SALE OPPORTUNITIES - Why wait until the very end of your renovation to sell it? Ask yourself, can we sell the property before it's finished or should we wait until it's completed so buyers can see and touch everything? We pre-sold our fourth renovation. We bought the property for $736,000 and pre-sold it as a "renovation off-the-plan" two days after we got the keys. We managed to secure a buyer and agreed to renovate the property for them within a four month timeframe at a sale price of $1,410,000. That meant there was no agent's commission and no marketing fees, not to mention the security of having a guaranteed profit at the end of it all. Happy days! It was a win for all. We walked away with a handsome profit and the buyers got a home customised to suit their tastes and desires in half the time that it would have taken a builder to do it.

SELECTING THE RIGHT AGENT - Finding a good agent is critical. The wrong agent will cost you thousands of dollars in lost profit. If you've mastered steps two and three (the market and property due diligence), you should already know who the good, bad and very bad agents are in your area. You need to find an agent who is a "closer", someone with the ability to get the deal done at the highest possible price but who is approachable enough to be liked by the buyer. You see, there are a lot of really nice agents out there but many of them are too soft when handling price negotiations or have difficulty counteracting lower price offers for fear of upsetting either the buyer or seller. When doing your homework on everything else, make sure you research agents as well. Some are great to buy from, others you would never sell with.

RENOVATING FOR PROFIT

TIMING THE MARKET - Did you know that some months are better for selling your property than others? In Australia, the prime selling season for real estate is in Spring and Autumn when the weather is pleasant for home hunters, lawns are green and flowers are in bloom. While this is the common theory amongst most people playing the property market, it's important to realise there are two sides to the coin. More properties are placed on the market during these periods, which gives buyers a larger pool to choose from. This can result in a drop in the number of buyers per property, thereby diminished competition and somewhat lower price offers. On the flip side, Winter and the Christmas/New Year holiday periods have fewer available properties so there's greater competition for the same number of qualified buyers. Competition between buyers is good because it will draw out their best price offers. Either way, the best time to sell your property is when the supply versus demand balance tips in your favour. When you look at this more closely, there are pros and cons to selling at any time of the year and there is definitely no right or wrong time. Some people search for a year or more before they find a property that suits them. As renovators, just give some thought to the time you go to market and your own personal circumstances at that point.

PROFESSIONALLY PRESENT THE PROPERTY - We've all heard the saying that first impressions count and it's crucial that the first impression your property makes strikes the right emotional chord with buyers. To do this, your property needs to be presented at its best to increase the speed of your sale.

The key here is property styling, sometimes referred to as property staging. Property styling aims to improve the overall appeal of a property by removing clutter, improving the sense of space, maximising functionality of rooms and bringing in furniture and accessories that make the property look new,

BONUS! FREE gifts at www.TGRProperty.com.au/Gifts

refreshed and welcoming. Believe it or not, many buyers have difficulty visualising how rooms within a property can be used. Quite often it's the styling that emotionally lures buyers into the property and it's what can make an ordinary property look extraordinary. On our very first renovation, we hired a property stylist. On settlement day the buyers came to the property for their pre-settlement check. They told the agent the property wasn't as appealing and looked different with all the furniture out. That's largely because they were drawn to the styling and not the actual house.

Property styling can be expensive. Depending on the value of your property, you can either do it yourself or hire a professional stylist (interior decorator) to do everything for you. Over the years, we've built up an inventory of our own furniture and furnishings by simply keeping an eye out for discounted decorator items in garage sales, on eBay, at store clearance sales and so on. If you're keen to renovate professionally and anticipate doing renovations on a regular basis, this is a great way to reduce your overall property styling costs.

If you're going to head in that direction, make sure you buy contemporary pieces. White furniture always looks great and can be dressed up with colourful decorator items such as vases, artworks and cushions. Always choose furniture that is modern and sleek to give the illusion of space in your property. Don't put nanna's big fat puffy lounges in your renovated property. It will reduce the sense of space and will do nothing to give your property a new, modern feel.

If you want to tackle the styling yourself, here are a few suggestions to keep costs low:

RENOVATING FOR PROFIT

1. Visit display homes to get an idea of how they style their properties.

2. Use your own furniture (if suitable) to style your property. In our early days, we substituted our own lounge for a couple of milk crates during our property marketing period.

3. Visit discount variety stores. You'll be amazed at how cheap you can buy decorator items in such places.

4. Garage sales are a great opportunity to pick up furniture or decorator items for next to nothing.

Property styling is unquestionably a great way to increase the overall desirability of your property, especially if there is an air of quality about it. Importantly, be smart enough to know that women have a stronger influence than their male counterparts on the decision to buy a property. Style the property with her in mind but don't go over the top.

Professional property styling in one of our properties. Note the use of contemporary furniture with neutral colour schemes. Furniture is kept to a minimum to give rooms a spacious, modern feel.

Unlike most other property sellers, we look for easy and effective ways to present our property in the best possible light. Apart from styling, we put up a small wall chart that details the key features in each room. These small signs are an effective way to

BONUS! FREE gifts at www.TGRProperty.com.au/Gifts

communicate all the positive aspects of the property without relying on the agent, who can sometimes get tied down answering prospective buyers' questions. We also produce our own "Property Fact Sheet" that is given to anyone who inspects it. This guide itemises all the positive features of the property, allowing buyers to see its true value.

THE TYPE OF SALE PROCESS - Think outside the square when selling your property. To make your property stand out, be different, creative or do something that really draws people when it's open for inspection. For our very first renovation, we held the auction at 7.30pm on a Friday instead of the normal Saturday auction time. We put 200 invitations in the letterboxes of residents within the surrounding streets, asking them to join us for a catered party and auction with waiters, drinks and hors d'oeuvres. We'd designed the house to be an entertaining home so this was a great way to highlight the property's key feature. It happened to be raining that night but we still managed to attract more than 150 people to the auction, which created an electric buzz of excitement through the property. People were overheard talking about how fantastic the property was; surely buyers would be hearing such comments. Our reserve was $840,000 and we sold the property for $955,000, breaking the suburb record at the time. The cost of the party was less than $500 but we believe it brought us at least $55,000 extra because it started a bidding war between three emotional bidders.

THE LEGAL EXCHANGE - Smart renovators know where they should and shouldn't spend money. Find yourself a good lawyer, one who specialises in property law and can professionally manage your legal dealings. Always have a rock solid contract that protects you, one that it's hard for buyers to get out of.

RENOVATING FOR PROFIT

CONCLUSION

Phew! Renovating may not be as simple as you first thought. Like anything, your first renovation project will be a huge learning experience. Just remember, there are always solutions to your renovating problems. And rest assured, the more renovation projects you do, the easier it all becomes. Practice truly does make perfect. Learn from each project by reflecting on what you did well and what you could have done better, then take that knowledge and use it to make your next renovation project even better.

We're honest enough to admit that renovating can be hard work, depending on how much or how little you want to be involved in your projects. We now choose to do only two structural renovations per year. We work four or five months a year and then take seven or eight months off. In effect, we're on holiday eight times longer than most people in salaried jobs. The reality is that our hard work is rewarded with huge renovation profits, the ability to be our own boss, extended holiday periods and free holidays overseas (from all the credit card points earned during our renovations). It really can give you a fabulous lifestyle.

Renovating has truly improved every aspect of our lives. We get to choose when we work and for how long. We get to be involved in something we truly love, rather than trudging every day into a job that we hate. We have the ability to share our wealth with family, friends and charities. When Steve's dad was struck down by cancer and unable to work, it was our renovation profits that allowed us to pay out his mortgage. Very few other jobs would have given us the ability to do that. There are so many benefits to renovating and you'll never really understand them all until you go through the process yourself.

BONUS! FREE gifts at www.TGRProperty.com.au/Gifts

Additionally, for us, there is nothing more fulfilling than standing on the street in front of our completed project, in awe of the amazing transformation that's just taken place. We've taken an unwanted, derelict dump and created a beautiful home for a family to enjoy for years to come. It's a level of personal satisfaction that can't be described.

As a renovator, it's important to create properties that make a positive contribution to the street and community you're in. Always try and do the right thing and don't negatively impact the lives of others in favour of greed. Be proud of your renovation projects and how you got there. Others will notice and will have more respect for you. They'll be keen to be involved with you on your next project.

Finally, to recap, our renovating success has come down to our precise ability to:

1) Know what types of homes are in short supply

2) Buy properties that can satisfy the market need

3) Renovate the property beyond buyers' emotional expectations.

Truly, anyone can be successful in property renovations. You don't need to be super intelligent or great on the tools. Renovation doesn't discriminate between male or female. In fact, more and more smart women are jumping on the renovation band wagon these days and capitalising on the male-dominated construction industry. Women have natural skills that men just can't match, which work perfectly with renovations. Regardless of whether you have a lot of money or none at all, renovating can build wealth for you – fast.

RENOVATING FOR PROFIT

Make sure you celebrate your successes and reward yourself appropriately. Good luck, may the force – trade force that is – be with you.

FREE BONUS GIFT

Stephen Tolle and Cherie Barber have generously offered two FREE BONUS GIFTS valued at $59.90

FREE **How to do a Renovation Financial Feasibility Tips Sheet** plus FREE **Trades Register Template** - Keep the contact details of all your tradies in one handy place for when you're in the thick of it on-site!

Visit the website below to receive these free gifts
www.TGRProperty.com.au/Gifts

Chapter 3
POSITIVE CASHFLOW PROPERTY

"Profits are better than wages."

SAM SAGGERS

SAM SAGGERS

Sam Saggers is a co-founder and CEO of Positive Real Estate, a leading buyer's agency and education company. A licensed real estate agent in every Australian city, Sam has personally brokered over 1,500 property deals in his 15-year career.

Having bought, sold and traded property for more than a decade, Sam established Positive Real Estate in 2003 to provide services for the thousands of Australian investors who lacked either the time or the expertise to locate, negotiate and purchase residential investment property. In recent years, the service has been extended to include educational seminars and programs that empower and teach clients to be successful property investors in their own right.

Through Positive Real Estate, Sam has helped to educate more than 5,000 people in real estate principles. His mission is to help ordinary people do extraordinary things! His company has worked hard to earn an excellent reputation within the Australian real estate market and is renowned for sourcing properties that offer high rental or capital yields at a low entry point. Many of Australia's top CEO's, as listed in *Business Review Weekly's* Rich 200, often call on Sam's advice to understand the trends and forecasts of the marketplace.

Sam has been featured in *Your Investment Property* and *Australian Property Investor* magazines. He is a world-class keynote speaker on real estate and has recently founded the Property Wholesalers Co-operative.

POSITIVE CASHFLOW PROPERTY

DISCOVER THE EIGHT FUNDAMENTALS TO MAKE EVERY PROPERTY IN YOUR PORTFOLIO CASHFLOW POSITIVE

There's a key phrase that's been embedded in my memory ever since I read *Think and Grow Rich*: "Anybody can wish for riches and most people do, but only a few know that a definite plan, plus a burning desire for wealth, are the only dependable means of accumulating wealth." The book has had a tremendous influence on me so it's a great privilege and pleasure to be asked to be part of this ground-breaking project.

For me, the greatest honour that can be bestowed on a person is that of serving others. It's my genuine hope that throughout this chapter you will start to sample some of the ideas, philosophies and fundamental principles that can serve your own wealth-creation. It was famous American motivational speaker Zig Ziglar who gave us the renowned quote: "If you give a man a fish he eats for a day. If you teach a man to fish he eats for a lifetime." My goal in this chapter is to teach you how to fish, direct you into a wider range of thinking and arm you with the knowledge, faith and – most importantly – the action to create long-lasting wealth through property investing.

First, though, I need something from you. I need you to walk into this with an open mind, accepting that anything is possible. I want you to recognise that no matter your background, be it rich or poor, the opportunities in this chapter apply to you and

BONUS! FREE gifts at www.TGRProperty.com.au/Gifts

can be used by absolutely everybody. I want you to be aware that there's nothing you can't do with a little bit of ingenuity. If you point to a person with drive and initiative you'll be looking at somebody who is no more than three to seven years away from a multi-million dollar self-sustaining property portfolio.

A study of history will reveal that the worst decisions were made by two kinds of people: those who couldn't swallow their own pride and those who became greedy. One of the most essential elements in wealth-creation through real estate is being able to manage your pride, while this is far from being a greed-driven chapter about getting rich quick. It's not so much about amassing an enormous fortune as it is about giving you the tools to live a good life.

When we reach the stage in our lives of reminiscing about our youth it becomes apparent why we were drawn to certain things. After toy soldiers my favourite game as a child was, without question, Monopoly. I would play this wonderful game for hours on end, not knowing I was establishing the framework for my later life. The game I now take part in is very similar, except that I'm playing on behalf of more than a thousand clients – including companies and even the occasional investment bank – and the dollars are very real. And I still love it. It's not just the economic reward that keeps me playing, though of course that is nice. What I enjoy most about the game is what I call "the art of the deal". I am fixated by deal-making and profit creation, both for myself and other people. Every day I get to take part in the grownup version of that same game I loved as a child, which is called the "Australian property market".

Just about everybody has played Monopoly and I still love the chance for a game. The simple reality is that even though it's meant as an entertaining board game its foundations are

POSITIVE CASHFLOW PROPERTY

very firmly set in reality. If you look beyond the dice and fake money you will see it's about the accumulation of assets and the monopolising of growth areas. It's adding value to real estate by accruing houses and hotels; it's mortgages, banks and real estate brokers; it's pitfalls and negotiation; it's a little bit of luck and lot of good personal management. Simply put, it's everything you see in the real market.

Since my childhood I've graduated from trading in Mayfair and Park Lane but the principles are still exactly the same. I help people buy assets that magnify their profits and put money into their pockets. Real money, that is. There's no fake paper cash in the real world.

ABOUT SAM SAGGERS...

For those who don't know me, my name is Sam Billy-Budd Saggers (yes, that's my real middle name but it's a story for another time). I own one of Australia's largest real estate buyer's agencies, called Positive Real Estate. I employ more than 30 full-time staff nation-wide and over the last seven years I've been personally involved in brokering over 1,500 individual real estate deals on behalf of more than 1,000 clients.

Next year will be my fifteenth in the industry, having started young and at the very bottom. I knew as soon as I finished high school that I wanted a career in real estate with the view of playing within the market. My first job was handing out pamphlets and letterbox-dropping homes for a sales agent friend of mine, which allowed me to tell people I was in marketing at the agency. Meanwhile, I studied real estate at college each night.

By age 19 I had become a senior property manager, which I greatly enjoyed. It was a fantastic learning experience and

BONUS! FREE gifts at www.TGRProperty.com.au/Gifts

it tested my skills, especially in negotiation. Early on in my twenties I recognised the direction I wanted to move towards, which was property sales, so I tried my hand at selling. I was an average sales person, neither the best nor the worst. I enjoyed that position as well but I knew I needed to start investing. I'd figured out that no matter what happened in my job or career, real wealth would come through owning property.

Young and naive, I bought my first property. I was so happy, honestly believing that all I had to do was buy property and watch its value increase. I had seen numerous friends make money through the process years before and I'd seen the pride it gave them to know their asset was a winner. I knew I could do the same so I raised the funds needed to invest.

I had found a property I thought ideal and was encouraged to buy the property by my workmates at my office, my licensee and my franchise. With their support I purchased it with great gusto. It was in the area I worked and that gave me confidence I was on to a winner. At the time of acquisition I was known as the "Unit Market Area Expert" - well that's what it said on my business card anyway.

I chose the property because it overlooked a park and was the most I could get for my money at the time in the area I lived and worked. I thought it was the right place to buy but of course I was totally wrong. We all pay for education in one way or another – the lesson that I'd bought the wrong property in the wrong market cost me $30,000 in hard savings.

Looking back, it was my naivety which resulted in me buying a dud. I obtained the property well after the growth cycle had hits its ceiling and I failed to negotiate well. I got caught up by my own emotions until I fell in love with the property and just had to have it. At the time of buying the property I didn't look at the true income and expense, I didn't conduct research at arms-length and I had no idea about the cashflow or growth potential. The decision to hand over my life savings of $30,000 as a deposit was entirely emotional. I soon discovered I was out of my depth and that I certainly wasn't the "unit area expert" that I had built myself up to be.

The property didn't go up in value and it began to take cash from my back pocket as it was negatively-geared in a heavy way. I could no longer save money because all my available funds were being diverted into the property. Effectively, my deposit was stuck and my money was not compounding. With no signs of growth, my only options were to cut and run from the investment or wait for the market cycle to start again. I assessed the situation and soon understood it would be years before the market regained strength. I decided to sell the property and ended up passing back to the market my life savings. The property was sold at a loss, leaving me both disgruntled and devastated.

Anyone who has lost opportunity or money begins to ask themselves, "How does this happen?" and "Why me?" I began soul-searching and looking at my peers within the real estate sector. I soon realised a fundamental problem. Real estate agents, my trusted peers and mentors, don't actually own real estate. Most of the agents I was associated with had no idea about investing. They didn't own property and, if they did, it was usually the family home rather than a wealth investment. They were not knowledgeable on property investments, deals or opportunities. Most of the salespeople were in the door one week and out the next, yet they were offering suggestions on what and where to buy. I was completely flabbergasted by a statistic I still find alarming: eight out of 10 agents in any office around the country don't own investment real estate but will happily sell or manage it.

I decided that's where I had gone wrong and asked the universe to deliver some people who knew the art of making money. That's when I met some business associates who had the idea of starting one of Australia's first buyer's agency groups. They had experience in owning real estate and building profit as well as funds, while I had time on my hands and the willingness to learn and create. When their guidance and finances combined with my determination we started Positive Real Estate and, as I have mentioned, to date we are privileged to have brokered over 1,500 real estate deals to help many, many people.

LET'S START...
Buying an investment property is a business decision, so it's important you treat real estate with the respect it requires. To maximise your profits it's wise to understand the fundamentals that will help you reach your goal.

At some stage every buyer is likely to suffer what is known as buyer's remorse. Questions pop into every investor's head when they ponder a property purchase. Have I bought well? Did I choose the best location? Will the property perform?

Psychologists would call this "uncertainty" but in property I think of it as a form of "illiteracy".

If more people took the time to understand the answers to these questions and actually schooled themselves in the art of buying property, wealth-creation wouldn't just be for the small percentile of Australians. It would be there for all to participate in, sharing the profits it can produce.

"PROFITS ARE BETTER THAN WAGES"
Here's another key phrase: "Profits are better than wages." The moment I understood this piece of philosophy I became rich

POSITIVE CASHFLOW PROPERTY

within the first seven years of my economic life. Here's the other key phrase that goes with it: "Anyone can buy a piece of real estate, but not everyone can buy a piece of real estate and make a profit."

If you fully accept that profits are better than wages it will serve you well for a life time. I wish somebody had taught it to me at school but I went for 12 years without hearing it once. It wasn't even mentioned at the real estate college I went to for a year and a half.

The goal of property investors in the market is to target optimistic returns. Understand that companies, banks and institutions are all hunting profits and that they're all hunting in the same safari park as you, called the Australian property market.

Of course, to learn how to create your own profits comes with time and experience. I can give you the benefit of my experience but you'll have to put your own time into it.

FUNDAMENTAL NUMBER ONE: UNDERSTAND EMOTIONS

The market place is made up of many emotions. The moment you let them enter your thought process when buying investment property, you spoil the deal. Don't taint the art of deal-making with your own personal tastes. Accept that most of us don't have the right tastes to return huge dollars. Property should be bought on the numbers and nothing more. If it "stacks up" and is feasible then it should be considered.

Avoid emotions at all costs. It's not the colour of the fence that makes your wealth, nor how big the kitchen is, nor even how beautiful the garden looks. What's really important is the numbers. Your only thought should be for how much profit is in a property or how it will perform over the long-term.

BONUS! FREE gifts at www.TGRProperty.com.au/Gifts

I like to explain it in this way. There are two buyers and two properties at the same point in the market. Person A in 2003, buys the worst looking property, a real dump of a place with a "horrible fence" in the Perth market. Person B, in the same year, buys a beautiful property with a magnificent kitchen and newly built fence in the Sydney market. Who made more profit? History tells us the Perth property market doubled after 2003 while the Sydney market went sideways. So Person A made the profits with an emotionless asset.

You need to divorce yourself from emotions, though you also need to understand they play a huge part in the market as a whole. The figure below shows the psychology of the market, from optimism to capitulation, all the way through to relief and hope. The market is a mixed bag of ups and downs.

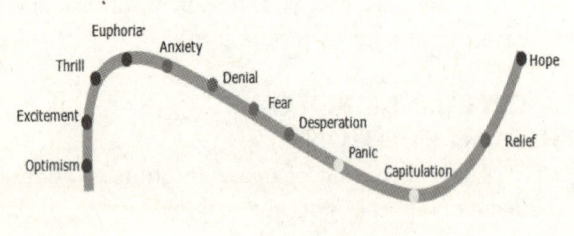

Market psychology

If you truly start to understand the market and comprehend its psychology you can make fabulous money. Most people buy when the market is "thrilled" or "euphoric", when the market has risen as much as it's going to and the chance to make massive profits has already passed.

You can make more money in "panicking" or "capitulated" markets, where there are a lot of cheap properties for sale. This is a good spot for another key phrase, this one from Warren Buffet:

"Show fear when everyone else shows courage and show courage when everyone else shows fear."

Everybody has that little voice in their head, the one that's designed to help them determine good from bad. However, it's not always accurate. Good can often turn bad and dreams can become nightmares. That's why you need to control your feelings. Acknowledge the market's sentiment, learn the vendor's emotions and you will start to profit from property. Move with your mind rather than your heart and you will develop the steely confidence that nothing is impossible.

FUNDAMENTAL NUMBER TWO: CASH ON CASH RETURNS

It's best to begin with a very brief explanation of what "cash on cash" actually means. When buying real estate, you need to find a deposit, which usually isn't provided by a bank or lender and generally has to come from your own savings. For a property transaction it can be anywhere between five and 30 per cent of the loan amount. The deposit is, essentially, your capital and it's never wise to invest capital unless you're sure you will get results. The formula that's used to measure the likely performance of your deposit is known as cash on cash return.

Cash on cash returns are the fundamental instrument to building a successful property portfolio. As you may now understand, when I started investing in property it was based on trial and error. The cash on cash investment principle was never explained to me. I bought a property with my life savings and injected $30,000 into the market that I couldn't afford to lose. When the market didn't grow I was unable to get that capital back in the form of equity.

BONUS! FREE gifts at www.TGRProperty.com.au/Gifts

Cash on cash is a term all investors should acquaint themselves with.

Seasoned investors measure cash on cash returns in 12-month increments. For example, if you were to put $30,000 in the market, accumulate the asset and achieve growth over 12 months to gain a further $30,000, this is considered to be a 100 per cent cash on cash return.

Put it this way: if you had $30,000 in the bank and at the end of 12 months you had your original $30,000 plus another $30,000, you would have a pretty good deal. Cash on cash is the same principle, only it's achieved through the property market. It allows you to secure and retain your asset but still have a readily available deposit to fund a new investment.

Control the Asset

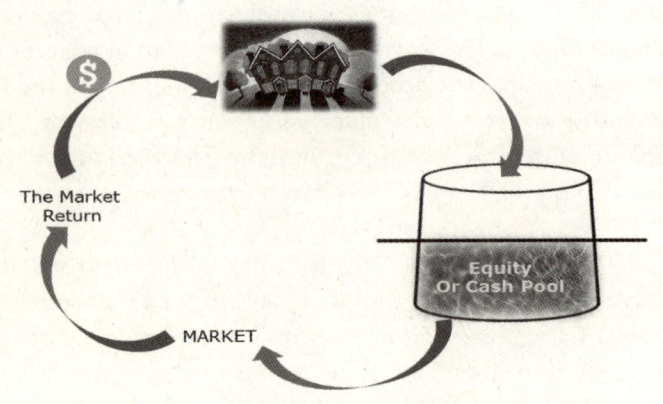

Know how much you intend to invest and recycle your initial investment within 12 - 18 months.

The cash on cash process

Return on capital is the true cornerstone of advancement. Never buy a property as an investment if you cannot get 100 per cent of your capital returned within 12 to 18 months.

FUNDAMENTAL NUMBER THREE: WHERE TO INVEST?

The words location, location, location seem to echo throughout the Australian property market. Beachside and waterside real estate, as well as those within a 10-kilometre radius of a CBD or major business centre, tend to be considered blue chip choices and over time have outperformed most other types of property within the market. Not everybody can afford a waterfront investment, though, so you need to learn about secondary markets as well.

Location is important but it's not the only fundamental, nor should it be the primary reason for purchase – even though the teaching faculty at my real estate college would have you believe that is the case.

One of the main points the lecturers would impress upon us ran as follows: "If an investor enters your office, your primary focus should be to assist them to purchase in the best location within their price range in your allocated area." I have no problem with this recommendation except when the area the investor is considering will not grow and cannot achieve a 100 per cent cash on cash return. The foremost problem with the Australian real estate industry is that it's run by shop keepers who are specialists in owner-occupied real estate and are determined to protect their patch of dirt. I can't imagine a suburban Sydney agent saying to an investor, "You know what? You're probably better off buying in Adelaide right now. It's really where the smart money is heading".

BONUS! FREE gifts at www.TGRProperty.com.au/Gifts

Not everyone can invest in premium localities, so if you're unable to get into the blue chip zones you should use the same fundamental principles in smaller secondary markets. Then, later, you can migrate your money to more premium growing locations. For years I've made money in secondary markets and transferred the profits to more qualified localities. Later in this chapter I'll show you how you can do it as well.

The six key market drivers

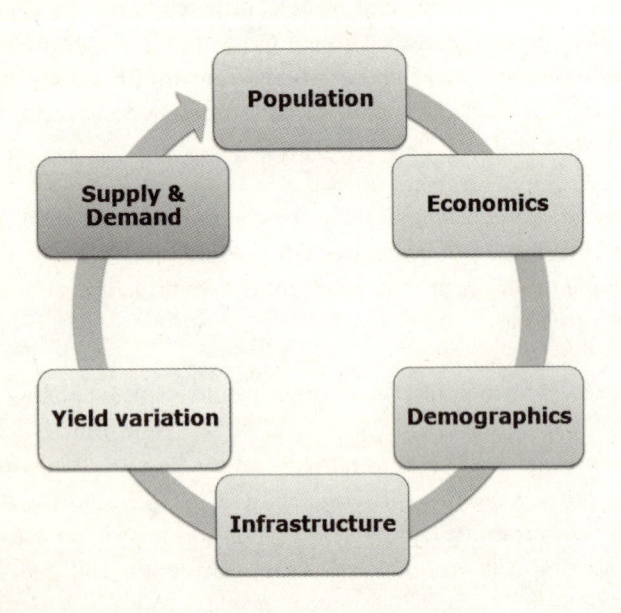

- Population
- Economics
- Demographics
- Infrastructure
- Yield variation
- Supply & Demand

Within any market, primary or secondary, there are indicators of the market's ability to perform. Understand the market drivers, become familiar with them and you will be able to forecast which areas will grow or trough. Whether it's from a suburb to a town or a city to a state, the same key market drivers exist.

POSITIVE CASHFLOW PROPERTY

The drivers are: population growth, economics, demographics, infrastructure, yield variation and supply and demand. Let's break it down with factual examples.

Population - Melbourne
By 2025 Melbourne's population is set to increase by over one million people, with more than 1,000 people relocating there every week. Last year's population growth was one of the city's largest rises, taking in both natural population increase and immigration. As well, the majority of overseas migrants are medium to high-income earners so they have the ability to buy and rent more properties. What effect do you think that will have on the Melbourne market?

Economics – February 2009
Interest rates are at their most affordable level since 1968. This will be a key driving point in house price growth and in sales volumes. The masses buy real estate in a 5.5 per cent interest rate market place.

Demographics
I always find demographics fascinating as the trends are constantly evolving with time. For example, changes in household structures mean Australians have an increased desire to reside alone. The higher divorce rate puts pressure on the property market because mum and dad both need separate homes.

Infrastructure
Developers and governments spend billions of dollars on infrastructure each year. If you can locate the infrastructure you will find the growth. Be sure the infrastructure is real and forthcoming, though, and not fictitious stories or fanciful hope.

BONUS! FREE gifts at www.TGRProperty.com.au/Gifts

SAM SAGGERS

Yield variation

This is a huge factor in the success of many areas. If yields are high, growth usually follows. Look for areas that are one to two per cent above their last five-year yield average and it's a sure sign growth is on the way. Yield variation is an instrument to gauge future growth of markets because as the yields expand, growth will follow and compress closer to already expanded yields. The further the yield advances, the more likely that a growth expansion phase will follow. Simply remember this: growth follows yields.

Supply and demand

At the time of writing, we are now in the middle of the biggest residential undersupply we have ever seen, some 180,000 dwellings short across Australia. The majority of the shortage is on the east coast of Queensland, New South Wales and Victoria. The Housing Industry of Australia believes that even if we started to build today at record pace – which was 17,000 houses per month when it peaked in 2001 – it would take years to return to an equilibrium. And we couldn't be further from record pace. In fact, right now our construction numbers are the lowest we have experienced in nearly a decade. In November 2008 we experienced the biggest decline in building approvals in eight years. All this information points to a scenario where demand significantly outweighs supply, meaning there will be a strain on the rental market over the approaching years. As consumer confidence returns, massive pressure will be placed on property prices. If you find the areas of undersupply you will be in prime position for growth.

Generally speaking, I look for a minimum of five out of the six key market drivers when I am considering investing in an area. Less than that and you won't have multiple factors working in harmony to fuel growth.

POSITIVE CASHFLOW PROPERTY

FUNDAMENTAL NUMBER FOUR:
WHEN TO INVEST?

"After expansion comes contraction but after contraction comes expansion." This is a simple thought but it can have a huge impact on what you do and a massive influence on when you should buy. Understand that 80 per cent of the market buys when the market is more than halfway through expansion, which is when I would sell rather than buy. You can make money no matter what the market is doing but investors will always make more by running counter to the cycle. For instance, in 2009 Sydney is the most majorly contracted market in Australia. Its economic emergence looms but buyers are wary. They shouldn't be. You can still buy well at a discount, assume your asset and position yourself for the start of the expansion phase of the property cycle.

Property investors should be aiming to buy at a discount when the property market is contracting and re-value the property when the market is expanding. Remember, profits are better than wages so buy low and sell high.

What I like about the Australian property market is that different states and cities go through growth cycles at different times, giving investors the opportunity to diversify their portfolios around the nation. We're able to use the varied growth cycles in the separate states and cities to always be investing in a market that's positioned for growth.

BONUS! FREE gifts at www.TGRProperty.com.au/Gifts

I'll give you a quick example. Five years ago Perth was in an opportunity phase on the property cycle, with lots of good indicators. Mining infrastructure was developing rapidly, the population was increasing, wages were high, unemployment was low and the city had not experienced a growth spurt higher than the four per cent per annum for more than six years (remember the seven to 10-year cycle). With these key market indicators aligned and the cycle poised for opportunity, investors who bought in Perth doubled their money within three years.

The property cycle over seven to 10 years

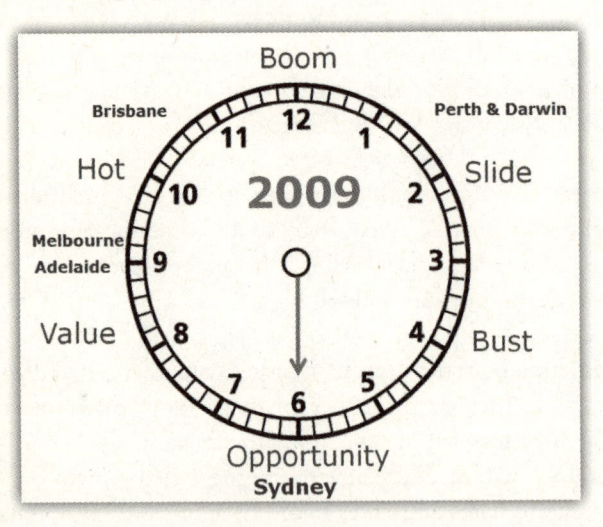

Property clock diagram showing 2009, with positions: Boom (12), Perth & Darwin / Slide (1-2), Bust (4-5), Opportunity / Sydney (6), Value (8), Melbourne / Adelaide (9), Hot (10), Brisbane (11).

Understand the property clock

Boom – This is the ceiling on market growth within any normal cycle. Its length is roughly six months and its corresponding psychology is euphoria.

Slide - After the expansion is over and the ceiling has been reached, property will slide in value by five to 10 per cent. This usually goes for a year and is accompanied by denial.

Trough - Property markets will flow above the Consumer Price Index (CPI) at a rate of three to four per cent growth. This can go for up to five years and the matching psychology is fear and desperation.

Opportunity – This is a risk market but also an opportunity market. At the bottom of the economic cycle there are small sale volumes but great value buying. This lasts for about a year and the corresponding psychology is capitulation.

Value – The market indicators are easy to read and they point towards growth, which is already happening with more certain to follow. This lasts for three years and the general feelings are of hope and optimism.

Hot – The expansion occurred and all buyers are believers. This is a fantastic market for selling but a poor one for buying. It lasts for a year and the psychology is excitement and thrill.

FUNDAMENTAL NUMBER FIVE: THE COMMODITIES

To make the most out of the market you need to arm yourself with the best tools. There are commodities in the property market you should buy, much like the commodities - gold, futures, stock, bonds, etc. – that exist in the stock market. Understanding how to best use the properties as commodities within the market is the key. First, though, let's discuss what the commodities are so we can consider how the categories relate to the market cycle.

THE FIVE RESIDENTIAL COMMODITIES ARE:

1. Discount
2. Renovation
3. Strata subdivision
4. Subdivision
5. Off-the-plan.

1. **Discount** – The commodity of discounting is as old as civilisation, with the last 3,000 years being a mixture of opportunity and adversity. Discounts follow a simple formula. If you take an existing property, understand the true value of it and the motivations of the sale you're sure to find opportunity and make a profit. As Napoleon Hill wrote, "If you can conceive it, you can achieve it".

Let me give you an example. In June 2008 I brokered a group of townhouse-style properties for clients and myself in Dulwich Hill, Sydney. Dulwich Hill is approximately six kilometres from the CBD and is considered to be a grungy, up-and-coming area.

The vendor had some unfavourable dealings and needed a fast sales solution. Rather than offering the properties at $500,000, which was the valuation price, he looked for a smaller price but a faster sale to help him overcome his challenges elsewhere. The properties were brokered for $400,000 and were purchased swiftly and accordingly. In this example the commodity – discount – offered the potential opportunity of $100,000 in recyclable value to the buyer and $100,000 loss to the vendor. In March 2009 the properties were revalued at $475,000, a $75,000 gain in just 10 months. The market didn't provide this increase, the gain was achieved by buying well in the first place and using the commodity discount.

POSITIVE CASHFLOW PROPERTY

Dulwich Hill

2. **Cosmetic renovations** – Adding value by carrying out some very simple renovations can often be done on a shoe string budget. Simple chores like painting a feature wall, replacing carpet, adding new blinds and manicuring lawns should be considered. The unwritten rule is that if your managing agent cannot co-ordinate the renovation for you or you can't do it yourself within a month, then it's possible you may overcapitalise. Because my personal preference is for strategies that I can handle remotely or quickly, I'm not into structural renovations or development.

Checklist - Some rules of renovation to consider:

- understand the market cycle for future growth by considering the six market drivers;
- buy well and secure the property at a discount;
- invest in rentable suburbs and towns where rents can increase;
- the underlying idea in a renovation is to gain a minimum of $3 for every $1 spent, so know your costing;
- grasp the cash on cash principle and forecast a deposit recycle time;

- don't get in above your head; for cosmetic renovations buy properties under $500,000 that appeal to the entire market when selling.

3. **Strata titling** – I call this adding paper value. When you first understand this commodity it can seem a bit too simple to be true.

There are a lot of duplex and triplex blocks of units, as well as townhouses, in the market that are still all owned by the one owner and often not yet strata titled. If you buy a property with multiple dwellings that is not yet strata titled, and if zoning allows strata title approval, this commodity can return huge profits, which, as we now well know, are better than wages. Strata subdivision can produce profits of up to 30 per cent or more.

So you hunt for, negotiate and then control a property that's on one title. You get council to "stamp it" and approve the new titles, then it's worth more money because you own more titles than you did initially.

Let me give you an example of a property I've been involved with, a block of 15 townhouses in the New South Wales town of Moree. The townhouses were on the market for $1,350,000 but I was able to negotiate a discount, securing the property on a six-month settlement with a five per cent deposit at an agreed value of $1,050,000.

That amounted to $70,000 per townhouse, which was good buying as four had three bedrooms and the other 11 had two. They were renting for $150 a week, making positive cashflow an extra upside. After sending the valuer into the property for what is known as a gross realisation valuation

POSITIVE CASHFLOW PROPERTY

I discovered the property was worth $1.7 million. Great profits indeed.

I then sent a surveyor to the site to give me a quote on arranging the strata subdivision. They returned with a figure of $12,000, with the development application likely to take about three months to complete. It ultimately cost me $19,000 and took six months to get the property strata approved and titled but that still amounted to $650,000 in profit from a small regional town.

Moree townhouses

4. **Subdividing** – This is a commodity that adds value. Simply put, buy a house with an extra big block of land and cut some off to either build another house or create a new block of land you can sell.

The first question you need to answer when looking at an area is the minimum size of a subdivision required by council? If 400 m^2 is required, look for 1000 m^2 to subdivide. You may need the extra size for roads and infrastructure such as water, power, phone and gas.

BONUS! FREE gifts at www.TGRProperty.com.au/Gifts

Corner blocks are very good to subdivide as you will have two street frontages, which makes the subdivision a lot easier and makes them more valuable as well. Many places in Australia (mainly northern states and country areas) have timber houses built in the middle of big blocks of subdividable land. I've seen investors jack the house up, move it over 10 metres and then subdivide down the middle. Other subdivisions have a driveway down one side to access the large block of land at the back, known as the battleaxe block.

Subdivisions cost more to complete than strata subdivisions, as you will have to complete planning requirements such as driveways, sewer and water pipes, electricity and phone line and many more council-directed requirements before you can get a new title issued.

5. **Off-the-plan** – Off-the-plan means entering into a contract to buy a property that is not yet built. It exists because of a need to eliminate a debt risk to those involved. Developers and builders are required to provide the bank with sales of their development prior to being given construction money. These off-the-plan purchases guarantee the bank that the market will buy out their risk, so they are not gambling on the back of the developer's project. Developers always have a certain pre-sale requirement prior to the banks offering money to develop the property.

We, as investors, can apply this commodity to create equity by using the market and time to add value. I like off-the-plan deals; they can give you great leverage for a small amount of money as a deposit.

Generally a builder or developer will need a deposit of 10 per cent. Let's say you are buying a property off-the-plan for

$350,000 (in a good location in an upward market cycle) so you would need to put down $35,000 as a deposit to hold the property. The benefit is that it can take years to construct and may increase in value by 10 per cent by the time you take out the full mortgage, making it a significantly better deal. In fact, I've personally done a number of off-the-plan deals where I haven't had to deposit any money at all, as the increase in property value during construction has covered the deposit at settlement and even allowed me to take some extra on to the next deal.

Off-the-plan is a great commodity as part of a whole strategy. Here's a checklist that will allow a smooth transition from plan to product:

- understand the market cycle for future growth and consider the six market drivers;
- choose boutique properties and don't get involved in estates with high density. Steer clear of high-rise or mid-rise units and try to buy in estates with less than 40 dwellings in the complex;
- always buy in stage one of a development, as this is always the best price, and don't consider any other stages because you will have already missed the boat;
- an 18-month minimum timeframe allows a property to mould well for profits and with just a deposit down you should secure 100 per cent cash on cash return;
- always have the plan valued at the commencement, so you know you are paying the plan's value in the beginning and not the value at the end;
- don't get in above your head - buy properties under $500,000 that will appeal to the entire market if you need to sell;
- always plan to settle and confirm borrowing capacity first before entering into an off-the-plan contract. Never buy to sell midway through the project's construction.

Now you understand there are commodities within the real estate market, you can use them to create profits. Let's practice understanding their effectiveness against the market cycle.

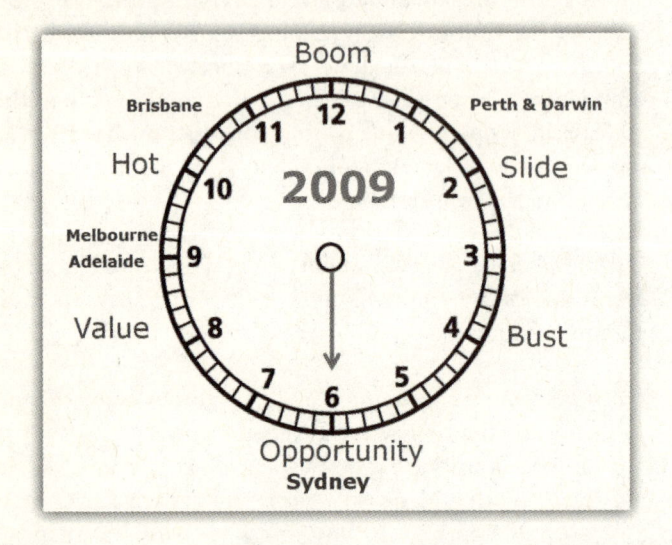

```
                    Boom
        Brisbane           Perth & Darwin
               11  12   1
        Hot                    Slide
            10    2009    2

        Melbourne
        Adelaide  9           3

        Value                  Bust
               8            4
                 7   6   5
                 Opportunity
                    Sydney
```

Understanding that Perth is, economically speaking, in the slide position on the cycle, would it be a good idea to buy off-the-plan? Would it be intelligent to renovate in Perth in 2009? The answer is no as you could very easily compromise your position and buy a problem property.

What about Sydney? Would it be a good idea to buy there for renovation? Opportunity markets are risk markets, as the growth can be held back longer than expected. Renovation might not be the best commodity to put into play here until there is further certainty, as you could run the risk of overcapitalisation. The discount commodity works best in opportunity markets.

Understanding that Melbourne and Adelaide sit in the value zone of the cycle, would it be useful to consider off-the-plan, discount or renovation? Yes, these markets can bring a return to all commodities.

Brisbane, meanwhile, sits in a hot market so it might be a bit risky to buy there off-the-plan.

"Time in the market and not timing the market" is more important but it helps to know what commodities to buy and how to adapt them to the property market cycles in each state. That is when you will truly grasp the concept of property investing.

FUNDAMENTAL NUMBER SIX:
PATIENCE IS A VIRTUE

An investor is like a farmer, in the sense that you can only reap what you sow and you won't see results immediately. You need patience, which is a rare commodity in the modern world. A key phrase that comes to mind is a quote from distinguished speaker and author Neil Eskelin: "Every farmer knows that you can't sow and reap on the same day. There is a timetable for your harvest that requires both working and waiting. Patience is a small price to pay for what you will receive."

Creating a deal that, as we say in the industry, "stacks up" takes endurance and commitment so don't rush into anything. Most real estate is sold in the market to illiterate buyers who are impatient, emotional and who consider themselves too time-poor to show persistence. The average buyer sees 10 properties and then purchases one based on their personal tastes. I, on the other hand, will make offers on over 30 properties subject to further and better due diligence. I'll then consider counter-offers, make counter-offers of my own and then put a target property under contract with the pre-negotiated due diligence terms and conditions. The more offers you have out there, the higher your chance of finding a better deal.

The Internet allows us to make offers on properties sight unseen, providing a level of liquidity that means real estate will never be the same again. People now buy real estate over the phone and Internet from right across Australia.

Offers, if structured properly, are not binding if the right terms and conditions are set out in advance, so consider it a sounding out process. Some terms that should always be standard in your offer document include being subject to building and pest inspection, subject to valuation and subject to finance terms suitable to you, the purchaser. Other more complex terms and conditions can be added according to the negotiations. Here are five clauses that can be prudent and helpful when making offers on property:

1. This offer is subject to and conditional upon the purchaser arranging financing suitable to themselves, such financing to be confirmed within 28 days from the time of receiving a contract.

2. This contract is expressly subject to and conditional upon the purchaser's solicitor's approval as the title, encumbrances, easement, and any other regulatory impositions that may relate to the subject property, such approval to be given in writing by the purchaser's solicitor to the seller's solicitor by no later than 5pm on the 28th day after receiving a contract.

3. This contract is expressly subject to and conditional upon the purchaser's approval of a building and pest inspection, such approval to be given in writing by the purchaser's solicitor to the seller's solicitor by no later than 5pm on the 28th day from the intended purchaser or their solicitor receiving a contract.

POSITIVE CASHFLOW PROPERTY

4. This contract is expressly subject to and conditional upon the purchaser's approval of a registered evaluation, such approval to be confirmed within 28 days from the date of intended purchaser or their solicitor receiving a contract.

5. The buyer(s) also requests a 28 day due diligence clause in the contract for buyer's investigations of the property as the buyer determines necessary. This contract is subject to and conditional upon the buyer being satisfied on or before the due diligence date with its due diligence. If the buyer is not satisfied with its due diligence then the buyer may by written notice to the seller, given no later than 5pm on the due diligence date, terminate this contract, in which case this contract will be at an end and the deposit holder must refund the deposit to the buyer and neither party will be under any further obligation to the other.

FUNDAMENTAL NUMBER SEVEN: DUE DILIGENCE

Without the adversity that investing of any kind brings, we would never advance. Sometimes we need small failures that will allow us to succeed in the long run. It's inevitable that all beginner investors – and even many experienced ones – will make mistakes. The trick is to limit them as much as possible and avoid the most obvious errors.

It amazes me how many purchasers buy a property after inspecting it themselves, without performing proper due diligence such as employing the services of a valuer, building inspector, pest inspector and surveyor.

It's pretty simple: unless you are qualified in these trades, you should not buy property until you have had experts analyse it. Think of it as buying intelligence, as it can tell you things you would otherwise never suspect. For me this is the final step; if all the boxes are ticked, I opt to purchase.

BONUS! FREE gifts at www.TGRProperty.com.au/Gifts

But remember, some of the best deals done in the market failed their due diligence. What better leverage in negotiation than the knowledge of weaknesses in the property, provided by an independent third party?

Due diligence costs money, so don't ever skimp on it. The few hundred dollars it costs to run due diligence can save you a lot more in the long run. Don't be put off if your due diligence finds a problem and the contract falls over. Don't feel betrayed because you have lost money, feel grateful that you have been saved from the loss of far more. Due diligence is a vital part of the process no matter the cards you're dealt.

FUNDAMENTAL NUMBER EIGHT:
ASSEMBLE A TEAM

Investment, if done alone, is a very tough struggle for success. Striking out on your own is a selfish and antiquated way to do business. Instead, surround yourself with family and close friends who can support you as you move through your journey to financial success, as well as a team of professionals who can guide your feet as you take each step. Among the people whose services you will need are conveyancers, finance brokers, buyer's advocates, solicitors, accountants and depreciation experts, to name but a few.

It's often preferable that these specialists be personally involved in the property investing game so they can better assist you in achieving property success. Surround yourself with merchants who are property-focused and who invest themselves. For example, a superior accountant will find you more cashflow to support your property portfolio.

POSITIVE CASHFLOW PROPERTY

> **FUNDAMENTALS CHECKLIST**
>
> 1. Emotions of market and the vendor
> 2. Cash on cash return
> 3. Where to invest – six key market indicators
> 4. When to invest – the property cycle
> 5. The commodities
> 6. Patience is a virtue
> 7. Due diligence
> 8. Assemble a team

Objectivism states that we can perceive the world through reason alone. It means that if you have an unachieved goal, you cannot blame your parents, your teachers, your friends or anybody else. Success and failure rest entirely with you. Now you have the key fundamentals and enough information to arrive at your goal, as well as the playbooks that will accompany you as you grow from real estate novice to real estate investor.

You are almost ready to start investing, so you now need to consider the science of cashflow and its relationship to the property market.

SHOW ME THE CASHFLOW...

The yield is the rental cashflow over the purchase price. It's prudent to invest in assets that carry high yields, as well as assets that carry large profits. Always consider assets that will grow in the long-term. The main objective is to create a balance of servicing and growth for equity within your property portfolio. Cashflow is the fuel that runs the engine and without it advancement is not possible.

BONUS! FREE gifts at www.TGRProperty.com.au/Gifts

A property portfolio can be cashflowed in various ways. Let's discuss a few, such as:

- Positive cashflow property
- Profits
- Tax cashflow (for real estate)
- Trading real estate for cashflow.

POSITIVE CASHFLOW PROPERTY

The reality is that about 80 per cent of portfolio investors don't buy cashflow positive properties, as they're happy with the family home and perhaps one other investment property.

Two per cent of the population invest in more than one property and 20 per cent of those are what I would call portfolio cashflow investors. This tiny group of people has ample cashflow investments to pick and choose from in the market.

For most investors, securing cashflow is a sensible means of providing serviceability to their property portfolio. Similar to running a business, a well-managed property portfolio needs cashflow. There are two types of cashflow, passive and non-passive. To put them in their simplest terms, passive income is derived from simply owning a property where the rent is higher than expenses, while non-passive income requires extra work.

To maintain and even increase serviceability, investors should consider returns or yields two to three per cent higher than the standard variable interest rate of the day. I would aim for yields starting from nine per cent for residential property. Off-the-bat passive returns are available in the market and are often found in small regional towns, university towns and mining areas. Exposure to these returns takes dedication. One would need to put in at least 20 offers a month on properties to secure a viable property with a nine or 10 per cent return in a medium interest rate market of seven per cent.

POSITIVE CASHFLOW PROPERTY

I have brokered around 1,000 positive cashflow properties, from small towns to secondary cities, and I know that commercially the formula is the same for my buyer's agency. Positive Real Estate makes over 200 offers a month to secure as few as 10 properties with these types of returns.

Passive cashflow returns are available in the market. When negotiating high yielding properties, remember to do the numbers and make sure you are truly buying positive cashflow. Genuine positive cashflow properties should give the benefit before tax and not be reliant on deductions. Figures should be calculated on 110 per cent borrowings.

Properties within the market that can't produce a pre–tax positive cashflow result are either positively-geared by tax deductions or still negatively-geared.

The best way to understand servicing is to know that yield variation and cashflow are very important to a bank or funder and make all the difference in running a property portfolio, as it increases your borrowing power and the range of what you can purchase. Consider this example:

> Person A is buying a property. Their wage is $50,000 per annum, the property they are buying is $350,000, the rent is $300 per week and the interest rate is seven per cent variable. The pre-tax cashflow - the yearly cost to run the property – is negative $5,000 per annum. They purchase the property and are content.
>
> The same buyer is now considering buying again to increase their portfolio. The funder looks at the wage of $50,000, as well as the annual return from the first property of negative $5,000. The funder considers the buyer's true combined

BONUS! FREE gifts at www.TGRProperty.com.au/Gifts

income to be $45,000 a year, meaning the buyer can only shop in the $250,000 range for their next property.

As you can see, Person A's portfolio is limited and will soon run out of steam.

Person B, on the other hand, is also buying a property. Their wage is $50,000 per annum, the property they are buying is $350,000, the rent $700 per week and the interest rate is seven per cent variable. In this instance the pre-tax cashflow is positive $5,000 per annum. The buyer purchases the property and is very happy.

Now when Person B considers buying again the funder adds that $5,000 cashflow to give them a combined annual income of $55,000. This allows the buyer to shop in the $450,000 range for their next property.

Therefore, Person B's portfolio can continue growing and, if structured well, will never run out of steam.

The number of great opportunities the open market passes by without full investigation is staggering. I'm amazed that some investors don't know how to create rent increases or add value to real estate to push positive cashflow returns higher. These are the non-passive cashflow investments as they require work to enhance the rental returns of the property. Here are some tips on increasing cashflow:

- rent out the property furnished
- make the property attractive to students
- add an extra bedroom
- carry out small renovations
- add air-conditioning

- fix obvious defects
- create privacy within the property.

I recently brokered a 14 per cent cashflow return. With only a small renovation and the installation of air-conditioning, the returns hit a staggering 30 per cent. This was made possible by treating the property as a non-passive investment. The fortune wasn't already sitting there, it had to be created.

You need to understand that vendors are often selling because they are finished with the asset bought in a previous property cycle, so they no longer see value in the property. Of course, there are other ways to create cashflow in real estate. I call this trading cashflow, which I'll explain a little later in the chapter. First you need to fully grasp what a margin or a profit is, to understand the process of buying, holding and selling property for the aim of providing cashflow for wealth-creation.

This property returns 14 per cent cashflow

PROFITS

I've alluded to the fact that individual buyers hunt in the same market place as companies, investment banks and massive hedged funds that are all looking for residential opportunities in the Australian property market.

The sole purpose of these institutions is to return profits that can boost the share price or be returned to investors. Individuals have the same goal posts to aim for, only on a different scale; the principle of profit is exactly the same.

Real estate is the only asset class that can be controlled by the people, it's bricks and mortar, and it truly is "capital in the hands of the people".

From time to time I am engaged to sell one-line assets to the likes of banks, fund managers and companies. These institutions understand that I seek out and find profits in the market. After 15 years of deal-making, they now know they should be attentive to the opportunities and products I can secure, thus they are always prepared to listen.

Let me give you an example of a property where capital was put in the hands of people who in turn profited massively.

In August 2008 I was engaged to sell 40 luxury waterfront properties that recently won a Master Builder's Award for their design. The properties were situated on a stunning beach and represented growth, growth and more growth. However, after trying for a year the developer/builder had only managed to sell 10 of the properties and couldn't sell any more because interest rates were hitting their peak and he asked that I find a group to buy the 40 properties as a one-line sale. A valuation was done and the properties were found to be collectively worth $40.2 million.

Naturally, such an award-winning waterfront asset was of interest to many institutions and within three weeks of being on the market an investment bank tied the asset up under instructions to purchase the property 33.5 per cent below its valuation. The

POSITIVE CASHFLOW PROPERTY

bank's internal credit committee approved the purchase for $26.75 million.

The bank's goal was to secure $13.5 million in profit, which represented the available profit margin the developer had in equity. The developer who acquired the land and constructed the asset was hoping to realise 33.5 per cent profit, or $13.5 million over the two years of building and one year holding.

The key phrase here is, "Every adversity brings with it the seed of an equivalent advantage".

So it was agreed the bank would vacuum the profit and the developer would pass on his risk. Documents were drawn up and capital was heading to the bank, to the finest and most intelligent minds and to their investors accordingly.

Then, in October 2008 the bank's share price was seriously affected by the international credit crunch. The bank was unable to continue the transaction and its credit committee, succumbing to international pressures, rescinded the property at the eleventh hour.

Persistence and a burning desire to win led me to realise that I didn't need institutional money to go through with such a transaction. I decided to put the profits in the hands of the people, as real estate is the only asset class that can be truly controlled by the people.

I divided up all 40 properties and began helping people buy them at the same agreed discount of 33.5 per cent. It reminds me of another key phrase: "If two or three people believe in a common purpose anything is possible."

BONUS! FREE gifts at www.TGRProperty.com.au/Gifts

I was able to arrange the contracts needed to eliminate the developer's risk, helping him out of a hole at the same time as I helped my clients and myself to huge profits.

The property I purchased within the complex is typical of those that other purchasers got. It's valued at $930,000 but I paid $618,450, an immediate gain of $311,550 that was confirmed by the valuation. That's a profit, which I never get sick of saying is better than a wage. I'm confident the $311,550 gain in 12 months is higher than most wages in the employment marketplace.

Now consider that within 12 months I will be able to borrow against some of the profit gained and turn it into equity. That profit will become a liquid line of credit, so I can cashflow many pieces of real estate in my portfolio for years and still have enough left to identify another property. This huge profit will allow me the opportunity to compound my capital by paying a healthy deposit on another good property purchase.

TAX FOR CASHFLOW
The next class of cashflow is tax for cashflow. It repeals the theory that there is no such thing as good tax and suggests that owning real estate in Australia can be very tax effective.

Most people have two large costs in their life, one of which is tax. Does anyone like tax? I don't. I don't mind paying because it means I've made a profit but I still don't like it. The other large cost is bad debt, through things like credit cards, car loans, plasma TVs and the loan against your home. Basically, any debt that doesn't create an income or give you a tax benefit is a bad debt.

POSITIVE CASHFLOW PROPERTY

By the way, before we go too far I want to make it clear I'm not promoting negative-gearing as an investment principle by itself, as to me, any potential tax deductions are simply a bonus of owning property. Without the assurance of significant capital growth, buying a piece of real estate to deliberately lose money, simply to get tax deductions, is not clever. I see deductions as a fringe benefit, not a fundamental principle.

For providing property to the rental market, the Australian Taxation Office (ATO) gives property investors a tax deduction. Real estate is a fantastic wealth-creation vehicle because there are two portions to it: the land and the building. While one goes up in value, the other goes down.

So when the building goes down in value – creating a paper loss only, that takes no money out of anybody's pocket - owners get to claim that loss as a deduction. It means investors don't have to lose money or have a negative cashflow to get massive tax deductions.

So, let me talk about tax first and put it in a way that will make more sense.

You go to work a certain number of days a week for a certain number of hours, giving your time in exchange for money. It's a system that's been around for eons and is the quickest way to make money, though you shouldn't get stuck in that process if you want to build wealth. Remember, profits are better than wages. Of course, I don't encourage anyone to quit their job until they actually are wealthy, as it's hard to become a property investor with no income because nobody will lend you money. The trouble with the system is that when you break it down into its separate days you'll discover that every hour of work on both Monday and Tuesday – and, for some people, Wednesday

BONUS! FREE gifts at www.TGRProperty.com.au/Gifts

as well – have benefited nobody but the tax man. You don't get a cent of it. So here's the thing you need to know. If you earn an income, PAYG, or are in business, the law states that as an investor you have the right to claim losses as tax deductions and reduce your tax legally when you invest in property.

If the average Australian bought between three and five properties – the newer the better and the higher cashflow the better – they could legally claim back 70-80 per cent of their tax for providing rental housing to the market. To put it more simply, the average Australian could actually claim back the money they earn Monday, Tuesday and Wednesday. Even more simply: stop working for free!

According to the company depreciation experts, 85 per cent of people who own property investments do not claim all the tax deductions they are entitled to. You need to get a Professional Depreciation Schedule, otherwise you're throwing money away by not claiming properly. The ATO will often refund between $1,400 and $12,000 even if your property is cashflow positive. So provide this schedule to your accountant because without it they will inaccurately estimate your claim through not knowing the costing of your property's fixtures, fittings, furniture, common areas etc.

Another question to ask is, do you wait until the end of the year to claim your tax? The answer is a resounding no. You claim your negative-gearing tax back weekly, fortnightly or monthly. It's called a PAYG variation and the ATO varies your salary to take into account the property investment losses. Talk to a property specialist accountant and they will help you apply to the ATO. For some this could be the key to unlocking some cashflow to move forward into real wealth-creation. We don't necessarily need a higher income, we just have to be clever with

POSITIVE CASHFLOW PROPERTY

what we've got. Claiming your tax weekly could change your entire financial position.

Unfortunately, the statistics reveal the average Aussie spends 121 per cent of their annual income. How can we spend more than we earn? It called bad debt and includes things like credit cards, hire purchase furniture, 1,000 days interest-free and so on. Even the loan on your home is a bad debt, as it doesn't create income and you cannot get a tax deduction on it.

THE DIFFERENCE BETWEEN GOOD AND BAD DEBT

Good debt is a loan on an investment property. The debt allows you to buy an asset that creates income (rent), gives you tax deductions and increases in value more than its costs.

Bad debt is the hire or purchase of a flat screen television for $10,000. It creates no income, you get no tax deductions and the product rapidly decreases in value. You end up paying $20,000 over five years for something that ends up being worth $500.

Bad debt can cripple you as an investor. It drains the financial life out of you on paper as well as sucking actual money out of your pocket. When you go to apply for a loan on an investment property (good debt) the banks do a special little computation called a serviceability calculation, which basically asks the question: have you got enough spare cash to cover your debts?

When you have a lot of high interest on bad debts (credit cards etc.) and a super large, low interest, no-income debt (your home loan), you blow the serviceability calculation up and can't get a loan (good debt) because of your bad financial cashflow position.

BONUS! FREE gifts at www.TGRProperty.com.au/Gifts

Many Australians find themselves in this position. They want to secure financial freedom and invest in the nation's safest asset, real estate, and they have equity in their own homes but they can't invest it because their serviceability is shot by bad debt.

Here's a question you have to ask yourself, is the home you live in right now as an owner/occupier your dream home? If you answered yes, well done. However, if you answered no the next question is, would you prefer to live somewhere else – at the beach, the mountains or closer to work, shops, cafés, restaurants, etc?

Ninety-nine point nine per cent of people bought the property they live in because it was all they could afford at the time they chose to nest. Somewhere along the line people have learned the idea that you have to buy and live where you can afford and then one day, when you have paid it off or get a higher paying job, you can move to somewhere you prefer. The problem with that is the rest of the market doesn't wait and grows in value at the same rate as your wage or faster.

Financially, we can all rent a better lifestyle than we can afford to buy, especially in the early years. So here's an idea: rent out the house that is not in your dream location and go rent somewhere that is. Instantly your bad debt becomes good debt. Abracadabra!

Live near the beach, reside in the city or move to the stylish place you love with all the cafés nearby that's walking distance to the kids' school. You'll kill two birds with one stone. Your lifestyle will change for the better and your serviceability will transform overnight. Your ability to access some of your equity to borrow and start buying investment properties will instantly open up.

POSITIVE CASHFLOW PROPERTY

Many people complain that the tax system is manipulated by the rich however, the rules apply to – and can be used by - everyone. There is indeed cashflow to be gained from the tax system.

TRADING REAL ESTATE FOR CASHFLOW

A largely unknown but highly effective strategy is trading real estate for cashflow. It's been a regular contributor to my personal cash stream for numerous years. I hold it in great esteem, yet many would like it to be abolished and no longer possible, for the fear of Capital Gains Tax. Its critics say it's impractical, passing judgement because of their own pre-conceptions. Their intolerance to it is caused by their naivety, as trading real estate for cashflow has a single core principle: keep it simple.

Those who still refuse to be open to it are going to be left behind. As Abraham Lincoln said, "We must plan for the future because people who stay in the present will remain in the past".

BUYING

The first step is creating what I call an "automatic acquisition plan". You must know your complete desires and focus on the plan. In my early years, my aim was as follows: "I am going to buy one property a year for the next 10 years." It's as simple as that. In fact, it's kind of like going to the dentist for a check-up. You put it in your calendar and once a year it pops up. "Hey, look. It says it's time to buy another property."

The thing with real estate is that you don't have to be tricky; you just have to be consistent. Those who are consistent make lots and lots of money. Those who try to be tricky often stumble because of their own stubborn pride or because they overcomplicate their portfolio through greed.

BONUS! FREE gifts at www.TGRProperty.com.au/Gifts

So, you buy one property a year for the next 10 years. It's pretty simple to calculate: at the end you will have 10 properties. When you do some simple calculations on Australian market averages, you'll find the median investment property is $250,000 and the average yield is seven per cent. You should be searching for an average growth of 10 per cent per annum, which is the hundred year average according to the Australian Bureau of Statistics. In 10 years you would have $3.6 million worth of property, $1.6 million worth of equity and $50,000 in positive cashflow. So, you get a million in cash if you sell them or $50,000 a year in cashflow if you keep them.

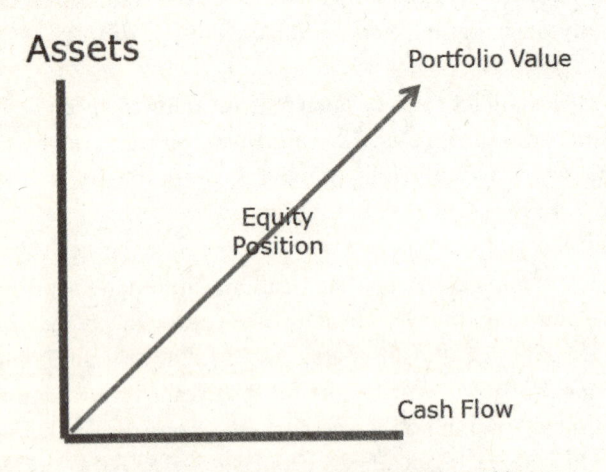

Being consistent, not tricky, increases your portfolio

It's a simple idea but don't underestimate the power of its simplicity and the compounding returns it will bring. As you can see, we all have the ability to secure a property portfolio if we keep it straightforward, and buy the right property with the appropriate rents. You can accumulate real wealth and live a good life within in a short space of time, even in less than a decade.

POSITIVE CASHFLOW PROPERTY

Creating cashflow through buying, holding and selling real estate demands dedication. It takes an understanding of just about every piece of information discussed in this chapter. It requires perfect harmony. To be sure of success you must construct a plan that is prudent yet simple in its design.

The automatic acquisition plan creates wealth, it's as simple as that. I completely support buying a property that will grow and return in the long-term. I endorse blue chip capital growth investments to be the main objective as a hold strategy. Cashflow or high yielding investments should be bought if there is an upside for profits and/or growth or to offset other high growth property. Some people buy high yielding assets purely because it covers the mortgage but without growth the purchase is truly meaningless. Yes, the asset is in your name but what is the quintessential purpose of the investment?

The automatic acquisition plan has been allowing investors to put high capital growth properties in their portfolio ever since its conception. However, can we all buy in blue chip? Do we all have the ability to purchase on Sydney Harbour or within the CBD ring? It's just not possible to add the finest real estate in the country to your portfolio, year in and year out, so you need to consider secondary markets. The idea is that the property you buy today can be sold later to send money to a premium location.

The property market has a ceiling, as we discovered earlier in the chapter. Generally speaking, value markets grow for three good years. During this time property can, in cases like the Perth property boom, double in value. For the balance of the economic cycle, property tends to be slow growing just above CPI.

Understand the cycle when selling, holding and buying.

An example of a property that hit its ceiling was a house I bought in Boulder/Kalgoorlie, Western Australia, in 2004 during the value period of the property boom there. I acquired an average four-bedroom home on a subdividable block of land as my add value project. The home was secured for $118,000 and valued at $130,000 at the time. The vendors were getting a divorce and, in a bull market, relented to my offer. The property was showing a nine per cent return and was rentable for $230 a week. My subdivision costs were $35,000. In late 2006 I sold the new property for $65,000 and in 2007, when the market hit its ceiling, I sold the original property for $220,000.

Logically speaking, having seen the property double in value and having extracted the value out of the property through the subdivision I could see that it was better to sell than hold. This was because I understand the property cycle and realise it may now be 2014 before the West Australian property market starts to represent value again. I could not see the asset going from $220,000 to $440,000 in that time. Therefore, I decided to sell and transfer the profits from this secondary location to a blue chip location and follow expansion rather than contraction. This is known as "migrating profits".

POSITIVE CASHFLOW PROPERTY

The principle behind money migration is that if you can find a better home for it in a more sustainable area, why not send it there? It doesn't make economic sense to form emotional attachments to property. You'll only watch it perform in thriving markets and then, as it runs out of sustainability, hold onto it for up to a decade before the patch of dirt the property sits on becomes popular again.

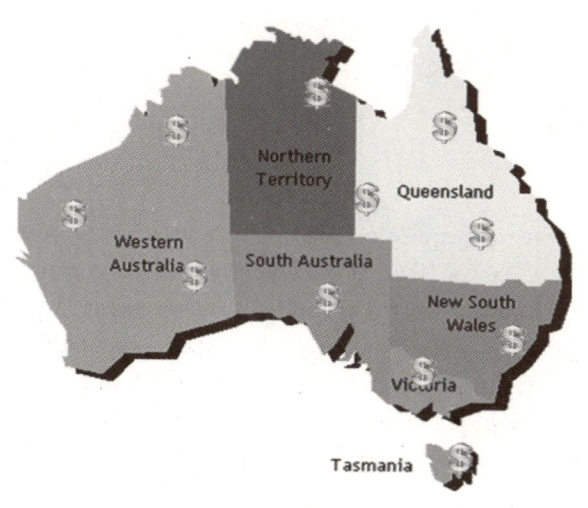

The migration of money

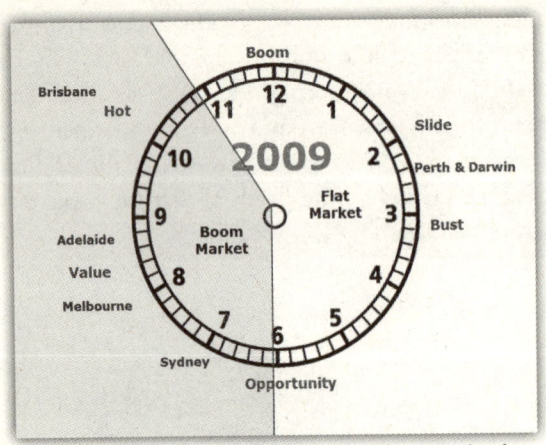

The property cycle in 2009 gives clues for years ahead

The automatic acquisition plan is to buy, at a minimum, one property a year for 10 years and hold the assets for compounding profits. However, what if we add a cashflow twist? What if we still bought a property with huge growth potential to hold, then added three properties a year to the plan and extracted the profits by buying, holding and selling them for the sole purpose of creating working cashflow?

Like in any business, you need a plan. In a few words, the aim is to buy low and sell high. If you were in charge of buying and selling stock at a huge department store, would you buy something on a Monday and try and sell it on a Tuesday? No, you would forecast the retail cycle ahead and endeavour to capture a product that would suit the market for the future time of sale. From start to finish, you would create the product, then import, market and sell it. You would buy in 2008 in order to sell in 2009. Real estate is no different.

POSITIVE CASHFLOW PROPERTY

To make a sale within a minimum of 18 months of buying a property, and to profit from its cashflow, you have to future pace your dealings. You need to know your objectives and you must start now, without expecting a result until the property is sold. I like to operate over 18 months and in this time period buy, hold and sell a property. My pattern is to buy four properties a year, one each quarter, hold one property and sell the remaining three. I control the stock and warehouse product. I draw down on the property and distribute it according to my cashflow needs. I have a plan and make great trading profits for cashflow. Later in this chapter I'll show you a recently completed example of trading real estate for cashflow. But first it's prudent to appreciate buying, holding and selling ideas.

The basic principle of buying property for cashflow is to buy, hold and sell. You need a minimum of 20 per cent profit to make the adventure cashflow positive and worthy of your time. Anything less won't work. How you create your profit for cashflow relates to the commodities: discount, renovation, strata, subdivision and off-the-plan or a combination of some or all. The strategy also involves buying in the markets within the opportunity and value zones of the economic cycle and selling properties within the late value to hot zones. You always want to leave a penny on the table for the next guy. Never buy in a hot or booming market for trading real estate and never shop in a market that's sliding or troughing.

If you buy well, the strategy is very low-risk. If you make your money when initially purchasing right, even if the market surprises you, you are still on top of your game through the commodities. For example:

- 15 per cent discount below valuation + 5 per cent capital growth over 18 months;

- 10 per cent discount below valuation + 10 per cent add value through renovation;

- 5 per cent discount below valuation + 15 per cent add value strata subdivision.

Buying property to sell again needs some checks and balances. Here are a few ideas:

- future growth – always buy during the opportunity and value phases of the market cycle;
- buy with a 20 per cent gross realisation;
- invest in suburbs and towns where rents can increase. Don't be slack here. If you don't increase your rents it can alienate the property from the market. For example, if you purchase a property with a five per cent yield and increase the value accordingly, but the yield variation doesn't increase, other investors won't be interested when you sell with a three per cent yield;
- the idea with renovations is to gain a minimum of $3 for every $1 spent, so know your costing;
- know the cash on cash principle and forecast a deposit recycle time;
- always buy real estate that can be sold under $500,000, as it's suitable and affordable to the widest audience;
- know your re-sale market demographic;
- always sell before the market reaches a ceiling.

HOLDING THE PROPERTY

Holding the property is fairly simple. Ultimately you want to control the asset, add as much value to it as you can and ensure the yields remain as high as possible.

POSITIVE CASHFLOW PROPERTY

I recommend the following:

- hold the property on a variable interest rate - never fix the interest rates as the loan will be expensive to break;
- choose a product with low breakage costs;
- never cross-securitise a trade property with another asset;
- always hold the property in a tax efficient entity;
- review rents every six months – choose a yield motivated agent and pay them well;
- watch the market monthly in the area of purchase;
- learn about agents practising within the area of purchase for resale needs.

SELLING
Presenting a property to sell

Owning and buying investment real estate is all about the numbers but selling is not necessarily so. Unless you're creative with your sale, through concepts such as lease option and vendor finance, you're more than likely going to need to sell the old fashioned way – by engaging a sales agent.

A good sales agent will help prepare a property so it creates an emotional attachment in the illiterate buyer or investor. Selling comes down to forward planning. If you have a game plan in place you will be able to master preparation, ambience and presentation to ensure you lock in your profits.

Effective selling takes a seven-question system:

- what are you going to sell?
- who are you targeting to sell it to?
- who will do the selling?
- how will the selling be done?
- who will provide after-sales service?
- what are the terms and conditions of the sale?
- how much will the sale cost and deliver?

BONUS! FREE gifts at www.TGRProperty.com.au/Gifts

EMOTIONAL BUYERS

Once you have answered the seven questions for your sales system, you may also like to address emotions in the market. Simple practical advice is often the best. If your target buyer is a non-investor, it's important that you offer the property for sale vacant but furnished.

In the lead-up to the property presentation, it pays to de-clutter the house as much as humanly possible. You need to understand what's in fashion. In 2009, the vogue is for sleek and minimalist. This will help to make the place look and feel spacious. Understand your target market demographic – be it couples, single, families or other investors – and dress the home accordingly.

When selling, it's prudent to know your price and not alienate your property by throwing out a high test price. It's also vital to be clear under what terms and conditions you are selling. It's essential that you know where you stand on these issues so you avoid confusing the market. If you are in a partnership, make sure you have a written agenda of sale done prior to arranging the listing to be market ready.

Make sure all offers are written up and that your agent presents you every proposal accordingly. Often buyers will make a contract subject to certain terms, finance, building and pest inspections. This is not an unreasonable mandate, so don't feel threatened in any way.

First impressions are critical. If you want to achieve the best possible price for your property, it needs to be in immaculate condition. You must be able to see your property through the eyes of a buyer and through the trends of the day. The outside of your property is the first aspect a buyer will see. Your property

POSITIVE CASHFLOW PROPERTY

needs to look appealing enough to entice buyers through the front door.

Consider dressing up the outside of your home in the following ways:

- clean, repair and repaint any fences and gates;
- give the outside of the house a fresh coat of paint;
- use a high-pressure hose on areas where you can;
- remove any weeds and manicure the garden;
- repaint your front door - maroon colour is often a warm look and shows class;
- place pot plants by the front door or on the front porch;
- store personal goods such as bikes and toys;
- be aware that buyers can be put off by the knowledge of pets, so do your best to remove animals during a sale period.

The inside of your property also needs to show ambiance, style and emotion that will relate to the potential buyer. Consider doing the following to the interior:

- position your furniture so rooms appear larger;
- throw out or store clutter;
- clean the property from ceiling to floor;
- ensure window dressings are clean and in perfect order, as clients will often gaze out windows;
- make sure doors and windows are operational;
- make sure lights and light bulbs are working;
- reorganise your built-in wardrobes to take away clutter and leave only sleek modern apparel that people will see themselves in;
- fragrance your home, trying coffee or flowers;
- remove all personal effects such as family photos, so as they feel like the property is their home rather than yours;

BONUS! FREE gifts at www.TGRProperty.com.au/Gifts

- hire artwork or funky furniture, if need be, which can provide good results at a low cost;
- let buyers wear their shoes, as the majority of Australians wear shoes inside and there's no need to frustrate buyers with insignificant hysteria.

SELLING TO INVESTORS

Often your target market will be other investors. The property you bought may have been a great investment, so much so that there's enough left for another investor to wring some more money out of it. If you have held the property well and increased rents often you will be approached by investors.

Investors, by nature, are hunters and they like to receive clear and concise communication. Therefore, it's important that the agent representing you is ready to act. Most sales agents in the market are educated in the technique of emotional sales but can fall apart with investors. Often as an investor you will already have a checklist in place that allows you to help the agent create a property investment report – if not, insist on this as it will help them sell. Otherwise their sales pride may get in the way and they may not be aware of the types of information investors require. For instance, selling a property in Brisbane to a person in Melbourne means that very thorough information is needed.

Here is some information you should arrange for your agent:

- property overview
- price details
- tenancy details - rental returns
- proposed finishings and inclusions
- location and surrounding details, such as schools, shops, transport etc
- location map/Google Earth map

POSITIVE CASHFLOW PROPERTY

- Google Street View
- comparable sales data
- valuation
- property financial details
- cashflow
- site plans
- floor plans
- capital growth rates
- demographic details
- investment reports and media information on the area
- lending criteria
- property management details.

Let's examine a recent property trade for cashflow.

Laverton is located approximately 20 kilometres from Melbourne's CBD. It's a lower socio-economic suburb and a secondary market but it is extremely affordable. In 2007, a one-bedroom unit was negotiated for $120,000 with a rent of $150 a week. As you would agree, for a capital city the yield variation was high and the affordability of the property suitable. The property had a registered valuation of $150,000, which gave a 19.5 per cent discount confirmed by valuation. The Melbourne market in 2007 lay in the value section of the property cycle, which, as you will recall, generally lasts for around three years and represents sales volumes and easy to read market indicators, with growth occurring and growth to follow.

So it was clear the market over 18 months would certainly provide the minimum growth of 0.5 per cent needed to reach a feasibility of 20 per cent. The property received a trading cashflow green light and was purchased accordingly after both the market fundamentals were studied and approved.

The eight fundamentals of the Laverton deal in 2007

1. Emotions – market was strong and "excited".
2. 100 per cent cash on cash return, with 20 per cent in and 20 per cent out 12 months later.
3. Where to invest – it was a secondary market in Melbourne and the key market indicators approved.
4. When to invest – the market cycle was set at value.
5. Commodity – "discount".
6. Patience is a virtue – all steps carefully carried out.
7. Due diligence – approved.
8. Assemble a team – done.

In February 2009 the unit in Laverton was sold, with the vendor's pre-conception that the property be purchased for the sole purpose of using property as the actual cashflow vehicle itself under mandate of trading real estate for cashflow. The results are listed below.

- Sale – February 2009 – $160,000 (sold in value phase that was nearing a hot market)
- Purchased 2007 – $120,000
- Gross profit – $40,000
- Sale costs – $3,800
- Stamp Duty – $2,800
- Legal and break costs – $3,500
- Holding costs – $3,000
- Capital Gains Tax – $6,725

Total net profit – $20,175

POSITIVE CASHFLOW PROPERTY

Laverton

This property was sold prior to reaching its ceiling value in a hot market. We believe its value will reach $180,000 but weren't willing to risk it and so got out early.

Trading real estate for cashflow is often misunderstood because it works on the theory of "fewer properties – more revenue". It's unlike its counterpart, positive cashflow property, which works on the theory of "more properties – more revenue".

Assume for a moment that our goal is a cashflow of $60,000 a year and then let's look at the two systems. To achieve this by trading cashflow for profits I would only need three properties like that in Laverton, where roughly $20,000 was cleared.

Positive cashflow properties, on the other hand, work on volume. At an average interest rate of seven per cent variable, for every $100,000 you inject into high yielding, positive cashflow property of nine to 10 per cent you receive about $2,000 in cashflow per annum before tax. So its relativity runs in volume. In order to reach the $60,000 per annum goal, we may need to own 30 properties valued at $100,000 each.

BONUS! FREE gifts at www.TGRProperty.com.au/Gifts

Our goal as property investors has always been to create an automated vehicle through the power of property to generate cashflow without consuming time. All the cashflow strategies are proven and work. Learn the purpose of each style and adapt the style of your choice to make it work for you.

Never lose sight of the real goal.

There is one recurring theme that dominates this chapter, crying out like a choir rejoicing in the grandest of cathedrals. Its extraction can be tweaked and well planned. It is as intriguing to me now as the first time I found it. The ability to use its influence is unmatched and it is marvelled by the masses. Its appearance commands the greatest of respect and it has come to symbolise power. It can create cashflow, which is the seed capital for investment. It's a universal principle, regardless of your religion. Its use is elementary, yet to obtain it requires unbridled passion. It is profit, which rules this planet entirely. Everybody wants it and is working in one way or another to get it.

You now have the foundation and fundamentals, as well as the ways and means that will allow you to take action. We've discussed the essential principles and the key signs of growth, the property commodities and cashflow properties, the tax ideas and market tools. You now have the road map for success, with real estate as your vehicle.

It's investing that inspires me to get out of bed in the morning, along with the understanding that "success requires no explanation and failure permits no alibis". At the basic level, everybody is offered the same opportunities in life but very few people take them. You need to decide whether you are going to.

POSITIVE CASHFLOW PROPERTY

Real estate wealth is available to everyone. Learn the currency that is real estate and you will soon be enriched with its power, able to provide certainty and enjoyment for yourself and your loved ones. You will construct a steady means of wealth-creation that isn't a fanciful illusion but a nutritious diet that is well controlled and passive in its design.

Your lifestyle will change accordingly but there's one thing you must always keep in your mind as you find success. The more your wealth grows, the more you will face the temptation for more and more and more. It can easily distract you from your purpose. You have to make sure you never exceed your limits. Be always productive but never greedy.

The best idea is to pick a goal that's both affordable and reachable, then resist the temptation to experiment with "maybes". Don't contradict the fundamentals but try wherever you can to remove the human element of emotion when buying. Income can often stagnate if we are too proud to remove our own weaknesses.

Your goal should be to create a passive business that is the architect of wealth-creation but you must never lose sight of what is real and what is just real estate. One final thought to leave you with: happier is the man who lives in a tent with the person he loves, than a man who lives in a mansion all by himself.

Understand that amongst all the sentiment of the market, profits matter. We are all surrounded and exposed to opportunities, the rewards of which must be worth taking advantage of. The ultimate reward is to live a good life.

So get ready. Decide to create your dream, become rich along the way and in doing so always remain happy.

FREE BONUS GIFT

Sam Saggers has generously offered a FREE BONUS GIFT valued at $495

FREE **Property Analyser Report** - This valuable tool enables you to accurately analyse any property in relation to its income and expenses by producing a cashflow projection.

Visit the website below to receive these free gifts
www.TGRProperty.com.au/Gifts

Chapter 4
PROFITABLE PROPERTY DEVELOPMENT

"If I can do it, I reckon anybody can!"

CARLY CRUTCHFIELD

CARLY CRUTCHFIELD

Carly Crutchfield is the founder and CEO of CCORP. However, she's not the average CEO, having travelled a very different path to the majority of those who find themselves at the head of successful companies.

Carly's career got off to a rocky start when she left school at the age of 12 and joined the workforce. By just 16, when most her age were idly considering what job they might like, she was already sick of the rat race and had developed an entrepreneurial streak, turning her attention to property.

The change of direction clearly worked. By 20 Carly had travelled the world, owned businesses, sold them again, volunteered for numerous charitable projects and gotten involved in the property and share markets.

Carly's adventurous path has made her what she is today: a self-made millionaire, philanthropist, author, property developer, business owner and more.

In addition to running her national company, CCORP, and its five subsidiary companies, Carly is one of Australia's top public speakers. She's also the nation's number one property development coach, having educated more than 22,000 people. Carly has been involved in property projects throughout Australia, New Zealand and the United States – with a combined value of more than $200 million – and she continues to develop today through her company CDevelop.

Carly is a true prosperity millionaire. She founded the non-profit group, CFoundation, to help empower lives and create change in the world. Giving more than just cash to this charity, she personally oversees projects such as school building, drug education, disaster response and youth education programs.

PROFITABLE PROPERTY DEVELOPMENT

PROPERTY DEVELOPMENT SECRETS OF THE WEALTHY

"Will you let me work for you? Instead of costing you a cent I'll pay you thousands of dollars." Looking back, it would seem I was more than a little crazy when I said those words. Still, it's funny how life can work out because it was exactly that sentence that has turned me into a multi-millionaire property developer and causes me to say:

"HALLELUJAH FOR PROPERTY!"

What other way – that's legitimate and legal – do you know of for a teenager who dropped out of school, moved out of home and had absolutely no credentials or money to become a millionaire?

For me the path to wealth was through property or, to be more specific, property development. I know it sounds ridiculous that a teenager could become a property developer but that is literally what I did.

It's helped a lot that I love the property game. I love everything about it. It's exciting, fun and challenging, with both wins and losses to always keep me coming back for more. Above anything else, though, I love the freedom of choice it has given me in my life. At just 27 years of age I'm a multi-millionaire with the entire world spread out before me. That's the main reason I'm still playing the property game and why I probably always will.

BONUS! FREE gifts at www.TGRProperty.com.au/Gifts

The good news for you is that property development is something just about anybody can do successfully and profitably. In this chapter I want to tell you exactly how I did it and how you can do it too. I will take you through the seven stages of property development so you can see what is actually involved in the process. My goal is to make you truly understand property development, to make it far more than a fuzzy and misunderstood subject, so you can best decide if it's the game for you.

HOW I GOT STARTED

Before we start talking about where you might want to go it's a good idea to discuss where I came from. I was born into a typical middle-class Australian family but I was something of a problem child. I was bored by school and didn't like it at all so, much to the dismay of my father, I left at the age of just 12. I thought I was all grown up and ready for life so I began working administrative jobs and trying to earn a living. By the time I was 16 I was already sick of the rat race. "Is this all there is to life?" I began to ask myself, "Clock in and clock out every day until I finally retire or die?" I was sure there had to be more and I was determined to find it. The only trouble was that I had no idea where to begin looking.

Rat race: Carly was sick of it by just 16!

PROFITABLE PROPERTY DEVELOPMENT

It was about that time when I was at dad's house and saw a book on his bedside table. It had money floating all over the front cover, which is what first drew my attention, so I picked it up and started reading. The book talked about making money through property and becoming something that I had never heard of before: an investor. I decided on the spot that was how I would make my money – I would become a property investor.

As I started investing in property my hunger for education on the topic intensified. I discovered you could buy properties directly from developers and get a big discount, so I started meeting developers and dealing with them directly. I would ask them a million and one questions about development and quickly discovered two things about them: they all loved what they did and they were all absolutely loaded. That's when I decided to promote myself from investor to developer.

All that was left then was for me to learn about development. Easy enough, right? Well, apparently not. It turned out that TAFE and local colleges didn't have any courses, while the university courses that were available cost around $75,000, took four years and only qualified me to work for a developer. That was no good. I didn't want to work for a developer, I wanted to *be* the developer.

My next course was to try finding a developer to accept me as an apprentice, which was also far easier said than done. When I found the one I wanted to work for he flatly told me he wasn't hiring anybody. Undiscouraged, I told him I would work for free if he would teach me the ins and outs of property development. He still wasn't convinced and simply laughed, saying, "You'd be too annoying." I guess he had a point about the young, over-eager school drop-out with far too many questions but I still wasn't ready to give up. "Fine," I said, in a smart tone, "I'll pay you."

BONUS! FREE gifts at www.TGRProperty.com.au/Gifts

It was an offer he couldn't possibly refuse. He looked at me for a moment with a smirk on his face and a twinkle in his eye, then said, "Done. You start next week." I'd actually been joking when I made the offer and clearly needed to do a lot of work on my negotiation skills. Still, it gave me a once-in-a-lifetime opportunity to learn the ropes and hit the ground running on real deals, not textbook theories. After learning from my mentor, I went out on my own and started applying what I had learnt. It wasn't long before I was doing my own deals and making fantastic profits, which is exactly what I'm going to show you how to do.

WHY PROPERTY DEVELOPMENT?

The fact that you're holding this book shows you've come to the same conclusion I did: that property is a great tool to create wealth. Before you take the first steps, though, you have to make a choice. What type of property do you want to deal in? Do you want to buy old houses? New? Units? Villas? House and land or land only? Which state do you want to buy in? Which suburb? Do you want it to be cashflow positive or negative? Do you want to buy and sell? Buy and renovate? Buy and hold?

What type of property do you want to deal in?

PROFITABLE PROPERTY DEVELOPMENT

All the choices can be very overwhelming, so much so that five years can pass while you're still thinking about it and not even in the market yet. The way around that problem is to take it back to basics and remove all the confusion by saying there are only two types of property – active and passive.

Passive property implies that you don't have as much involvement in the process and simply sit back to wait for the results. It is also known as buy-and-hold and is one of the most common types of property investing in Australia. You buy the property, get a 30-year mortgage and then you either live there or rent it out. Many Australians have made fantastic profits from doing this and it's a good strategy if you're willing to wait the 10, 15 or 20 years it can take to make a good profit.

Active property, on the other hand, is exactly what it sounds like: you take a more active role in the process and get directly involved to make your profits far quicker. It means doing something to increase the value of the property, rather than waiting for time or the market to increase the value. It's looking at an existing property or plot of land and working out what you can do to it to make it more valuable. Could you increase the use? Could you split it up (subdivide) and sell it off in pieces? What other deals could you put together? The only limit is your own imagination. Active investing puts you in control and gives you the ability to plan how much profit you want and how quickly you want to make it. It is less of a guessing game than passive investing and, in most cases, much more profitable.

None of this is meant to suggest that one form of investing is better. Passive and active are both fantastic ways to invest in property and, as a rule, I wouldn't recommend one over the other. The decision ultimately depends on how fast you want to see the profits and how much involvement you want to have. If you aren't that interested in getting involved with property and you don't mind waiting a decade or two to see a profit, then passive property investment will absolutely work for you.

However, if you are a bit more motivated or excited about playing the game of property and if you want to see the results in the next few years, then I would absolutely recommend giving property development a go.

WHAT EXACTLY IS PROPERTY DEVELOPMENT?

To start making money in property development, you first of all need to understand exactly what it is and what a developer does.

When many people think of property development they get images of skyscrapers, huge cranes floating on the skyline and, of course, construction. However, construction does not define property development – construction is what a builder does.

The main role of a property developer is to put deals together. As the developer you are the mastermind with the motivation and vision to think up the project in the first place. You find the potential property, you work out how to increase the value of it and you create the plan to make that happen.

The magic of property development is in the deal, not in the pouring of concrete or the laying of bricks. I've done development deals where I sold my part of it and made a large profit before construction ever began.

There are some deals you will take through to construction but even then you are not the one who actually goes on-site and starts building. You are still the deal-maker who drives the deal through, the co-ordination point between the builder, the architect and the bank. It might help you to think of that trio as your three wise (wo)men. They are the team that will gather

PROFITABLE PROPERTY DEVELOPMENT

around you and work together to achieve the end result of a profitable development site. Your job is to lead them.

You are the deal-maker who drives the deal through, the co-ordination point between the builder, the architect and the bank.

It's the exact reason I managed to become a successful property developer in the first place. When I started there was no way I could have worked out the finance on my own, let alone managed a team of tradespeople or drawn up blue prints. Even now I wouldn't be able to juggle all of that. However, by having the team, my three wise (wo)men, I am able to keep my mind on putting together the deals and making sure they are profitable.

The real trick is to know from the very beginning how long a project will take and how much it will cost, then to stick to those predictions. Any blow-out in time-frame or budget will start eating into my profits so I have to make sure my three wise (wo)men keep everything on track. It helps a lot that they have a vested interest in seeing me succeed, as they pay financial penalties when they don't meet targets and get significant rewards when they do. It puts us all on the same team, striving for the same goals. All I need to do is check in once or twice a week to make sure they're on track.

BONUS! FREE gifts at www.TGRProperty.com.au/Gifts

The nature of the process means it's possible for you to create a lucrative new revenue stream while maintaining your current job or lifestyle. Best of all is that property development works on a number of different levels of involvement, all of them profitable, so you are able to choose the one that works best for you.

THE SEVEN STEPS OF PROPERTY DEVELOPMENT

There are seven steps to each successful property development, which you need to learn before you can start playing the game. You don't have to do all seven – you can easily make money from doing just one or two – but you do need to understand all seven so you know where your own actions fit within the broader context.

The first money I ever made in property development was by doing just the first step. I didn't buy or build anything, yet I still made thousands of dollars. I simply found a potential development site, then I found someone else who needed it and put the deal together. This is where you can see that playing the game of property development does not always mean building something. You can get involved in different areas of the development process and make fantastic profits or you can do the whole seven steps of the dance and make even more profit.

Once you know the seven steps and understand the whole process of property development it's up to you to choose which part of the game you like best and how deeply you want to involve yourself. So, let's get started with the first step…

STEP ONE:
FINDING A SITE

The first step is obviously to find a potential development site – you can't do anything until you have a potential property. Finding the site doesn't actually mean buying the site; that comes much later. You just want to find a property or some land that has the potential to be more than it currently is.

First you must find a potential development

There are many types of development sites. For instance, you might find an old house on a big block. You could build another house in the backyard, put a fence up between the two and get approval from council to split the property into separate titles. Suddenly you will find yourself with two houses, which hold far more value than a single house with a big backyard.

Alternatively, you might come across a farm of 100 acres in southeast Queensland or regional Victoria. You could call council to find out the minimum size of farms in that area and if the answer comes back as 25 acres you could split the property into four separate farms. Instead of selling to a single buyer you would sell to four separate ones, which usually brings far more money. This process is called subdividing.

So, the very first step is to go out and start looking for a property you can increase the value of. There are many ways to find a suitable development site. These are some of the best:

1. **Newspaper** - Your local newspaper will list many development site opportunities. You won't find them in the normal "property" section, though. Instead you should look for something along the lines of "investment opportunities", "commercial and investment property" or "development sites" that will be separate to the usual property lift-outs.

Your local newspaper will list many development site opportunities

You see, there are two different property markets: the retail market and the active market. The retail market is generally for passive investors, people who want to buy a property that somebody else has already done the work on. That's a valid option, though it does mean that whoever did all the work has also taken the best profit.

PROFITABLE PROPERTY DEVELOPMENT

Therefore, you look at the active market where developers and savvy investors get involved. This is where you will find the development sites and value-add properties that are exactly what you're looking for. In fact, many of the people in this field are so savvy that a lot of properties sell before they even make it to the newspaper. That's why you will also need to use the next method of finding sites.

2. **Development agents** - Development agents are different to real estate agents. They think differently, are paid differently and generally know a lot more about advanced real estate and development. About the only thing they have in common with the average real estate agent is that they tend to specialise in specific suburbs, which gives them an excellent understanding of the local area. They know what has been there, what is coming, what new properties have sold for and what they will sell for in the future. They also make it a point to find potential development sites in their area.

Development agents have their finger on the pulse of a market and generally know when a development site exists in the area. However, they rarely advertise this information as they will usually have a list of developers to whom they supply sites. They will get in touch with these people and the site will often sell before anyone even knows about it and long before they have the chance to make an offer.

You've probably seen this phenomenon in your own local area. You'll be driving through your suburb when you see a big block under construction and think to yourself, "What's going on there? I didn't even know that was ever for sale… and now they're building!"

You will want to find development agents who cover the area in which you would like to begin a development or get a deal happening. You can find them by typing "development agents" into Google or by asking your local real estate agent if they know of any in the area. The real estate agency may even have a department that deals in this area.

Once you've tracked down a development agent, give them a call, let them know what you're looking for and ask if you can be included on their list. They will then inform you when they find sites that match your criteria. You may need to call a few times and build up a relationship with the agent so they know you're serious.

3. **Council resources** - Another great way to find development sites is by using council resources. These are free to use and quite easy. There are two tools in particular that most Australian councils have and which are a great help when looking for potential sites: zoning maps and planning schemes. A zoning map is an actual map of a suburb or area, which shows every single property, road, beach, park and so forth. Each property has a specific colour that shows the "zone" that property is in. A commercial zone means it could be used for shops or restaurants, while a parkland zoning would mean no buildings can go there. The map will also show density levels, such as a low-density zoning that means only houses with big backyards can be built and no dense unit blocks are allowed.

So, as you can see, the zoning map will help you understand exactly what the purposes and potentials are for every single property.

The planning scheme, on the other hand, is a report issued by council that defines more about the zoning maps. It tells you

PROFITABLE PROPERTY DEVELOPMENT

exactly how high a building can be built, how far back from the road it must be, how much of the land you can actually build on and so forth. With these two documents you can look for and find potential development sites, then know exactly what you can do with them.

Once you find a development site that has potential you can move on to the next step, though you don't necessarily have to. If you would like to cash in and take your profits now, before anything has been bought or built, you are able to. This is called site-finding and it's how I made my first money in development.

I had just started learning about property development and was researching sites, getting used to the language and the process of it all. I was speaking to an experienced developer when he asked me how it was all going. I told him I hadn't really done anything yet and I was just finding sites for research.

"Well, have you found any good sites?" he asked.

I told him that I had and, right there on the spot, he offered to pay me for them. At that point I was confused and didn't really know what he was talking about.

"But I don't even own the properties. What would you be paying me for?"

He replied: "I'll pay you a site-finder's fee, a reward for doing the research and finding the deal. I don't have time to go look for properties and I need my next development to move into soon."

I didn't even hesitate. "You're kidding me," I said, "right, I'll go find you one!"

BONUS! FREE gifts at www.TGRProperty.com.au/Gifts

I looked in an area where I knew there had been some development recently and found a street that had rows of houses alongside a few blocks of units. It made me wonder whether those houses could be turned into units as well. I looked at the council zoning map and the planning scheme and, sure enough, discovered all the houses had the right zoning.

I then hit the footpath and went door-knocking to see if any of the owners wanted to sell. Imagine it: I was young, five-foot-nothing, very green to development and showing up unannounced on people's doorsteps to try developing their property. Needless to say, I had some interesting responses.

Still, it was only a few houses in that I got the answer I was looking for. I found an owner willing to sell, who I was able to put in touch with the developer. After a little more research it turned out to be a great deal. The developer bought the property and paid me the site-finder's fee.

It was at that moment I fell in love with property development and realised it really was the game for me.

STEP TWO:
SITE ANALYSIS

Once you have a potential site you need to do more research so you know everything about the property that will help you put together a deal with the right amount of profit. This is one of the most important steps, yet it is often brushed over or forgotten about by inexperienced developers. In this step you are really building a foundation for the rest of the process. This is where you will do a lot of the preparation and find many of the answers that will propel you through the entire project.

When researching a property there are several things you should

PROFITABLE PROPERTY DEVELOPMENT

be looking for. First of all you need to find out the demographics of the local area. Who lives there? What is the general age bracket? Are there families or is it a population of mainly students? Is it primarily an old or young area? Are there high, medium or low quality properties and finishes? Who wants to live in the area? What is the migration into the area – are people moving in or out? The questions go on and on. To answer them you will find the Australian Bureau of Statistics is an excellent resource, with many up-to-date statistics, figures and demographics that you will find very useful.

This information will help you understand who is likely to buy your property, as well as giving you an understanding of what exactly they're looking for and how much they might be willing to pay. Knowing these things will help you decide what to build and let you know how much you can spend and still return a profit once the property is sold.

Something else you need to research is the environment and amenities of the area. You need to know what shops, transport, schools and hospitals can be found near your potential property. This information will also help you decide what to build and how to price it. If there aren't any amenities or services nearby it may not be a good place for a residential development. Or, if you decide to go ahead with a residential development, you may need to also build a couple of retail shops for the new houses. Another scenario could see you investigating an old farm block on a main highway with absolutely no amenities for miles – this might be a good site for a service station.

When conducting this type of research there's really no substitute to simply getting out there and actually having a look at the area. Just drive around and take note of what you see. You can also speak to local agents, though their information is generally going

BONUS! FREE gifts at www.TGRProperty.com.au/Gifts

to be based on opinion and shouldn't be relied upon too heavily. It's always best to double-check what you've been told with your own eyes. The zoning maps at local council will be able to show you what sort of properties surround your potential site but will not give you specifics about the types of amenities or shops.

Finally, one of the most important things you need to research is the local property market. You want to find out how many properties there are for sale, whether properties are selling fast or slow, what sort of properties are for sale, what the prices are, which developments have recently gone through council, which development applications are currently waiting to be approved, what is currently being constructed and so on.

There are a few research tools you can use to do this. Property advertising websites such as www.realestate.com.au will show you what is on the market and what the asking prices are. If you call the local council they will be able to give you a report stating which development applications have been approved and, in some cases, what is awaiting approval. You can also find out a lot by simply driving around the local area to see what is being built.

When it comes to research you should put together a list of all the above things you need to do. Go through and check them off, one at a time, and collect all the research results in a file. You will need this information when carrying out steps three and four.

If you have done your research and still think it looks like a good potential site, then it's time to move on to step three and make sure there is profit in the deal.

PROFITABLE PROPERTY DEVELOPMENT

STEP THREE:
FINANCIAL FEASIBILITY

This is where we really start to talk turkey and get down to the nitty gritty. At this stage it is very important to throw hype and opinion right out the window and just look at the facts and figures.

Feasible simply means the project is workable. The "feasibility" of a property means how "workable" the deal is, which is another word for profitable. In this business everything is dictated by how much profit you can make and this step is all about making sure there's enough profit to move forward.

Feasible simply means the project is workable and profitable

A Financial Feasibility for a development is a report that lists all of the costs of the development site: the initial cost of the site, the time it will take to develop, the taxes, the interest, the fees – everything. This is weighed against the amount of money the development is expected to make.

BONUS! FREE gifts at www.TGRProperty.com.au/Gifts

The report generally has two columns of numbers, one down each side of a page that lists the costs and income of the project. At the bottom there is a percentage and a final amount. The percentage is how much profit you are making relative to the overall costs of the development. The amount – the really exciting part – is how much money you can expect to walk away with once it's all finished.

It's very important that you look closely at this report and consider it carefully before deciding whether or not to move forward. You should be looking for a minimum profit of 20 per cent, which is the level that developers and development bankers generally expect. Of course, anything over that is also more than welcome.

If doing one of these sounds like hard work you needn't worry, as there are many types of feasibility software that will work it all out for you. The software lists all the potential costs, then you research the specific amounts for your project and enter them into the software. The computer does its magic and spits out a report that lists all the items and sums before coming up with a profit percentage and the amount in dollars you could make.

There are two versions of the software that I use, a simple one for doing quick calculations and a more advanced version when I really want to get down to business and double-check everything.

At the feasibility stage you will sometimes find that the deal is not actually profitable. That doesn't mean you should just walk away and leave it for dead. Deals will sometimes need to be massaged and worked out before they become profitable, so you need to put on your deal-maker hat and start looking for ways to make it feasible.

PROFITABLE PROPERTY DEVELOPMENT

One way to make a site more profitable is to maximise the usage of the property, which simply means increasing the number of ways a property can be used. For instance, you could have a block of land that you intend to put two freestanding houses on but you may decide instead to maximise the usage by putting four townhouses there. Before you do so you need to make sure you are within the council guidelines and that the profit from selling the extra properties outweighs the cost of building them.

A few years ago I was developing a site in Sydney and had to do exactly this. The site was designed for about 25 dwellings but no matter how I did the numbers I just couldn't make it profitable. In fact, the project was going to put me out-of-pocket. I knew I had to change the design so I could fit more dwellings but I had no idea how to go about it. I approached several architects, none of whom were able to help me, before I finally found one who thought outside the box enough to come up with a solution. He came back to me with a design that gave us 32 dwellings, maximising the usage to an excellent degree. The cost of building the extra seven dwellings was nothing compared to the income from selling them. When I punched the new numbers into the computer it came back with a profit of more than 20 per cent, which amounted to over $2 million in cash. Beautiful!

The important thing to know in this step is that you shouldn't let a deal slip through your fingers because it doesn't look good at first glance. Take your time and see if you can find a way to maximise the usage. You could end up with a little gold mine on your hands.

STEP FOUR:
FINANCE

In property development finance is handled in a completely different way to anything you may have experienced before. One of the things I love most about property development is that the sky is the limit. There are no rules, so you can be as creative as you like when putting together deals and carrying out projects. This applies to the finance as much as any other part of the industry, which is lucky because if we all had to put together a normal finance application, save our 10 per cent deposit and hope for the best, property development would be a dead-end. Unlike those who are chasing money for personal use or a passive investment, property developers have a multitude of options they can choose from when seeking finance.

In most cases you won't want to deal with a normal mortgage broker, who will have limited experience putting together finance for development projects and, in my experience, tends to offer the wrong sorts of loan. Nor would I suggest you go directly to a bank, which will only be able to offer you their own products.

Imagine the situation in the context of shopping for a car. If you have no idea what you want, it's important you get a feel for all of the options out there. If you go to a Toyota car yard, you will find some fantastic cars – but they will all be Toyotas. You might end up getting the best Toyota but that doesn't mean it's the best car for you. There could easily be another brand they didn't have that would have suited you much better. However, if you go to "Bob's Car Yard" you might find that instead of specialising in a single brand he stocks 15 different brands and can give you an unbiased opinion about all of them.

PROFITABLE PROPERTY DEVELOPMENT

It's a similar scenario with a finance broker. They can offer you all the loans available from all the different firms they represent, which in most cases will amount to around 30 different banks or lending institutions.

To stretch the analogy a little further, you wouldn't go to "Bob's Car Yard" if you were looking for a truck or van. For that same reason you shouldn't pick just any finance broker. This part of the game is not simply about finding a broker, it's about finding one that deals in development finance or – as it is often called – commercial finance. You should be aware that commercial finance in this context does not mean loans for commercial property such as shops and warehouses but refers to any loan that has a business use. Banks and lenders see development as a business rather than a simple investment, as they know you aren't sitting at home waiting for the equity to grow over time – you are taking action, putting a deal together and actively increasing the value of the property. They also know that the income stream of a development is different to normal business. Rather than a steady stream of income coming in every week or month you tend to see all of the profits at the end of the deal and then you see big profits.

Commercial lenders take all of this into account and are able to offer you a different type of finance that is perfect for developers, called commercial finance. It offers something called capitalised interest, which means you don't need to pay back the interest monthly as with normal residential loans. Instead the lender or bank adds up the interest over the term of the whole loan and you repay it at the end, along with the capital of the actual loan itself.

The beauty of this is that it frees up your cashflow when you need it most, making it possible for novices to get started and established developers to complete very big projects. A residential lender will not have a very good grasp of commercial loans or capitalised interested products and may not be able to offer them at all, so you need to look for a lender who offers commercial finance. The best way to do this is by searching on Google or by asking your local broker.

When you get commercial finance the lenders will usually loan you anywhere from 50 to 70 per cent of the value of the property. For a property worth $1 million that would mean the bank loans you $700,000. That leaves at least $300,000 in cash you still need to come up with, which isn't the kind of money most people have lying around.

To cover that shortfall you need to get creative. Luckily, there are plenty of options still open to you, including a fantastic tool called "vendor finance". The vendor is the person you are buying the property from, so vendor finance means getting a loan from the person who is selling the property you intend to buy. I know it sounds crazy – why would somebody lend you money just so you can buy something off them? – but it does happen and can work out extremely well.

Here's how it works. You approach the owner and explain that you would love to buy the property from them, but not for $1 million they're asking. Instead tell them you want to buy it for $1.2 million. Straight away you're going to get their attention. They may think you're crazy but they're definitely going to listen to you. Explain to them that you've been approved for a loan to buy their property but that you are short $300,000 of the asking price. Tell them you are looking to develop the property and then sell it for $1.4 million. That gives you a $400,000 profit, which you can offer to split with the vendor if they agree to the deal.

PROFITABLE PROPERTY DEVELOPMENT

If you explain this properly and gain the vendor's trust there is no way they will refuse. So they sell the property today for $700,000, you sign a separate contract agreeing to pay them the remaining $300,000 as well as another $200,000 upon completion of the development, and you're left with a profit of $200,000 despite the fact you didn't put a cent of your own money into the deal.

At about that point you might start thinking, "That's all well and good but I gave away half my profit". That's not really true, though. If you hadn't offered that deal you wouldn't have had the deposit for the loan, the bank wouldn't have lent the money, you wouldn't have developed anything and you wouldn't have any profit. Instead you made other people's money work for you and walked away with $200,000. Not bad, right?

Vendor finance is one of your best tools in putting together property deals and if you ensure that there is a win for both parties you will be successful in negotiating deals exactly like this. I have successfully negotiated many vendor finance deals. The trick is to be patient, ensure that the vendor understands exactly what is happening and feels safe; you can do this by putting everything in writing on signed contracts. If you try to cheat the vendor it simply won't work so you need to stay honest and look for a scenario that delivers a win to both parties. You'll end up with a workable deal that makes everybody happy.

STEP FIVE:
PLANNING APPROVAL

Council approval is crucial to your project

Before you build anything you need approval from council, which is what this stage is all about. This is where you seek planning approval or, as it is properly known, a Development Application (DA).

A DA is something that your architect can help you put together. It contains the blueprints and plans of your proposed building and will be designed based on the council guidelines and regulations. Once it is completed you give it to the council and pay a fee for them to look at it and grant approval if they agree with what you're proposing.

Submitting a DA does not guarantee approval. The council compares your plans against their own master plan for that suburb or city and then they take a number of factors into consideration to decide whether they think your development is best for that particular plot of land. It's rare for a DA to be

PROFITABLE PROPERTY DEVELOPMENT

approved by council the first time it goes through. You will usually be told to make small changes to the plan, which your architect can easily do before it is resubmitted. Once all the kinks have been ironed out council will agree to your proposal and issue a development approval.

Once a property has development approval from the council its value instantly increases. You have clearly defined the way in which you intend to maximise the value of the property and gotten approval for your plans. That alone is enough to raise the worth of the property, meaning you could actually sell the property with the successful DA attached and potentially make a profit before you even lay the first brick.

If you want to ease your way into property development and gradually increase your involvement, completing DAs and on-selling them can be a great first step. It gives you the chance to use development tools, get the hang of the planning process and still makes profit – all without the hassles of actual construction.

If you're looking to do this but you don't have the money to actually buy a property in the first place, you needn't worry. There are still paths open to a person who is willing to think creatively. You may have heard of something called a "property option". It's a legal contract that can be a simple and powerful tool in the hands of somebody in the situation I just described.

Having an option means you have the right to buy a property at an agreed price on a specified date in the future. It gives you time to do further research on the property, get your finance together or get a development application approved before you ever actually purchase the property. It also gives you the peace of mind that no one else can buy the property while you are doing all of this, because the property cannot be sold to anyone else until the option contract expires.

BONUS! FREE gifts at www.TGRProperty.com.au/Gifts

To put an option in place you will need to have a contract. A good option contract should be drawn up by a qualified solicitor with property experience and could cost approximately $10,000. You will also generally need to pay an option fee when you place an option on a property, which will be decided based on your own negotiations. Generally an option fee is one to three per cent of the property's purchase price. Therefore, if you have a property that is worth $300,000 and you agree to pay a one per cent option fee you would end up $3,000 out-of-pocket.

The length of an option also depends on the negotiations. It could be six months, one year or even a number of years. Generally speaking, though, 12 months is the standard term. The longer the option period being negotiated, the harder it can be to make a deal. This is because you're locking in a purchase price, despite the fact that property values generally increase over time and the vendor will tend to think they could get more money for the property if it is sold in the future.

There are two basic types of options; one that gives you the right but not the obligation to purchase the property and another that gives you both the right and the obligation. With the first type of option you have a bit more freedom, as you can pull out of the purchase at the end of the option period. In this scenario you would generally lose your option fee, unless otherwise negotiated, and any other money you may have spent on research. In the second type of option you have to go ahead and purchase the property at the end of the option contract, regardless of where things stand. It doesn't give you as much room to move but there is one advantage in the fact it makes the vendor feel more secure knowing they have a guaranteed purchaser.

You may be wondering why a vendor would want to let you option their property. To understand it fully you need to put

PROFITABLE PROPERTY DEVELOPMENT

yourself in their shoes and look at it from their point of view. They may be strapped for cash, with no money to pay the school fees that year. If you offer them an option to buy their property in one year's time they get the $3,000 from the option fee but they don't have to move out of the house for another 12 months. Incidentally, this is one of the best negotiating tactics there is. If you can discover the wants and needs of the other person you will be well on the way towards creating a deal that works for everybody.

One of the benefits of an option is that it doesn't just buy you time, it also gives you the chance to make big profits – and I do mean big profits – through property without ever actually buying a single piece of land. You might find a property that is in the right zone for you to maximise its value but doesn't yet have council approval. You could negotiate an option to buy the property for $500,000 in 12 months' time. Next you contract an architect to draw up plans subdividing the property and splitting it into two separate blocks, then you go to council and get DA approval for those changes. The moment that passes the potential value of the property increases from $500,000 to $700,000, which is nice enough to know but doesn't make you any money yet because you still don't actually own it. At that point you have two choices: go through with purchasing the property and develop it yourself or cash out early and take the profit you've already created. To do that, you don't need to sell the property – you can simply sell the option. There are plenty of developers out there who don't have the time to look for properties and complete DAs, they prefer to jump onto a project once it's been approved and is ready to roll.

So, you take your option and the DA to a developer who would like to buy the property – you can advertise for this in your local paper – and you sell the option for the extra value that you

BONUS! FREE gifts at www.TGRProperty.com.au/Gifts

created in the property, which in this case is $200,000. After subtracting the cost of the option fee and the DA you are still left with $175,000 profit. The best part about this deal is that nobody loses. The developer goes on to pay the $500,000 option price on the property, then carries out the approved plans before finally selling both houses for $1.2 million.

Just in case all those numbers got a little confusing, I'll give them to you again in a clear list:

House valued:	$500,000
House optioned at:	$500,000
Option fee paid by you:	$5,000 (one per cent of the purchase price)
Cost of DA paid by you:	$25,000
New value of property with DA:	$700,000
Developer pays you for option:	$200,000
Developer pays vendor for house:	$500,000
Developer builds extra house:	$200,000
Developer sells both houses for:	$1,200,000
Your profits after expenses:	**$175,000**
Vendor's profits:	**$500,000**
Developer's profits after expenses:	**$300,000**

Property options are fantastic tools and I often use them when creating deals. When you really grasp the concept and start to understand how they work they are extremely valuable.

Another fantastically creative way to do a development or make money from property without actually buying the property is through a joint venture, which is simply a business partnership that has two or more partners.

BONUS! FREE gifts at www.TGRProperty.com.au/Gifts

PROFITABLE PROPERTY DEVELOPMENT

It works when you find somebody who owns the potential property and wants to make money off it, yet has no idea how to develop it, get a development application approved or carry out any of the steps required. Once you understand the entire process you will be able to help other people complete development applications on their properties and then charge a percentage of the profit you have made for them.

To give you an example, let's say you find a couple who owns a large farm. They know that developers have started moving into the area but they don't want to sell to one because they would like to make some of the profit for themselves. However, they don't know what to do or even how to get started. That's when you approach them and explain that you can help them through the development process of splitting their farm into six smaller blocks to be sold off individually. There's relatively little work involved, mainly the fencing off of the properties and a little clearing so roads can be built to access each new farm. You tell them you can get all that done for them and also obtain development approval, without charging them anything upfront, in return for a 20 per cent share of their profits at the end. That may sound like a lot but if they had simply sold their land to a developer they wouldn't have made nearly the same amount. Also, the fact that you are charging a percentage means they will feel secure in the knowledge you are going to go out of your way to get the best deal possible for them.

These are just some of the many creative and exciting ways that you can put deals together and start creating profit through property development without needing money to get started. As you learn more about the subject you will see how easy these deals are to put together and you will find that they really are everywhere.

BONUS! FREE gifts at www.TGRProperty.com.au/Gifts

Step six:
CONSTRUCTION

By now you should have your deal locked away, finance approved and plans stamped by council. Unless you've already cashed in your profits and moved on to the next deal it's finally time to start building. Taking a project through to the construction stage adds a significant amount of time and work but it also exponentially increases your profits. It's up to you to decide how much effort you are willing to put in and what level of return you expect.

Construction adds a significant amount of time and work but up go your profits!

Personally, I love bringing deals right through to construction. It's an amazing feeling to see your deal come to life and become a lasting product that others will share. Of course, it goes without saying that the larger profits at the end also help to make it a pretty sweet experience.

The great thing about the construction stage is that you actually don't do any of it yourself. Although I've been behind the construction of numerous buildings I've never actually hammered a single nail into a piece of wood or come close to pouring a slab of concrete. Your job as the developer is not to do the construction work but to create the team that will go in and do it for you. You hire the builder, giving them the approved plans and a contract that has very tight clauses related to cost and timeframe targets, then they hire the tradespeople who finally get the show on the road.

When it comes to the construction stage there's a very simple formula for success. It comes in the form of a flow chart that spells out the hierarchy of the project and makes sure everything goes smoothly. The real trick is to take your time and make sure you find a builder you can work well with. Crucially, he needs to have experience building similar projects to what you are asking. The last thing you want to do is pick a house builder to do a high-rise development, then become the guinea pig project he makes all his mistakes on as he gains experience. You want someone who has references and can show you similar projects they have done.

The hierarchy for a development site looks like this:

Developer (you)
|
Project manager
|
Builder
|
Site manager
|
Tradespeople

DEVELOPER

This is you. You are the dreamer, the creator, the entrepreneur and the deal-maker. You're the one who went out, found the potential deal and put it all together. You are the co-ordination point and the driver. You don't go on-site every day to see what is happening but stand back a little, liaising with the project manager to ensure the site is running on schedule and on budget.

PROJECT MANAGER

A project manager can be a godsend in any development, especially larger projects. If you are doing a smaller site such as a duplex or a few houses the builder can double as the project manager but on larger sites you will need both a project manager and a builder. The project manager should have experience in managing and co-ordinating projects. It is his job to run a tight ship, to co-ordinate with the bank and the architect and get the project done on schedule and on budget. He is on-site daily and inspects everything to ensure it's as it should be. He communicates and reports directly back to you and is accountable for the progress and profitability of the development. If you are doing a project for the first time, it's a great idea to get an experienced project manager and work closely with them. Once you get the hang of it you could be the project manager on your own sites and pay yourself a salary as you move towards the big profits at the end of the project.

BUILDER

The builder is responsible for construction according to the approved plans. He hires the team, schedules the tradesmen to work in accordance with each other and gets your property built. Some builders will have more than one project going at once, in which case they will not always be on-site. I suggest you find a builder that does one project at a time so you get maximum attention. Either way, the builder co-ordinates directly with the site manager who is always on-site and directly managing all of the tradespeople and sub-contractors.

TRADESPEOPLE

These are the guys that are in there doing the hard yards. They're the electricians, carpenters, plumbers, bricklayers – you name it. They're the foundation of your development and the ones who will literally bring your plans to fruition. They are co-ordinated and managed directly by the site manager and you don't want to get in the way. If you arrive at the site and start issuing instructions you will only create a mess. Understand each of the above roles, know what each person does, and know who manages who. The only reason you should talk to the tradespeople is to say thanks when you arrive with a carton of beer on a Friday afternoon.

One of the key factors of my success has been my ability to understand the above formula and respect the chain of command. It's made it possible for someone like me, with absolutely no experience in construction, to become a property developer. I know who does what and I let them get on with it. My job is simply to keep an eye on progress and make sure everybody is keeping to the budget and timeframe.

STEP SEVEN:
SALES

Once you have built a property you will finally have a product you can sell. This is the final stage of property development and is an interesting step because it can actually be done concurrently with the others. You can start selling your properties long before they have been built, which is called off-the-plan selling. It basically means selling a property based on the plan you have drawn, rather than by walking someone through the finished product. It's a fair question to ask why anybody would buy a property they haven't even seen. The answer is that, as you now know, the value of property goes up over time and tends to double every seven to 10 years. This works out to be an increase of about 10 per cent every year, so the buyer will take possession of a property that is worth more than the price they paid for it. For instance, if construction takes two years the property will be worth 20 per cent more than what they paid for it.

Off-the-plan property sales can be a great tool if they are done in the right way, which is to sell the property for what it is worth on the day you sell it. Don't price the property according to how much you think it will be worth once it's completed – this is not fair and is one of the reasons off-the-plan property sales have gotten something of a bad name. Unscrupulous real estate agencies have been adding large commissions to the purchase price of off-the-plan properties, preventing the seller from getting the profit they deserved and turning many potential buyers off the idea.

When done the right way off-the-plan sales offer a great opportunity for you to secure property sales during construction and not have to worry about selling them once built. It also allows buyers to invest in a property where they can lock in today's price without having to pay until the property is built a year or two down the track.

If you price your properties correctly and employ an honest and ethical sales strategy you should be successful in selling your product. Remember, at step two you already did your research and site analysis so you have good information that will help you price your properties and know how to market them.

PROFITABLE PROPERTY DEVELOPMENT

Whether you plan to sell all or just some of the properties you have built, ideally they will be sold before the end of construction. This decreases the time until the end of the whole project and minimises the amount of interest you pay to the banks, which in turn makes you more profit. So get your sales strategy pumping as soon as you start building.

No matter what your sales strategy is – whether it's selling off-the-plan or upon completion of the building – you need to figure out who is going to sell the properties for you and how they are doing to do that. There are three basic options for selling your properties:

1. **You** - This is as straightforward as it sounds, though it means you have to gain an excellent understanding of the market and formulate a sales strategy. The advantage of selling your own properties is that you don't have to pay anyone else a commission on the sale, which effectively gives you extra profit. However, you also have the extra work of actually selling the properties. This involves the creation of marketing and brochures to inform your buyers, placing advertisements to generate interest and using others methods to find potential buyers. If you only have a small development site selling through your own network can sometimes work well.

2. **Real estate agent** - This is probably the option you are most familiar with. A real estate agent is the avenue most people go down when buying and selling property. They will generally charge a commission of anything from one to three per cent of the property's purchase price, as well as a marketing fee for the placement of advertisements and the creation of brochures.

BONUS! FREE gifts at www.TGRProperty.com.au/Gifts

Most people still use a real estate agent when buying and selling a property

Real estate agents can be a good option because their commission rate is low, they understand the local area and they are experienced in selling properties. The downside of real estate agents is they don't always have a lot of experience in selling off-the-plan, which can be a very different game to selling properties that already exist. You need to ensure your agent understands off-the-plan sales, has a good knowledge of the area and will be proactive in finding potential buyers.

3. **Project marketer** - Project marketers are similar to real estate agents. In fact, they are real estate agents and will generally hold all the same licenses. The difference is that they usually deal only in developments and sell mostly off-the-plan, creating a direct link between the buyers – who are mostly investors – and developers. They are known for being very proactive about selling and will carry out an enthusiastic campaign to find potential buyers for your properties. This could involve brochures, billboards, even television advertisements – it all depends on the size of the development.

PROFITABLE PROPERTY DEVELOPMENT

Project marketers will generally charge double the rate of a normal real estate agent, anywhere from four to six per cent of the property's purchase price. However, they will not usually charge you the marketing costs, which come directly out of their own pocket. Another thing to keep in mind is that you don't pay them a cent until they've secured a sale, so you are only paying for the results you get. Ultimately, a project marketer will cost you more but they may sell your properties quicker and could have all your properties sold by the time you finish construction. This is one of those areas where you need to weigh up the cost versus the benefits.

By choosing the right sales strategy – and putting it into action as soon as construction begins – you can help minimise the risk of being stuck with an unsold property. That's why it's so important to have control over this step of the development process.

RECAP

Well, now you understand the seven steps that make up what we know as "property development". As you start to play the game you will realise it's just a matter of following the steps and playing it out. Simply put: if you don't follow the steps you won't get the results.

Once you really get a feel for all the steps you can start jumping around and mixing them up a little. Remember, you don't always need to do all steps. On some deals you will only do the first few steps, with others you might come in at the middle or you may jump in on the end of a deal and make your profit that way. It's entirely up to you.

When you're first starting, though, I suggest you begin with step one and move forward through the other steps in sequence. Jump in at the beginning and start looking for potential deals and development sites, then move onto step two and do the site analysis on the site you have found. At step three you will bring all your research together and decide if the venture will be profitable, then step four is all about finding creative ways to finance your project. Once that problem's been solved you can move on to step five, planning approval, then begin the construction of step six. All of it leads up to the most exciting part of all, step seven, where you will get to reap the big rewards of your work.

SOME REAL DEALS
It's one thing to hear theoretical examples but it's quite another to examine how the things we've discussed work in the real world. I thought you might like to see some of the deals I've done that have started at step one and went right through to step seven, using some or all of the above strategies.

29 UNITS
This was one of the first projects that I ever worked on. I needed $3 million to buy the land but I simply didn't have the money at the time. In fact, I don't think I had a spare $3.

Undeterred, I approached some private investors and proposed they pay enough for the deposit on the land, in which case the banks would lend the rest. In return I offered them 10 per cent interest per annum, which was a good opportunity because the banks were offering only five per cent at the time.

So I now had enough for the deposit, while the banks would pay the rest. However, I still needed to get the DA approved, which for all 29 units turned out to be quite expensive. I needed another $150,000 and we all know by now that it simply wasn't lying around my house.

PROFITABLE PROPERTY DEVELOPMENT

I went back to the developer who had mentored me, told him what I was doing and asked for $150,000 in cash upfront. He agreed but wanted a big split of the profits at the end of the deal. I had to think carefully about that but I finally said, "You know what? That's fair enough". I needed his money more than he needed to invest it, as I couldn't have gotten the deal rolling without that extra cash.

The development ultimately took 18 months to complete and brought in profits of over $2 million. At no point did I spend any of my own money. I simply put the deal together, brought all the parties together and made sure they all walked away with a healthy profit.

8 TOWNHOUSES

This is a smaller and more recent deal that I particularly like because the project involves three people I've helped mentor and it's great to see it all come full circle.

There was a big block on the market for $660,000. Through negotiation I got it down to a purchase price of $500,000 that I had to pay in cash, with no options or joint ventures. There was already an approved DA on it to build eight townhouses, each of which would be worth $370,000.

The three people each invested $250,000, which was enough to purchase the land and cover the extra costs of development. In return for their investment they would each get a brand new villa valued at $370,000, thus giving them the option of taking the $120,000 in profit or hanging on to a property that will increase in value over time. The best advantage of all, though, was that they got a real insight into the way a development works, day to day, from beginning to end. They were hands-on in the management of the development, giving them both real development experience and real profits.

My role in the process was to run the whole project and manage the builder who, because it was a small project, was also the project manager. My reward for putting it all together was a profit of $370,000, making this another example of a creative no-money-down deal that allows everyone to walk away as a winner.

MAKE EVERYONE A WINNER

Ensuring that everyone is a winner at the end of a deal is one of the most important things you need to remember when creating wealth for yourself, no matter what vehicle you use. You can't make money on your own – there have to be other people involved and it's up to you to do the right thing when dealing with those people. You have to take their situations and expected outcomes into account. If you only look for ways you can win, your game is far too small. However, when you think about how you and the others around you can win, your game becomes bigger and you will inevitably have the chance to win a bigger prize.

MY NUMBER ONE TIP

As long as I'm giving you the secrets of property development that have brought me success, I may as well include the number one tip that has been the driving force behind my journey.

Creating wealth has a lot to do with the purpose you create it for. If you don't really know why you want to make the money, if you just think it sounds pretty cool to "be rich", then you need to sit down and work out a real purpose. Money itself is not a motivation. Money is an energy that is created through having a purpose and a motivation – it can't be that purpose or the motivation.

My purpose is philanthropy. My mother imprinted on me from a very early age the importance of charity and giving back, a lesson I've never forgotten. For as long as I can remember I was always doing charity walks, taking collections and volunteering for just about everything that was going. As I got older I started to see real problems in the world that I wanted to change. I helped a lot of organisations and did a lot of volunteering but I still felt like I wasn't really making a difference, that nothing was really changing. I remember thinking I'd need to make a lot of money to start bringing about the changes I wanted, so that's exactly what I did.

By now I've volunteered thousands of hours of my time and donated hundreds of thousands of dollars to charity. I've created a charitable organisation and this is the purpose that continues to motivate me. It's why I get up every day wanting to do bigger and better property deals, as I know I need the money for my real life's work.

That's my purpose but yours may be different. It doesn't matter what it is, so long as it's real and you make a conscious effort to live by it. There's one thing you might want to keep in mind: the bigger your purpose and the more people it reaches, the more power, success and freedom will be coming back your way.

GETTING STARTED

So, there you have it. You now know the seven steps of property development, which is an excellent start to your wealth-creation journey. The question is, what should be your first personal step?

After reading this chapter you may have a little fire burning in your belly and a little voice inside your head saying, "I reckon I could give that a shot". If you are feeling that way and think this game sounds like something you want to try, then all I can say is, "Give it a shot".

That is exactly what I did. I remember very clearly my state of mind when I first got started. It seemed like such a big game that I felt overwhelmed and was actually very confused. However, at the same time I had a feeling of, "I just really want to give it a go". So that's what I did. I started by picking up the Saturday paper and looking for development sites. I would then call the people who placed the ads and ask questions about the properties. If you think all of this makes me sound superhuman or special in any way, you're dead wrong. The first few calls I made were an absolute disaster. I had no idea what to say or which questions to ask, I didn't understand the language and I didn't even know what I intended to do. On a few calls I became so tongue-tied and embarrassed that I simply hung up mid-call.

Crucially, though, after those bad experiences I would pause for a moment, catch my breath and then pick up the phone to make another call. I knew I just had to start associating myself with the deals and get into the developing environment. I kept making calls and researching sites, then it wasn't long at all before I started to get the hang of it. That's when I started meeting contacts and began probing them for more information on the subject. I'm not going to lie to you and say it was easy. In fact, it was damn hard, particularly as there was nobody around at the time to show me the best way forward. I guess I took the rockier path, and stumbled a few times because of it, but you're a lot luckier today than I was back then. These days there actually are some courses around that can teach you the ins and outs of property development in a few days, which is far better than the experience I had of piecing it all together over a period of years. There have been times when deals were tough and life was hard.

PROFITABLE PROPERTY DEVELOPMENT

As you know, I didn't come from wealth so I literally had to start with nothing, but it's been an incredible experience and it continues to be just that. I can't even describe the amount of love and respect I have for the game of property and, specifically, property development. The best part is that it's indiscriminate and has given me a world of choice and freedom I would otherwise never have had. If you are willing to throw your hat in the ring, to believe in yourself and persevere against all obstacles, I have no doubt it will do exactly the same for you.

Do you want my ultimate, guaranteed-to-succeed magic trick? It's simply this: just give it a bloody good go and never give up.

If you are willing to throw your hat in the ring, to believe in yourself and persevere against all obstacles, property development will being you great rewards.

FREE BONUS GIFT

Carly Crutchfield has generously offered a FREE BONUS GIFT valued at $147

FREE Audio Download – **"Property Secrets of the Wealthy".**

**Visit the website below to receive these free gifts
www.TGRProperty.com.au/Gifts**

Chapter 5

CREATIVE CASHFLOW

"When it comes to property of course I'm negotiable on the price... but why would you want to pay more?"

RICK OTTON

PROFILE

RICK OTTON

Rick Otton is one of the original pioneers of creative property strategies in Australia and the United Kingdom. He is internationally recognised by the property industry for his property transactions using positive cashflow and little or no money down.

Rick is founder and CEO of We Buy Houses, a leading property enterprise which he has successfully expanded into the international markets of the United Kingdom, New Zealand, United States and Australia. Starting in 2001, Rick has been buying, selling and trading property, using little or none of his own money and structuring transactions to create positive cashflow. Since then he has taught 23,700 people to buy, sell and trade residential property using his strategies.

Rick's mission is to transform the way people buy and sell property, to empower them where the traditional real estate system has failed.

He is creating an international community of investors who combine the goal of making money with the higher purpose of solving other people's problems. These include problems such as potential buyers who can't get on the property ladder and sellers who are facing financial difficulty as a result of owning property.

Rick believes that "things don't change, people change things". He relishes the challenge of looking at standard practice and asking, why is it this way and is it working?

His philosophy has been highlighted in various Australian TV shows. He's appeared in the 2004 ABC documentary *Reality Bites; Today Tonight; Insight* on SBS; and *A Current Affair*. In October 2007 Rick gave away a house on national TV during two episodes of Channel 9's *Hot Property*.

He's also been featured in *Australian Property Investor* magazine and in the Australian books *The Secrets of Property Millionaires Exposed!* and *Ideas: Original Perspectives On Life and Business From Leading Thinkers*, as well as the American book *Walking With The Wise*.

CREATIVE CASHFLOW

HOW TO BECOME A PROPERTY ENTREPRENEUR USING OTHER PEOPLE'S MONEY

Imagine buying a house without getting a bank loan.

Imagine buying your home without using any of your own cash.

Imagine buying a house even if your credit isn't perfect.

It is possible to buy property using little or none of your own money. And it's possible for both the buyer and the seller to get what they want at the same time. I'm Rick Otton, and in this chapter I'll show you some real "no money down" property transactions that my students and I have done.

My mission for the past 20 years has been to transform the way people buy and sell property in Australia and New Zealand. Thousands of people are already buying and selling property the easy way but there are still many more people doing it the hard way. I'm here to show you that there is an easier way. In fact, there are many easier ways.

THE PROFIT IS IN THE TERMS, NOT THE PRICE

In traditional price-led negotiations, where sellers want the price high and buyers want the price low, nobody wins except for agents, banks and lawyers. My strategies take the focus off the

BONUS! FREE gifts at www.TGRProperty.com.au/Gifts

price, and onto flexible and convenient payment terms. This is how I can structure transactions where both the buyer and seller get what they want, as you'll see in the examples.

In the current financial climate, we're facing a crisis that most people haven't ever experienced in their lifetimes. In many ways, today mirrors the savings and loans crisis in the USA of the late 1980s and early 1990s.

While the media spreads gloom and doom, you'll see that these are actually great times. While it's always a great time to buy, the best time to buy is in a falling market, when hardly anyone is buying, and everyone needs to get more flexible with their priorities and reshape their processes. As you'll see later on, that's how I got started, in one of the worst falling markets of all.

While most people buy and sell property one way only, there are actually many strategies that enable buyers and sellers to *both* get what they want, without the usual headaches and hassles that have become so commonplace for most Australians. That's what this chapter is all about.

IT'S ALL ABOUT CHANGING PROCESSES

People say that I'm a property guy, or that I'm the creative finance guy. But really I'm a processes guy. I look at processes that have been accepted and unchanged for a long time, and I ask:

> **"Is this the best way? Or is it just a hand-me-down process that no-one ever changed?"**
>
> **"Is this the most efficient process?"**
>
> **"Just suppose we did it another way…"**

I apply this way of thinking and changing process to everything, and I recommend that my students do, too, as soon as possible.

CREATIVE CASHFLOW

But I'm most passionate about changing processes with property because property affects everyone. It's such a big part of our lives. Whenever I change part of the process of buying and selling property, it unlocks hidden opportunities for people, solves problems that old processes simply couldn't, and has ripple effects that can help so many people and improve so many lives.

OPTIONAL HASSLES

When selling property, most people accept the following hassles as an unavoidable part of the process:
- agent commissions and advertising fees
- having the house on the market for months on end
- nobody showing up to open houses
- agents can't sell it so the price keeps dropping
- market fluctuations make it harder to sell.

Similarly, most buyers accept the following hassles as an unavoidable part of the process:
- Stamp Duty and legal fees
- saving up a 10 per cent or 20 per cent deposit
- qualifying for a bank loan
- dealing with real estate agents.

However, all of these hassles are entirely optional. Most of my students have done deals that avoid some or all of them. In fact, among my students, the following situations are much more common:
- selling a house in an hour, a day, or a week
- no agent commissions or advertising fees
- no deposit, just move in and start making payments
- get the price you want fast, in any market.

Everything's optional, and everything's flexible. Once you accept that as a principle and fact of life, everything will change for you.

BONUS! FREE gifts at www.TGRProperty.com.au/Gifts

Questioning convention and creating new processes are valuable skills. Especially today, when the pace of change is faster than anyone could have dreamed of just a few short decades ago.

Traditional processes can often create problems. I'm into solving problems, and creating processes that solve problems by default. I'm always finding easier ways and more efficient ways to do things. I'm always asking, why does it have to be hard? The answer is that it doesn't.

Most of us unconsciously make things hard for ourselves because along the way we've learned that good things require hard work. This isn't true in all cases, but we apply it to all cases anyway. If you work hard at school, then you get to go to university. If you work hard at university, then you earn your degree and go on to get a job. When you work hard there, you go on to get a promotion. The good things always seem to come after knuckling down and working hard. So when good things come along, even if they're really simple, we tend to unconsciously overcomplicate processes and make them harder than they really need to be.

Let's say two guys meet at the side of the road. One has a six-pack of beer, and the other has a bottle of scotch. They start talking and decide they want to swap the beer for the scotch. Nobody thinks anything of it. They agree, they swap, they're both happy, it's no big deal. It's simple and it's easy.

But if you change that same simple swap from drinks to houses, all of a sudden it seems a lot harder. The truth is that it's no different at all, but we've all learned to make it more difficult –

for ourselves and everyone else. When houses are involved there are a lot of extra rules in people's heads and suddenly every man and his dog has an opinion. All you hear is: "you can't do this" and "you have to do that".

Most of the time you won't be told the most efficient way and, trust me, there is definitely more than one way to do things. It's just that there is a most commonly accepted way, which usually hasn't been improved or made any more efficient for a few hundred years or more. The conventional processes usually make things easier for the solicitors (because they don't have to think, they just photocopy the same form that was used in the 1800s) and make things unnecessarily complicated and expensive for the buyers and sellers.

Here's what I believe, and I've seen it work in practice thousands of times: if two people want to transfer an item or two between them, those two people should be able to agree over coffee or ice-cream and come to a simple arrangement that works for them both.

WE DON'T HAVE TO BE TOLD WHAT TO DO
Farmers used to do it all the time before the banks got involved, swapping sheep and grain for pieces of land or paying instalments over a number of years instead of paying the full amount up front. They were flexible. They were open to different ideas. When the usual process wasn't going to solve their problems, or before a "standard process" had been invented and accepted far and wide, they thought things through, talked one-on-one and created a process that worked.

Creative financing is all about creating processes that solve problems. Talking one-on-one like the farmers, with the buyer talking directly to the seller, is part of making these strategies

are talking to a real estate agent, you aren't
story. If you're going to solve someone's
terms of a deal, you need to talk directly to that
so you can find out exactly what problems need to be
solved.

Here's something I've always found fascinating:

**The majority of self-made millionaires
in any country are new immigrants.**

New immigrants can't go back to the old country, so their backs are really against the wall and they have to deliver results to survive. They have ideas, perspectives and habits from the old country, not the new country, so they automatically think differently to everyone else around them. They don't have a group of "that'll-never-work" friends influencing them or holding them back or trying to get them to *stop* thinking differently. They don't have anyone to lose face in front of. They didn't grow up being told the same version of "that's-just-the-way-things-are" as all the people around them.

As a result, they ask obvious or awkward questions that others don't; they challenge unquestioned processes and accepted conventions. They find a better, more efficient way. They think differently and do things differently. They've got nothing to lose – not money, friends, reputation, status…not anything. And usually, they *do* have themselves and their family to take care of, and everything to gain. With no fallback plans, they have to make it or die trying.

CREATIVE CASHFLOW

It's never too late to think like a new immigrant.

You see, it's not actually *being* a new immigrant that makes the difference. It's *thinking* like one. And anyone can do that. Anyone. Anytime.

It was actually thinking like a new immigrant that helped me get started in property in the first place.

When my wife and I were living in the USA in the early 1990s, our backs were against the wall, and we couldn't go back. I noticed that the real estate in Dallas, Texas, was really cheap – actually, too cheap. After doing some research I found out that the whole savings and loans mess was unravelling before my eyes.

I originally started in property because I hated my job. Everything in my life seemed to take money out of my pocket, and nothing except my job brought money in. I was looking for something else to bring money in so I could escape from my job. I read in a book that only five things increase in value over time, and property was one of them.

So I went out and bought a bunch of books and tapes so I could learn how to make money in real estate. Because I didn't have any friends in Dallas yet, there was nobody to tell me all the reasons that those books and tapes don't work. I didn't have any friends or support system to show me the old ways and talk me out of it. I didn't know any better. My ways simply made more sense. So I just started doing as the books and tapes said.

In fact, I'd already bought a dozen houses from banks before I'd made enough friends who tried to convince me that the banks didn't have anything worth buying. The property was being sold at ten cents on the dollar, but the locals wouldn't touch it because they would say, "We've seen values drop 80 per cent, what makes you think it won't drop further?" This was a great opportunity for Australians, who are familiar and comfortable with real estate, and who think differently from the locals. So we invited some of our Australian friends over for our wedding, and they got to cash in on the real estate opportunities while they were there.

Looking back now, I can see the new immigrant thinking in action.

Friends are great to talk to but terrible to listen to.

So that's how it started. I saw an opportunity where everyone else saw a problem, and I changed what needed to be changed to make it financially viable. From then on I could see that houses can be money machines that spit out more cash than you put into them each week. So I kept buying more houses.

The more deals I did, the more "problems" (a.k.a opportunities) I saw, the more ways I found to do things a little differently. Without friends around to tell me all the reasons it wouldn't work, I just looked at each problem and said "what if we did it this way?"

If you just start to ask this one question, it'll change your results and your life forever:

"Is this the best way, or simply the hand-me-down way that no-one has ever changed?"

There are generally two kinds of people in this world: the people who say "you can't do that," and the people who say "let's find a

CREATIVE CASHFLOW

way". Both of them are right but I've always been someone who "finds a way". I'm often inspired to find a way when I hear "you can't do that". It feels almost like a dare, like they're saying, "I bet you can't do that", to which I reply, "Watch me!" and I go off and make it happen.

If someone says, "It'll never work", is that based on the process that they know, or is it based on the process I'm about to create? You see, there's no such thing as "you can't do that". You can do anything, it's just there are some things you just haven't figured out the process for yet.

I don't know about you, but whenever there's a new challenge or opportunity that needs a new process to be created, I'm excited to figure it out.

I have a friend called Geoff who I've known since we were kids. Geoff has over a dozen real estate offices around the world, is a private lender, and owns well over a hundred of his own buy-and-hold properties. If there was anyone in the world that I would want to impress with my new-found property skills, it was Geoff.

When I came back from the USA, after I'd done all these deals over there, I told Geoff that I wanted to do the same thing in Australia. Geoff said, "It might work in the States, but that won't work in Australia". That just inspired me to prove that it *would* work in Australia.

So I started doing property deals in the western suburbs of Sydney: Blacktown, St Marys, Mount Druitt. I did the deals the same way I had been doing them in the USA. I brought my results back to Geoff to prove to him that it worked in Australia. It should have been obvious. He had to admit that it worked because I'd already done it. But Geoff said, "It might work out in the west, but that won't work in the rest of Sydney". Which inspired me to prove that it would work *anywhere* in Australia no matter what – regional, suburban, or mid-city.

Geoff was very specific about which suburbs he thought it wouldn't work in. So I did deals in those suburbs. He was specific about which kinds of houses and units and price points it wouldn't work for. So I did deals with those kinds of houses and units and price points. Everything he said wouldn't work, I did. And it worked. So then Geoff said, "It might work for you, but it wouldn't work for anyone else". I knew from the start that if I could do it, anyone could. But that last piece of "you can't" inspiration from Geoff was what got me to start teaching these strategies to other people.

CREATIVE WAYS TO GROW WEALTH

There are a few keys to growing wealth, but the one that seems to be most important (and often overlooked) is cashflow. To grow wealth you need to own something that grows in value, like property, and to hold it – and generate cashflow from it – while it grows.

Buy-and-hold investments will make you wealthy eventually, but "buy-and-fold" is much more common. According to the Australian Bureau of Statistics, 70 per cent of Australians who buy an investment property sell it within five years because it's not giving them what they want. And 47 per cent of those who sell will either lose money or barely break even.

Before they have grown in value enough for you to live on them, buy-and-hold investments will usually take money out of your pocket every month. This can cause problems. Cashflow solves this problem.

CREATIVE CASHFLOW

Everything in life takes money out of your pocket. Family commitments, investments, health challenges – everything. Because of this, I didn't have any money to put into property when I started. I needed property to bring money in, not take it out. So from the beginning, all my strategies had to create more ways to bring in money. And that's exactly what they do.

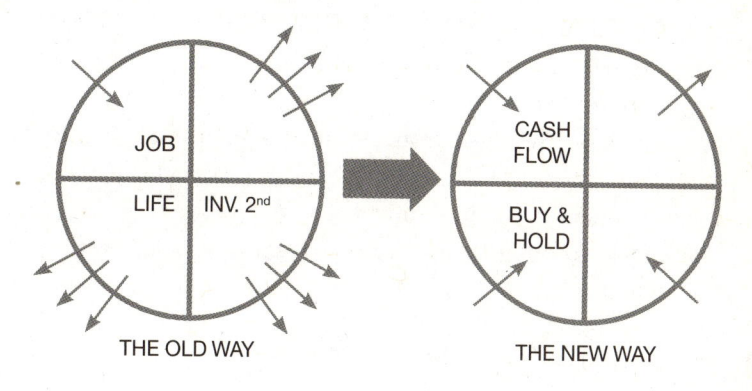

THE OLD WAY: JOB / LIFE / INV. 2nd

THE NEW WAY: CASH FLOW / BUY & HOLD

Here's what I learned to do early on:

Use some properties to generate cashflow, and use other properties to grow wealth.

This is why all the strategies I teach in my live trainings enable people to generate cashflow from property. Cashflow solves lots of problems. With these strategies, instead of price-led negotiations, we get a little bit flexible with how we swap property for money. And both the buyer and seller end up better off.

It's all about convenience, not price. I buy and sell houses with flexible finance terms, the same way major brand retailers sell over 60 per cent of their home theatre systems – pay some now and some later, with no interest and easy terms. When you get creative about the way a transaction is financed, there's no need

BONUS! FREE gifts at www.TGRProperty.com.au/Gifts

to haggle over price. As a buyer, you can pay some of the price now and pay the rest later. As a seller, you provide convenience at a premium, so you don't need to drop your price.

Let's take a look at the main strategies right now.

CREATIVE FINANCING = CASHFLOW

You can only have so many negatively geared properties taking money out of your pocket before you send yourself broke. Even just one negatively geared property can cause enormous problems and stress. The solution is cashflow. So the main strategies that I show my students (and I'm about to show you) are strategies that enable you to generate cashflow from all of your property transactions.

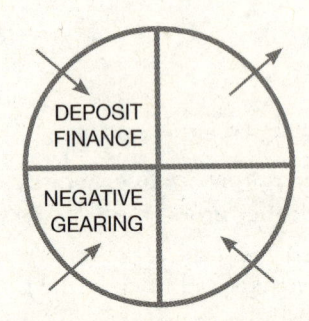

All three of these cashflow strategies are various forms of vendor finance, which is also known as seller finance. With seller finance, the seller provides more convenient ways for the buyer to purchase the property than conventional bank finance. Every situation is different. It's also referred to as creative financing because you can get creative with whatever specific terms best suit the buyer and seller.

CREATIVE CASHFLOW

When you use any of these creative finance strategies to on-sell a property, you make it easier for buyers to buy. You basically make it possible for buyers to buy now and pay later, just like retailers do with computers and big-screen televisions. And when you make a property easier to buy, it will sell faster. My students often buy houses for a dollar, then on-sell them in under a day, without paying fees or commissions to agents, and without dropping the price.

This is great news if you have a property you want or need to sell, because when you want to sell, you usually want three things: to sell fast, to get the price you want, and to pay as little in fees as possible.

"That's great, Rick," I hear you say, "but I don't have a property to sell, I can't even buy one." That's just fine. All these strategies are designed to solve buyers' problems by making your property easier and more convenient to buy. This automatically solves sellers' problems because they can sell fast without dropping the price. You can use the same strategies as a buyer and a seller. Once you have the skills to sell a property fast for a great price, you will find countless properties out there just waiting for you to buy. Just like my students, you can keep some and on-sell the rest – fast!

EASY TO BUY IS EASY (AND FAST) TO SELL

Legal professionals use technical terms to describe these strategies. I prefer to use what I call "mums and dads language" instead of professional jargon. So, in the explanations that follow, I'll define the jargon for you, but I'll be using this simplified language most of the time. Now let's take a look at some of the most common creative financing scenarios in detail.

BONUS! FREE gifts at www.TGRProperty.com.au/Gifts

DEPOSIT FINANCE

The professional jargon name for this strategy, and the paperwork that supports it, is a Second-Mortgage Carry Back. But deposit finance is a much simpler name that perfectly describes what's actually happening. The seller simply finances the deposit for the buyer, so the buyer doesn't need to pay the full deposit upfront.

Three trends in today's market make deposit finance not only appealing, but often necessary in more and more cases:
- out-of-reach property prices
- tough economic times
- poor saving habits.

People simply don't save the way they used to. Nobody uses lay-by anymore. Whenever we buy furniture and electrical goods we all use the buy now, pay later option. And retailers have had to provide these easy finance terms to compete. They provide convenient finance terms which enable their customers to have a big-screen high-definition movie experience in the comfort of their own home today, without saving up the money first. And if they didn't (if they had to wait for people to save now, buy later), they would lose more than half their sales.

Obviously, if people aren't saving for the small things, then coming up with a deposit for a house is going to be a big challenge. Many people have great incomes, but they just don't save. These same people can and do, however, reliably pay things off over time.

House prices have been rising for quite some time, so much so that the price of an average house has become out-of-reach for the average buyer in some cities. Because banks will only loan 80 – 90 per cent of the value, the higher the price of the house, the bigger the deposit required.

BONUS! FREE gifts at www.TGRProperty.com.au/Gifts

CREATIVE CASHFLOW

Let me ask you something: how many people have a lazy $250,000 sitting around in a cheque account to cover the deposit, Stamp Duty and legal costs of buying a house? Fewer than one per cent of Australians. Which means that even if they can qualify for finance with a traditional lender, fewer than one per cent of Australians would be able to buy an average house in Sydney.

House prices may not continue rising in tough economic times, and interest rates might drop and ease the mortgage burden a little. But other constraints come into play at such times. Banks have been known to reduce the amount they will lend on property. So instead of getting a loan for 90 per cent of the property value, you can only get 70 per cent or less. In the savings and loans crisis of the late 1980s, banks in the United States wouldn't lend money on property at all. We had to get very creative in those times. We even got finance on a car and threw in the house for free.

Things may not be that extreme, but you can see how helpful providing deposit finance can be. The biggest benefit is that it will enable you to access many more buyers, and sell your house fast without dropping your price.

VARIATION ONE:
DELAYED DEPOSIT

Let's say you're selling a property worth $400,000. The property has been on the market for six months and it hasn't sold. The agent has already dropped the price by $10,000 every month, but it still doesn't entice buyers and you're not sure if you want to take an offer as low as $350,000.

You know a couple that would love to buy a house like yours, have their finance ready to go for $320,000 (80 per cent of the $400,000 value), but they just don't have $80,000 in cash for a deposit.

BONUS! FREE gifts at www.TGRProperty.com.au/Gifts

Based on getting your $400,000 price, would you be willing to allow this couple to pay 80 per cent now and pay off the deposit over the next 10 years at the same interest rate as their bank loan? Of course you would: $320,000 in the hand now is better than the possibility of $350,000 someday. And based on the agent's track record, the price will probably be dropped to $320,000 in the next three months anyway.

If you finance the deposit, you'd get $320,000 now, and the $80,000 "deposit" paid back in instalments over the next 10 years (or however many years you and the buyer agree upon). By being willing to accept delayed gratification with the deposit, not only would you sell your house faster, you'd receive about $950 per month for the next 10 years, or until the buyer refinances and pays you the rest of the $80,000 in full.

By putting paperwork in place by which you finance the deposit, you can get the price you want now, and you're creating an opportunity for the buyer. When buyers compare all the properties they've seen, and yours is the only one that says "no deposit required, move in now, pay later", they'll naturally find your house more attractive than any of the others they've seen because of the payment terms.

If you make these terms available in the first place, you won't have to wait months to find a buyer. They'll find you and you'll usually be able to sell within a week or two.

VARIATION TWO:
EXTEND THE GRANT

You have probably seen some of the advertisements on television recently for various property builders or developers that say either "no deposit" or "increase your first homeowners grant to

CREATIVE CASHFLOW

$32,000". You've seen above how they finance the deposit so it doesn't have to be paid up front. Now let's look at how you can increase the first homeowners grant for your buyers, and make your property more attractive to buy (and faster to sell) as a result.

Recently a lady had her house on the market for months. The agent had discounted the price down to $525,000 but she didn't receive a single offer over $500,000. She didn't know why, and the agent didn't offer any reasons. At the time she was trying to sell, first homeowners in her state were entitled to an additional $3,000 grant for any property up to $500,000. If they paid $500,001, they no longer qualified for the extra $3,000 grant. Knowing this, the seller could put the price back up to the full retail value of $580,000, offer $3,000 cash back, and end up with a net sale price of $577,000.

You would often be better off to increase the first homeowners grant for a potential buyer than to discount your price. If you discount, you have no control over how many tens of thousands of dollars the discounting strategy will cost you, or how many months your property will stay on the market. If you offer an "extra $7,000 grant", for example, you know that the strategy will only cost you $7,000 off your full retail price. You can offer this to first homeowners or to everyone. Putting money into people's pockets always sounds better to them than simply discounting the price.

Note: The full first homebuyers grant expired in December 2009. It's important to check which grants - state or national - apply at the time that you're selling, because these grants could be affecting the actions of your potential buyers.

BONUS! FREE gifts at www.TGRProperty.com.au/Gifts

VARIATION THREE:
HONEYMOON PERIOD

When you make something easy to buy, it becomes easy to sell. The key is to differentiate your property from the other properties that your buyers are looking at. This is especially important if there are a lot of very similar properties for sale at the same time, such as in an apartment block or housing estate. If all the houses are the same, only the terms will set you apart and make yours sell faster than the rest.

Put yourself in the buyer's shoes. If they can get into a house without paying a big deposit, that would make their life easier. In most cases they'd be grateful to you for the opportunity that no one else offered them, they'd pay full price for the house, and they'd never miss a payment.

You can also make your house more appealing and easier to buy by offering a "honeymoon period" of some sort. When everyone else is trying to discount to make their property more attractive than the one beside it, your honeymoon period would actually *be* more attractive to buyers. Based on getting your full price, there are many creative variations on the honeymoon idea. You've probably heard a few from retail chains. Anything the electrical and furniture stores can do, you can do too.

You can offer a reduced interest rate, two per cent less in the first year, and one per cent less in the second year. You can offer three per cent interest for the first twelve months. You can offer whatever you like. Just go through the numbers to make sure it works, and make sure your offer will be enticing to buyers.

CREATIVE CASHFLOW

The paperwork for the honeymoon period interest rate simply states that the buyer pays the first three per cent and you make a payment to offset the rest. This is all processed at settlement, the offset amount is either paid to the bank up front or sits in an account to be drawn down on each month. Let's look at an example.

If you're selling a property for $600,000, and you offer a two per cent reduced interest rate for the first twelve months, here's how it would work:

If the buyer has a 25-year bank loan for $540,000 with an interest rate of 7.25 per cent, their full monthly payment would be $3,903.16.

If they were to pay only 5.25 per cent, their reduced monthly payment would be $3,235.94, making the offset amount $667.22 per month that you would pay for them.

$667.22 per month x 12 = $8,006.64 for the first twelve months.

So, you can see from this example that the real cash out of your pocket is only $8,006.67. But the appeal of a two per cent reduction in the interest rate would mean that you wouldn't need to drop the price of your property, resulting in a faster sale and a far better price. If you must discount, discount the interest rate. By selling faster and getting the price you want, a strategy that discounts the interest rate would leave you much better off than any strategy based on discounting the price.

BONUS! FREE gifts at www.TGRProperty.com.au/Gifts

VARIATION FOUR:
HANDYMAN SPECIAL

There are many people who would love to renovate a run-down property and make it their home, but they simply don't have the deposit to get started. Renovations invariably improve the value of a property. Just suppose there was a way that the renovation itself could be the deposit.

I call this strategy "Sweat Equity" or the "Handyman Special". There are a few details to be aware of, but the main gist of the strategy is that buyers use their elbow grease as the deposit.

It's very important that they cannot live in the property while they're renovating it under any circumstances. They have to have their finance, the renovation must meet certain standards, and they must be motivated to turn my house into their home. Most people redecorate anyway. This way they get to renovate and redecorate before they move in.

Here's how the numbers work:

A rundown property in Penrith, NSW, was valued at $278,000. With a renovation it would be valued at $340,000. So if the property was already renovated, the sale price would be $340,000. A 10 per cent deposit on that property would be $34,000, so I offered to accept a deposit of a renovation worth $34,000. We agreed on the price of $340,000. The buyers qualified for a loan for the other $306,000 and got to work renovating.

When the renovation was complete, it was better than I had imagined. They bought the house, paid me the $306,000, and moved in. The new owners then got the house valued at $395,000, so their hard work actually enabled them to grow $89,000 in equity. Let's look at a couple of examples from my students:

Deposit Finance Examples

The Winnebago Deal

Student Ben

I call this the Winnebago Deal, because this guy was selling his house in Craigmore, South Australia, to buy a Winnebago. I didn't know this at first. We were negotiating how much money he'll take now and how much he'll take later. He was definitely open to flexible terms, but the whole time I was struggling to figure out what he really wanted. As soon as I found out that he wanted a Winnebago, we got the catalogues and looked them up online. He was so excited! He was in his mid-60s, and he'd decided it was time to drive around the country and live off his pension. And he also wanted a little extra cash to help for maintenance and repairs to his Winnebago.

When I started doing property transactions, I connected with a few accountants and finance brokers. Interest rates were on the rise at the time, and the only people buying properties were investors. So each time I got a house, I'd send a few photos, and they'd broadcast it to their clients. They helped source investors interested in buying the houses I found, and they never had any problems getting finance.

So, I on-sold this house to an investor. The house was valued at $290,000, and he owed $110,000. The Winnebago cost $75,000, so he took $203,000 up front, leaving him with $18,000 in the bank to cover repairs and maintenance. We even got the cheques made out directly to the Winnebago dealer. The investors then rented the house back to the guy on a three-year lease.

He was content to wait three years for his "deposit" – the $87,000 balance – that's how happy he was with the deal.

BONUS! FREE gifts at www.TGRProperty.com.au/Gifts

RICK OTTON

No Deposit in Wyoming, New South Wales

Student Rob

Knowing what I do, a couple asked if I could buy them a house. They had no deposit, but said they could get this house really cheap. It was an unadvertised mortgagee in possession property on the Central Coast, NSW. It was selling for $160,000 plus Stamp Duty, so I borrowed the money short-term for a week for a fee of $5,000.

I on-sold the property to the new owner (the guy who had asked me to buy it for him) for $213,000 plus Stamp Duty. It was valued at $215,000 at that time. He gave me an upfront deposit of $8,000. He got a bank loan for $160,000. He owes me a deposit of $47,200, which he's paying back over 30 years with interest. He'll probably refinance and pay me out in a couple of years.

Upfront: $8,000 cash deposit.

Monthly: Instalment payments of $363/month.

Backend: If the buyer refinances before 30 years, I'll get the rest of the $47,200 deposit that has not yet been paid off.

CREATIVE CASHFLOW

Stamp Duty in South Australia

Student Ben

A few years earlier I had sold another house in Craigmore to a family of four on a rent-to-own. They paid me $5,000 to move in, and then paid me $300/week. At the end of the lease term, they went ahead and got their bank loan approved, and had the rest of the deposit saved up to buy the house. The solicitor rang them two days before the settlement to ask for the rest of the funds to cover the Stamp Duty. They asked: "What's that?" True story, they had everything ready, but they didn't know they needed to pay Stamp Duty. It was going to cost another $15,000. They called and asked me what they should do.

I had made a profit of $29,000 on this house, so I said I could loan them the money for the Stamp Duty. We drew up some paperwork for a loan, I charged them 8.5 per cent interest, and they were able to buy their own home.

SELLER FINANCE
(OR SOME NOW, SOME LATER)

When people talk about vendor finance, they're most commonly referring to this one particular strategy. The modern professional jargon name is an Instalment Contract, or I.C. for short. In years gone by this strategy has also been known as a Terms Contract, Vendor Terms or Seller Finance. The slang term is a Wrap-around Mortgage, or a Wrap. Simply put, the seller finances the whole purchase price, and the buyer pays instalments to the seller instead of the bank.

BONUS! FREE gifts at www.TGRProperty.com.au/Gifts

Just as the seller was able to creatively finance the deposit in the previous examples, you can also creatively finance the full price of the property. This is helpful for people who may have a deposit, but have trouble qualifying for a loan from a bank.

Fewer than 54 per cent of people can qualify for a bank loan today in Australia. I'm not talking about people who shouldn't get approved for finance because they genuinely can't afford it. I'm talking about good reliable people, with money coming in every month, that just don't fit the criteria for the computer modelling approval process, and hence can't get finance. These people might be self-employed, new immigrants, or have moved houses or jobs too many times in the past three years. One bill that got forgotten years ago while you were in the middle of a relationship breakdown can ruin your credit history. Someone who owns 17 fruit shops, or who has too many properties, usually can't qualify for finance for the next one.

Any of these things can prevent a perfectly good potential buyer from getting a loan from a bank. But before there were banks we figured out how to transact between ourselves. And we can do that again.

WHAT ARE THE BENEFITS OF SELLER FINANCING?

As a seller using seller financing, you nearly double the number of people who can qualify to buy your property. Your property would appeal to 100 per cent of the potential buyers out there because the financing is already in place. You've made it easy for everyone to buy.

You can get the price you want and receive the full retail value for your property. You make money three ways: the upfront deposit, ongoing monthly payments, and a big chunk of money at the end when the buyer either sells or refinances the property.

CREATIVE CASHFLOW

You pay no agent's commissions or large advertising expenses. You also pay no running costs associated with the property.

You will also reduce your property holding costs, because finding a buyer for a seller financed property is much quicker than a conventional real estate sale.

As a buyer, it is easier to qualify for seller finance than a bank loan. The buyer can buy a house with a reduced deposit, and move in more quickly than with bank financing.

The buyer benefits from the house appreciating in value, because the purchase price is written into the Instalment Contract upfront. And the buyer has time to pay off the house.

VARIATION ONE:
THE BABYSITTER

Let's say someone is trying to sell a house worth $400,000. Different problems arise based on how big their loan is. People only ever sell for one of three reasons:
- to get their hands on the cash
- to stop paying mortgage payments
- to solve a people problem (divorce, inheritance, etc.).

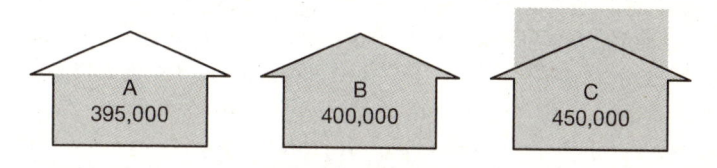

A	B	C
395,000	400,000	450,000

Houses A, B and C are all worth $400,000 but each house has a different loan amount against it. This means each seller has a different motivation, a different reason for selling. When you ask why they're selling, they'll all say "we need the money". But you need to dig deeper than that. What money they need and why they need it is very different in each case, so they'll each need a different solution.

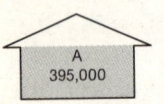

Why are the owners of House A selling? The mortgage payments aren't a hassle, but something happened in their life and now they need to get their hands on the $5,000 cash that's sitting in their house. And they need it as soon as humanly possible.

A traditional real estate agent would charge an advertising fee and maybe get them access to their cash (or less) in four months (or more). If I could write them a cheque for $5,000 in 60 seconds and then have paperwork systems handle the rest of the details, do you think they'd prefer that? Of course, because they just wanted to access the cash bit now. They'd get instant peace of mind, plus their $5,000 cash.

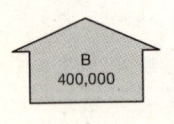

Some people, like the owners of House B, don't have a cash problem. They just want the debt to go away so it stops killing their marriage and their joy.

So I can go in there with a form, and start to look after the debt for them. I don't have to give the seller any money in exchange for their house, I just start to babysit their loan. How much money have I just used to buy my first home? None. I would end up with a payment of about $4,000 a month, and my first home. Or I could use another strategy to turn that payment into positive cashflow for myself (as you'll see in the following examples).

CREATIVE CASHFLOW

The point is they didn't have to wait four long months while losing money and sleep. I could make the seller's whole problem disappear immediately with the right paperwork system, so they get instant peace of mind and no more mortgage payments.

Why are the owners of House C selling? Obviously it's not about the cash, because there isn't any. Even if they sell the house today for market rates, they'll have to find an extra $50,000 to settle their debt. They want the pain and the problem to go away. Just selling the house doesn't make all that disappear. But my systems will.

You can see how this problem is also created when someone in the House A or B situations discounts their price. The lower they drop the price, the worse it gets. But they don't even have to discount it much before there's trouble. This is exactly how the old system creates more problems than it solves.

So, I can babysit the loan with a form, just like I did for Houses A and B, but to solve the $50,000 dilemma we'll have to add another step. This is where I use the phrase:

"I can't transfer the problem from you to me because I didn't create it. But here's what I *can* do. I can come in as a transaction engineer to create a solution and help you find someone as fast as humanly possible."

Then I'd either find a rent-to-own buyer, or do a handyman special or use one of the other cashflow strategies that work equally well to turn negatively-geared property around.

BONUS! FREE gifts at www.TGRProperty.com.au/Gifts

VARIATION TWO:
THE 10.10

Over 38 per cent of homes in Australia are owned outright, with no debt against them. When someone sells one of these houses, it's not usually about getting their hands on the cash bit, or about ending the pain of the mortgage payments. Usually it's about funding a lifestyle instead of being asset-rich and cash-poor.

Most people think they need to sell their house and put the money in the bank or some managed fund or investment scheme to create an income. But with a 10.10 it's a lot simpler than that. With the 10.10 I just pay 10 per cent more over 10 years. Here's how it works:

ME: "Why are you selling?"
SELLER: "I need the money." *(That's what they all say)*

ME: "What do you need the money for?"
SELLER: "I need it to retire, take holidays, have a decent lifestyle."

ME: "You're asking $400,000 for it. I'll give you $440,000."
SELLER: "Sure, what's the catch?"

ME: "If I agree to give you $440,000, that's 10 per cent more than you're asking for, would it be ok if I gave you some now and some later?"
SELLER: "I suppose. How much now? And how much later?"

ME: "Well, I could give you the full $440,000 in monthly instalments over, say, 10 years. How would you feel about that?"
SELLER: "How much would that work out to?"

CREATIVE CASHFLOW

ME: "Could you punch in the numbers?" *(I give him the calculator)* "440,000… divided by 10 years… divided by 12 months a year. How much is that?"

SELLER: "3667."

ME: "So that's $3,667 per month. How soon would you like the first cheque? I can give it to you right now. How does that work for you?"

SELLER: "Sure, that's great."

Of course, we'll come to arrangements with a different number of years, and different instalment amounts, but it's the same basic framework. Sometimes they want to calculate how much they'd get if they sold the house and put the money in the bank – my deal's better for them. Sometimes they ask why I'd pay more. I pay more for the flexibility of paying it off in instalments – just like at major retail stores. Everyone knows you pay less for cash.

Here's how it works out for me. At the end of ten years, I've paid $440,000 and I own a house outright. At the end of a normal 30-year mortgage on the same house, I will have paid over $1 million in payments for the same house. I like the 10.10 deal better. I win, the seller wins and, for a nice change, the bank doesn't win.

A student of mine was working with a pensioner who wanted to sell his house. Now, when a pensioner sells a house for $435,000, it's not about selling the house, it's about what it will do for the pensioner. Here's how the dialogue went:

STUDENT: "Why are you selling?"

SELLER: "I need the money." *(I told you that's what they all say)*

BONUS! FREE gifts at www.TGRProperty.com.au/Gifts

STUDENT:	"What do you need the money for?"
SELLER:	"I need money to live on in retirement."
STUDENT:	"What will you do with the money from the sale?"
SELLER:	"Dunno, probably just put it in the bank."
STUDENT:	"So, are you more interested in getting the most money for this house, or do you really want as much income as possible every month when you retire?"
SELLER:	"Well, as much income as possible every month."
STUDENT:	"How much interest can you get at the bank?"
SELLER:	"About five or six per cent, I guess."
STUDENT:	"Would you rather get five per cent or eight per cent?"
SELLER:	"Well, eight per cent of course."
STUDENT:	"And if you were getting eight per cent, would you really care which bank it was with?"
SELLER:	"No, of course not."
STUDENT:	"Why don't you let me buy this from you, I'll pay you 50 per cent more than the bank was going to give you every month. It's like I'm the bank."
SELLER:	"That'd be great. Why didn't anyone ever offer me this before?" *(They all say that, too)*

So the seller wins because he gets income stream that I pay him monthly. As a buyer, my student got to buy the house, no money down, no stupid bank loan forms, just move in, and simply start making monthly payments.

CREATIVE CASHFLOW

Are you starting to see the possibilities now? How many doors could this open up for you? Understand that I'm just giving you the basics here. These strategies are pretty cool, but they're just the fundamental scaffolding, so you get the idea of what's possible. Like I said before, once you get your head around this, it's amazing what you can do! Here are some transactions that my students have done:

Instalment Contract Examples

Bankrupt in Maryborough, Queensland

Student Steve

I put the normal advertising up, a couple of signs, some flyers, and a line-ad in the local newspaper. I got a phone call on a Thursday from a lady. She said: "I hope you can help me, I'm in real trouble. I have a house in Maryborough, and if I don't sell my house I'll be bankrupt or homeless on Wednesday. Or both."

This lady and her husband had gotten into financial difficulties because they couldn't afford the house they were living in. They were living beyond their means, but they put their head in the sand and hoped things would just work out. Eventually they realised that it wasn't going to work out unless they did something, so they put the house on the market. But they listed it at a very unrealistic price. As time went on they started to get further in arrears on their loan and the bank took them to court. She rang me only five and a half days before the court case. She said: "I'm either going to get blacklisted, kicked out, or go bankrupt on Wednesday."

BONUS! FREE gifts at www.TGRProperty.com.au/Gifts

I said: "You've really left me no time to do anything creative. I'll make some calls and see what I can do." I called some people I knew, and I put together the funding through private money from two lenders. I let her know that because she had left it so late to call me that I could get her out of trouble, but I couldn't make her any money. With the money from the private lenders, I could clear her out of her debt and her arrears, and leave her some money leftover so she could get re-established in a rental property. The total cost, including the private lenders fees, was $156,000. I paid her arrears up to date, and settled in 10 days.

Then I re-advertised the property, and within a month I sold it on an instalment contract for $230,000. I took a $5,000 deposit in the hand, and put an instalment contract in place for $225,000. I then took out a bank loan which covered the $156,000, because I had to repay the private lenders in six weeks. So, the new buyer is paying $225,000 to me, I'm paying $156,000 to the bank, and the buyer will finance me out in three years.

Upfront: $5,000 cash deposit.

Monthly: The buyer pays me $1,950 and I pay the bank $1,355, so the difference is a monthly positive cashflow of $595/month.

Backend: When the buyer refinances in three years, I'll get $225,000, repay my loan and be left with a backend profit of $69,000.

CREATIVE CASHFLOW

New to Australia and cashed up

Students Julie & Dave

A guy had a house in Dandenong, Victoria, on the market, but the agent could not sell it. He'd started at $240,000 and had dropped to $220,000 over time. I said, "I can buy it today, how much do you need?" He needed $200,000 to clear his loan. I bought it for $200,000 with a $40,000 deposit just as a normal purchase.

I sold it four weeks later to a couple who were new to Australia, and had not been in their current jobs long enough to get a loan. They both worked and earned enough. I asked them about the deposit. They had $50,000 of their own, and qualified for the homeowners grant. So they paid $65,000 deposit, which meant I got my $45,000 profit up front, and they pay me $402/week, which is $207/week positive. They've been in the house for 18 months so, as well as the profit, that's $16,133.58 in positive cashflow so far.

Upfront: $65,000 cash deposit. $45,000 profit + recouped $20,000 of my invested funds.

Weekly: The buyer pays me $402/week and my loan and fees are $195/week, leaving a weekly positive cashflow of $207/week. After 18 months, that's $16,133.58 so far.

Backend: $0, because I got all the profit upfront.

BONUS! FREE gifts at www.TGRProperty.com.au/Gifts

RICK OTTON

Bankrupt in Deception Bay, Queensland

Student Rob

This guy was going bankrupt when he found me. I paid $2,500 of his arrears payments, and put joint venture paperwork in place which said I would guarantee to babysit his loan while other people bought the property. The loan debt was $178,000. I on-sold the property on an instalment contract for $250,000 to an air-conditioning guy. He then spent $50,000 on it, did it up and increased the value by $120,000. I got a deposit of $10,000 upfront and monthly instalments. After two years he cashed out, and I made a profit of $72,000 on the backend. Now he's got the place on the market for $370,000.

Upfront: $10,000 cash deposit.

Monthly: Instalment payments from the buyer.

Backend: When the buyer refinanced in two years, the rest of the $250,000 that was remaining, for a backend profit of $72,000.

CREATIVE CASHFLOW

Lots of calls from Taree, New South Wales

Student Brett

My wife and I spent a few days in the country town of Taree, looking for a house to buy and then on-sell for a profit. We bought a place for $125,000 with a six-week settlement, and access to the property for four of those weeks to put signage up and show people through.

We used the normal yellow signs that said "no bank qualifying, for sale by owner, low deposit, $325/week". We put ads in the local paper as well.

We put signs up, and began driving back to Sydney. The phone started ringing before we hit the freeway. We got a lot of inquiries, a lot of people on welfare who didn't qualify as buyers. We on-sold it to a first homebuyer with a $10,000 deposit plus the $7,000 grant upfront. They bought it for $152,000 on an instalment contract. They paid us instalments of $325/week. And paid out a lump sump of $100,000 12 months later.

Upfront: $10,000 cash deposit + $7,000 grant.

Monthly: Instalment payments of $325/week.

Backend: When the buyer refinances, there will be a backend profit of $27,000.

RENT-TO-OWN

A Lease Option or Rental Purchase Agreement is the name of the legal paperwork used with the Rent-to-Own or Rent-to-Buy strategy. There's also another strategy that utilises Lease Options called a Sandwich Lease, which is also known as a Back-to-Back Lease Option.

A lease option is an abbreviation for "lease with an option to purchase" or "lease with an option to buy". If you have an investment property, you can either rent your house to a tenant, or on-sell the house to a new buyer using a lease option. With a lease option, the buyer can choose to buy the property at any time before their lease expires, which is the exact same duration as their option period.

At the time of this writing, in NSW you must wait 42 days before exercising the option, and in other states there is no waiting period. It's important to check for the updated ruling in your state or territory.

The paperwork used is a *lease* (Residential Tenancy Agreement) combined with a document called an *option*. In NSW you'll also include a *contract for sale*.

Because of the flexibility of these strategies, the babysitter examples can be done using either a lease option or seller finance. The main difference between seller finance and a lease option is that the tenant/buyer has the opportunity to "rent before they buy".

With seller finance, the buyer chooses to buy immediately by making instalment payments to the seller. The buyer pays a deposit to the seller, and the seller provides finance. With a lease option, the buyer rents first with the option of buying later. The

CREATIVE.CASHFLOW

buyer pays an option fee upfront, and makes rent payments to the seller until the end of the lease term or until they decide to buy.

You will most likely get more money upfront as a deposit from a buyer using seller finance than you would from an option fee from a tenant/buyer using a lease option. The buyer on seller finance is making a 25 or 30-year commitment right now. The tenant/buyer is only signing a one to two year lease with the option to buy later, and is more likely to have a tenant mentality.

A lease option is a very fluid and flexible piece of paperwork that can be written for any length of time. Every rent-to-buy agreement will be different, depending on the needs and desires of the buyer and the seller. The buyer and the seller negotiate the terms between them.

The option fee is the "getting started money" that the tenant/buyer pays to get into the rent-to-buy property. You can think of it as upfront money, just like a deposit. The sale price is agreed and fixed at the start of the lease option term.

Some sellers write a long lease option of 25 to 30 years and structure it similarly to seller finance. Other sellers choose a shorter term, and review the sales price and collect another option fee every time the lease is extended. Depending on your circumstances and your reasons, it is important to consider the different benefits when structuring the length of a lease option.

WHAT ARE THE BENEFITS OF LEASE OPTIONS?

As a seller using lease options, you make it easier for everyone to buy your house. You can get the price you want and receive the full retail value for your property. You make money three ways: the upfront option fee, ongoing monthly rental payments and a big chunk of money at the end when the tenant/buyer buys the property.

BONUS! FREE gifts at www.TGRProperty.com.au/Gifts

You pay no agent's commissions or large advertising expenses.

You will also reduce your property holding costs, because finding a tenant/buyer for a property is much quicker than a traditional sale.

As a buyer, it is easier to qualify for a lease option than a bank loan. Also, the buyer has time to save up a deposit, and try out the house before they buy.

Many tenant/buyers prefer a lease option over a traditional rental arrangement because they have more control over the property, and they're able to renovate and change the living style to suit themselves. The buyer also benefits from the house appreciating in value, because the purchase price is written into the option contract upfront. And if they can sell it for a higher price at the end of their lease option term, they can keep that profit.

Another benefit of using lease options as a buyer is that you can build up a whole portfolio of these rent-to-own properties and it's a hidden asset. Some people like that for various reasons. Also it's a lot quicker and easier than buying the usual way. You can usually move into the property in three days or less, and it costs you a lot less cash to get in.

VARIATION ONE:
FIRST HOMEOWNER STEPPING STONE

Many first homeowners have trouble getting over the psychological hurdle of making the transition from renting to buying. They get stuck thinking, "What if it's the wrong house?" It's not only financially a bigger commitment than what they're accustomed to, it's also a bigger step emotionally.

A lease option can help serve as a stepping stone between renting and buying. First homeowners can "try before they buy" and lease the property for a year or two or three before committing to buying it.

CREATIVE CASHFLOW

Women's shoes are pretty expensive. There's nothing worse than paying a lot of money for a pair of shoes, then learning after a couple of weeks that they hurt your feet. Wouldn't it be great if you could rent the shoes for a while to see if you like them? Then when you've decided that the shoes are right for you, you can come back and buy them.

I once bought a beautiful south-facing waterfront property. What I didn't know when I bought it was that the house didn't get any sun and it was absolutely freezing all through the winter. On a lease option a buyer can try out the house and find out all they need to know, and then commit to buying the house when they're ready.

Another way this strategy works for first homeowners is to help them save up a deposit. Tenant/buyers can pay extra rent that goes towards saving a deposit. It almost works like a forced savings plan. Then after the first year or two, their savings record is proven and they can go to the bank and get a loan to finance the rest of the price and buy the house.

This is how it is possible to get higher than market rent with a lease option. Some transactions result in the seller receiving rental amounts that are more than double what tenants would pay in a conventional rental tenancy.

A lease option is also a great stepping stone from private finance to bank finance. If someone doesn't qualify for traditional bank finance for some reason, this can be a great way for them to get into their own home straight away. Then a year or two down the track they can refinance and get into the traditional banking system. Take a look at a transaction one of my students has done:

BONUS! FREE gifts at www.TGRProperty.com.au/Gifts

First Homeowner Stepping Stone Examples

Gold Coast in three days

Student Brett

A couple in Lower Beachmont on the Gold Coast, Queensland, had been trying to sell their house for over six months. They had already dropped the price a fair bit. They were motivated to sell, and found me through my website. We met at a local coffee shop one Saturday morning. I suggested: "How about I give you your current asking price? Would you be happy if I can look after the loan payments until I'm in a position to go through with buying it?" They jumped at that idea, because it had been vacant and eating a hole in their pocket for so long. Their asking price was $370,000. I started paying them $575/week straight away on a lease option, with two years to get finances together.

I knew I had a buyer to on-sell this property to. I had someone looking in the area. This couple had even looked at a house in the same street. They were very keen and although they were both on very good incomes, and they had a reasonable deposit, it wasn't good enough for the bank. The lady was self-employed, so they could only go on the husband's income. I knew this house would suit them. I made a phone call and explained that I might have a house for them. They drove by the place on Sunday and got excited. We met on Monday and I gave them the keys.

I on-sold the place to this couple. They paid a $15,000 deposit upfront and $855/week, with the option to buy it at $418,000 in two years. Only three months later they refinanced. This was the perfect stepping stone they needed to get into their first home. Houses in their street are easily worth $450,000. After they moved in, they were so grateful they invited us around for dinner. They put on an amazing feast, with a three-tiered platter of seafood, and cut out pineapples and pina coladas. I got a call from them the other day. They still love it!

BONUS! FREE gifts at www.TGRProperty.com.au/Gifts

VARIATION TWO:
PROFIT WITHOUT FEES

A normal pattern for people is to buy a house, live in it for five or six years, then move. They buy another house, live in it for five or six years, then move again. They do this over and over again. Every time they sell they get to profit from the increase in the value of the house. But every time they buy and sell they incur all kinds of fees and rates, obligations and liabilities that come with ownership.

Lease options enable you to get all of the profits without the hassles.

With a lease option, you can move into a property within a few days, so it's a lot quicker than waiting for a sale to settle. Also, with a lease option the sale price is set when you sign the paperwork. So if the price goes up, you have already fixed the purchase price and you can sell it for a profit.

With a lease option a buyer can get control of a piece of property and do things with it before incurring all the normal ownership costs. Contractors do this a lot. They'll use a lease option to get in, use their skills to renovate and increase the value of the property, and then sell it for a profit without taking on the ownership costs upfront.

It's also possible to do a joint venture with the owner of a property. In the above example, I fix the price, pay the owner rent, and I take the full profit when I sell.

Here's another way to profit from the property: I could move in rent-free, renovate the owner's property over time, and we can agree to split the profits that are created when I increase the value of the seller's house. The possibilities are endless. See for yourself. Here are some transactions my students put together:

Profit Without Fees Examples

Single mum renovation joint venture

Student Dave

I got a call from a single mum in Singleton, West Australia, with teenage kids. She was a chef, and her work hours had been slashed by two-thirds. Her house was run-down. It needed floor tiles, fresh paint, landscaping, and a new kitchen. Because she was only working one-third of her regular hours, she couldn't do any of it. And if she had to sell the house as it was, she would take a hefty loss.

She rang after hearing about me through word of mouth. She sounded like a seriously motivated seller, but I wasn't sure what I could do to fix her situation. Based on my research, if I was going to buy it I would have to offer $250,000, but houses were selling in that area for $310,000 - $330,000. I could fix it up, but there wouldn't be much for her.

This was my first no money deal. I had an idea. Why not do a joint venture with her? My dad could do all the work, and we'd pay for materials and labour. We agreed to split the profits over $250,000.

It took dad a month to fix the place up. We put it back on the market, and it sold for $310,000. After the expenses, I made $7,500, dad made $7,500, and the lady got $265,000 instead of $250,000. It was great!

BONUS! FREE gifts at www.TGRProperty.com.au/Gifts

CREATIVE CASHFLOW

Positive cashflow without ownership

Student Rob

I only completed this deal today. Some of the local real estate agents know to bring me properties that need to move fast so an agent called me and said there was a guy who really needs to sell. He first listed at $270,000 and has dropped the price to $225,000. I offered $210,000, which he refused. I said I'd pay $225,000 if the seller pays the $5,000 commission to the agent. I pay $300/week on a two-year lease option.

I on-sold it to a new tenant/buyer on a lease option for $250,000 at $430/week. It's not a bad weekly cashflow, and I've got no loan debt and no fees. The old owner pays for insurances and rates, and the new owner takes care of maintenance.

Upfront: $8,000 cash deposit.

Monthly: I pay $300/week and I receive $430/week, so I net $130/week.

Backend: If/when the tenant/buyer buys the property, I'll get $25,000 profit.

BONUS! FREE gifts at www.TGRProperty.com.au/Gifts

VARIATION THREE:
NEGATIVE-GEARING TURNAROUND

Based on average rental rates and average loan rates, average investment properties will usually end up being negatively-geared. But we want positive cashflow. If you have a negatively-geared property, getting a tenant buyer in on a lease option instead of normal lease can turn your cashflow situation positive overnight. A lease option is much faster to put in place than a traditional property sale. On a lease option, the tenant/buyer has bought into the idea of home ownership, so they generally pay much higher rent and they take care of any maintenance or renovation expenses themselves.

Different sellers use long and short-term lease options depending on their needs and preferences. A longer-term lease option can secure positive cashflow from your property for as long as possible. A shorter-term lease option will encourage your tenant buyer to refinance sooner. Let's take a look at some transactions where my students have turned negative gearing problems into positive cashflow in just a few weeks:

CREATIVE CASHFLOW

Negative-Gearing Turnaround Examples

Long-distance investment turnaround

Student Dave

The investor had a negatively-geared property and needed cashflow relief. We agreed to put a rent-to-own buyer in the home and split the positive cashflow and profits if it sold for more than $230,000. The property was in Cairns, I was in Brisbane, and the investor was in country Queensland.

This was a long-distance deal. I put an ad in the local newspaper and I faxed a flyer through to the local supermarket to be stuck on their community noticeboard.

I spoke to the existing tenant, who hated the agent and the owner because of late repairs after a cyclone a while back. I got the tenant a referral and helped them find a new place and get released from the terrible lease. In return they showed people through the property for me, all at one convenient time.

In a couple of weeks we found a suitable buyer, who bought the place for $300,000, and paid a $3,000 option fee and $500/week for two years. Ironically, this buyer had been knocked back as a tenant by the agent six months earlier because they had dogs. I never even saw the house until I flew up for the day to get all the paperwork signed, have a swim and then fly home for dinner.

Upfront: $3,000 cash deposit.
Weekly: Rent $500/week, minus loan and outgoings of $330/week = Positive $170/week.
Backend: $70,000.

BONUS! FREE gifts at www.TGRProperty.com.au/Gifts

RICK OTTON

Car deposit turnaround

Student Geoff

Another investor found me through word of mouth via an investors group. He had a property and wanted to turn his negative cashflow positive. We agreed to put a rent-to-own buyer in the house and split the profits over $250,000.

The buyers found me in a few days from a newspaper ad for the property. This couple rang up and viewed the home on Saturday morning, then signed the paperwork and had the keys to the house on Saturday afternoon. They bought the place on a two-year lease option for $300,000 and $550/week.

The buyers were talking about selling their second car to get the money for a deposit, so I suggested (for speed and convenience) they just give me the car. They signed the car transfer papers as well as the lease option papers all in one meeting and moved in that day.

Upfront: Car (I got $3,000 cash from a wrecker on Monday morning).

Weekly: Rent $550/week, minus loan and outgoings of $410/week = Positive $140/week.

Backend: $50,000.

VARIATION FOUR:
BACK-TO-BACK LEASE OPTIONS

By using two lease options back-to-back, you can give this opportunity to someone else, and they can rent before they buy. So you buy a property as an investor on a lease option, then you on-sell the property to an end buyer on another lease option at a slightly higher price. You make sure that you're receiving more money than you're paying so the deal generates cashflow each month.

BONUS! FREE gifts at www.TGRProperty.com.au/Gifts

CREATIVE CASHFLOW

Lease options are the most flexible of all the creative strategies we've talked about, and there are countless ways you can use them. You can use lease options in combination with pretty much every kind of strategy. Back-to-back lease options enable you to build up a portfolio of properties and benefit from positive monthly cashflow capital gain profits, without taking on the usual fees and obligations of ownership. Here are some more examples from my students you may find interesting:

Back-to-Back Lease Option Examples

Investors and car accidents

Students Julie & Dave

Dave took the phone call. This lady told us about two investment properties in Berwick, Victoria, one of the nicest suburbs in the outer east in Melbourne and asked, "Are you interested in buying them?" She and her husband had bought house and land packages a few years before and had them built. But neither being a landlord nor negative-gearing were suited to them. That's the plain simple truth of negative-gearing: you lose a dollar to get back 25 cents. So, they were struggling financially because of the burden these properties had put on them.

They actually sold one already at $302,000, but the loan was $318,000. At settlement they had to write a cheque for $24,000 of hard cash out of their own pockets. They simply didn't have enough money to sell the other two the same way.

We did the paperwork to take over the properties on a lease option for 10 years. We paid up their rates, and guaranteed to take care of the loan payments. We advertised the properties just by using the usual handwritten signs and newspaper ads.

BONUS! FREE gifts at www.TGRProperty.com.au/Gifts

We on-sold one to a young couple from Beaconsfield. She had been in a car accident, and they had lost their house when they were down to one income during her recovery. They had plenty of money, and could maintain the payments, but they couldn't make up the arrears that occurred during the accident and recovery time.

They moved in on a rent-to-own basis and have never missed a payment. They bought it at $350,000 and the house is worth $385,000 now. It's great that they've got all that capital growth out of it.

They just needed somebody to giving them a chance when the banks wouldn't. They've paid $600/week since they moved in. If I'd just tried to rent that out on a normal rental I'd only get $300/week. We're cashflow positive because the loan is only $486/week.

We on-sold the other one on a lease option as well to a single mum. She had a lot of money, but life sometimes gets in the way. She told us it wasn't working out and it was too much of a commitment for her, so we released her from the paperwork. We're keeping that property as our own buy-and-hold, and we didn't need any bank loan, or a deposit. We've just taken control via the paperwork. It's perfect for us.

It's not unusual for people to get into this situation. They don't get told everything. Real estate agents just want to sell them a house. People get in over their head, and they can't get out. This is a no-fees-no-charges way to fix those problems.

Back-to-back moving for work

This couple needed to move towns for work. They needed $7,500 for moving, and were happy to leave the rest of the money in the house for a few years. We bought the house on a lease option for $285,000, and we pay $350/week.

Students Julie & Dave

BONUS! FREE gifts at www.TGRProperty.com.au/Gifts

CREATIVE CASHFLOW

We on-sold it on a lease option to a lady who runs a truck company for $345,000. She had $25,000 to put towards her own home, and pays us $700/week. She only needs 15 months before she will refinance and pay me out the rest.

Upfront: $25,000 cash deposit − $7,500 for the seller = $17,500 cash in hand.

Weekly: Positive cashflow of $350/week.

Backend: $30,000.

Back-to-back in an hour

Student Brett

The buyer and the seller both found me via referral.

At 11am I met the seller, who was absolutely stuck. He had already moved out, and was renting somewhere else. Then the sale of his property fell over, and he was stuck making payments on two places. He was asking $340,000. I bought it on a lease option at that price and paid $640/week with $50/week credited to the sale price, and I agreed to pay one mortgage payment.

At 12pm I met the buyer. The buyer had a decent income but didn't have enough of a deposit to buy the traditional way. He scraped together $10,000 for a deposit. I on-sold the property to him on a lease option for $385,000 at $725/week. Win/win/win!

BONUS! FREE gifts at www.TGRProperty.com.au/Gifts

THE NEXT STEP

These strategies aren't that difficult. Once you get your head around them, and you have the right people on speed dial in your phone to make it happen, results start to snowball. You'll find yourself looking at things a little differently, and you'll start to find opportunities everywhere. Every property problem is an opportunity.

If any of these strategies sound interesting to you, you can get started straight away and do this yourself.

There are two ways to do anything in life – the slow way and the fast way. If you are the kind of person who wants to do things the slow way, and go through all the trial and error yourself, I don't think you would have picked up this book in the first place.

If you want to do things the fast way, go to the bonuses page and book into one of the live events right away. Obviously there is way too much information to cram into one book and this chapter was designed to open your eyes to new possibilities, to give you a glimpse of what everyday people like you are doing with property and creative financing strategies every day. And the possibility that you can do the same.

If you want to start building your own property portfolio today, if you want to buy property for a dollar, or you need to sell fast, or turn negative-gearing into positive cashflow overnight, I can teach you more in person at the live events.

I hope to meet you personally very soon, and see what deals we can do together.

Do it for the lifestyle!

CREATIVE CASHFLOW

FREE BONUS GIFT

Rick Otton has generously offered a FREE BONUS GIFT valued at $147

FREE Audio - **"Why You Can't Use Old Systems to Solve New Problems!"** Listen as Rick and his mentoring students challenge conventional wisdom in this closed-door training.

Visit the website below to receive these free gifts
www.TGRProperty.com.au/Gifts

Chapter 6

RENTING SHARES

"Everything's easy when you have the right tools!"

AUSSIE ROB

AUSSIE ROB

Rob Wilson aka Aussie Rob is an internationally-recognised trading expert and educator.

Headquartered in Surfers Paradise, Queensland, Aussie Rob's trading education company teaches thousands of students each year how to trade the easy way.

His early days, however, were far from easy...

Born in a small South Australian river community and raised without a mum, Aussie Rob ran away from home at 16 and commenced a diesel mechanic apprenticeship in Darwin. He later joined the Australian Army and served four years, during which time he developed strong leadership skills and self-discipline.

On the downside however, his earning potential was capped, his efforts went largely unrecognised and his work was nothing more than what he called a JOB – Just Over Broke.

Determined to reach his full potential and make a difference in the world, Aussie Rob tried a number of entrepreneurial careers before turning his attention to trading.

Self-taught, Aussie Rob became a successful global trader in his own right and mentored fellow traders. Since 2000, and in partnership with an established software company, he has developed several software programs to educate and empower "mum and dad" investors – the most powerful being *Lifestyle Trader*, launched in 2006.

He has appointed licensees throughout the country to promote *Lifestyle Trader* and establish Traders' Clubs to support and mentor investors.

Aussie Rob and his wife Kerry have also established The Aussie Rob Foundation, whose mission is to "empower people to eliminate poverty".

RENTING SHARES

HOW TO TRADE ONLINE AND PROFIT IN ANY FINANCIAL CONDITIONS

G'day, my name is Rob Wilson, or, as I'm known in the industry, "Aussie Rob".

I, just like you, had been looking for the Holy Grail in business to enable me to get my money working for me instead of me working for my money. However, I didn't just want my money working for me on a casual basis, I wanted great, regular, consistent CASHFLOW!

It is really important for you to understand that I am an online trader and since 2000 I have been teaching hundreds of thousands of traders/investors in the US, Canada, Australia, New Zealand and the UK about global markets.

I retired from the Rat Race to live in the Bahamas and traded online for a living. Now don't feel sorry for me, someone had to do it! I travelled the world undertaking every course I could get my hands on, subscribing to all of those newsletters and buying countless pieces of software, books, CDs, videos blah, blah, blah. I'd been trading since 1984 but once retired, I really wanted to take my trading to the next level and at that time, I had the luxury of having plenty of time on my hands.

Thanks to the Internet, trading is now so, so simple and best of all, the only tools you need are a laptop and an Internet connection and you can run your online trading business anywhere in the world. Now that's what I call "lifestyle".

I finally found my calling in life - teaching others how to set up an online trading business. In each of my training sessions the same old stumbling block kept raising its ugly head, "Analysis Paralysis". Virtually every trader I came across was spending hours and hours analysing trades. As if one computer screen covered with streaming data wasn't enough, many had two screens on their desks and some had three and even four.

Those days are now over; the new way to trade is here!

But before we get ahead of ourselves, let's rewind, as it's pretty important for you to know my background. I'm gunna keep it short, in a summarised form, but with enough detail for you to understand where I am coming from.

ABOUT AUSSIE ROB

I wasn't born with a silver spoon in my mouth and I didn't get a university degree. I am a self-made person who has learnt from The School of Hard Knocks.

I was born in a small South Australian country town to a mother who was just 16 and a father who was the ripe old age of 19. I guess you know where this is heading…

That's right, it was pretty tough for my parents in those days and their marriage obviously didn't last. The odds were certainly stacked against them. My mum left when I was young so I grew up with my dad who was an interstate truck driver. I didn't get to see much of him either because he was on the road most of the time. So from an early age I learnt life survival skills. I had to, I had no choice.

RENTING SHARES

My dad remarried when I was 14 and at the mature age of 16, I decided to run away from home and start my own life. In hindsight it was the best thing for everyone. Imagine my poor step mum at the age of 21 having a 14-year-old step son!

At 2am one morning, I snuck out the back door, pushed my motorbike down the driveway and rolled it about a mile down the road before I built up the courage to start it up. With my heart pounding with both fear and excitement, I headed north to Darwin.

There I became an apprentice diesel mechanic and then subsequently joined the Australian Army. Wow, what a decision that was!

The army was the best thing for me for many reasons. It put me on the straight and narrow by teaching me the discipline that I now contribute to most of my online trading success. You see, trading is something like 20 per cent technique and 80 per cent discipline. Actually, it's probably more like 10 per cent technique and 90 per cent discipline because if you don't follow the rules, you can end up losing your shirt.

The other great lesson I learnt in the army was that the "system" totally sucked when you worked twice as hard as the bloke next to you but earned the same amount as him. I then declared that when I got out of the army I would never work for a boss ever again.

I lasted four years and then my natural entrepreneurism took over. Growing up without a mum, I learnt many survival skills; skills that have proved invaluable my entire life. So in essence, I am so glad that I had the childhood that I did as it made me the person that I am today.

BONUS! FREE gifts at www.TGRProperty.com.au/Gifts

My business ventures have been extremely diversified including financial planning, franchising and even the president of a private bank in the Bahamas (I'll leave that story for my memoirs).

It just goes to show that your background or education does not need to limit your ability for success! If a high school drop out from country South Australia who grew up without a mum and ran away from home at 16 can become successful, then anyone can.

I'm writing this now in Los Angeles as I've just finished an awesome training session teaching at Tony Robbins' *Wealth Mastery*. I've also taught with other greats like T Harv Ekker, Chris Howard, Zig Ziglar and of course, Stuart Zadel, on some of the biggest stages in the world!

I've proven that success does not have to come from a classroom. It doesn't have to come from having rich parents. You don't need a university degree nor do you have to be a genius. All you need is the gut-wrenching desire to become successful. I attribute mine to wanting to prove myself to my father.

My real turning point came when I realised that I didn't have to prove anything to anyone. I still have that burning desire that no matter what I do, I REALLY want it to be mega successful. I have always done whatever it takes to get it done, but always with two considerations:

1. I have to be able to look at myself in the mirror every morning; and

2. Whatever I do, it has to add value to someone else's life.

RENTING SHARES

So I guess I could summarise this last couple of pages by saying, "Get rid of the story, just make it happen!"

My personal story is a lot deeper than what I've written here; you're just gunna have to wait till I publish my autobiography one day. No doubt you have a "story" too. We all do. We can all say, "But you were lucky, you had (such and such)" or "But it won't work for me because…" All I can say about that is "BS"!

We all have stories. Get rid of them. Get over it and make a decision to make an impact with your life.

What I'm gunna be introducing you to here in this book has worked for thousands of people around the world so there is absolutely no reason why it can't work for you too. Actually, there is a reason why it may not work for you. It won't work for you if you don't want to make it work.

You see, I've discovered that there are two types of people:

1. Those who look for all of the reasons why something WON'T WORK; and

2. Those who look for all of the reasons why something WILL WORK!

Which one are you?

I'm gunna finish this intro with a little success secret…

> *The difference between success and failure is minimal. The starting point is the most crucial, and that is simply getting off ya butt and doing SOMETHING.*

BONUS! FREE gifts at www.TGRProperty.com.au/Gifts

WHY TRADE ONLINE?

I'm so excited to be contributing to this book as the world's financial markets continue to be unpredictable. You may be wondering what financial markets have to do with the Internet. Well, my objective in this chapter is to open your mind to the incredible cashflow and investment opportunities that are right in front of you with online trading.

So why consider online trading as a business? Well think about this…

Question: How many employees do you need for an online trading business?

Answer: NONE

Question: How much money do you need to spend on advertising, Google AdWords, pay-per-click campaigns etc. for your online trading business?

Answer: NONE

Question: How much rent do you have to pay for your online trading business?

Answer: NONE

Question: How much inventory would you have to hold for your online trading business?

Answer: NONE

RENTING SHARES

Question: How many widgets would you have to sell for your online trading business?

Answer: NONE

Question: How much time do you have to spend each day on your online trading business?

Answer: Less than 30 minutes per month. NO, not per day, per month!

Question: How much money could you make with your online trading business?

Answer: I'm gunna teach you, step-by-step, how it is extremely realistic to be earning 10 per cent plus per month. YES, PER MONTH. You know what that equates to? Yes, greater than 100 per cent per year.

Question: Can I run my online trading business through my self-managed superannuation fund to capitalise on the incredible tax benefits?

Answer: ABSOLUTELY. Most of my students run two accounts.

1. Super Account: To save for their future retirement.

2. Instant Gratification Account: This is the account to use to fund your day to day living.

OK, do I have your attention now? I do? Great, then let's get into it…

BONUS! FREE gifts at www.TGRProperty.com.au/Gifts

AUSSIE ROB

It's currently early 2010. The share markets in both Australia and the US have shown solid improvements since March last year which some feel is a blessing after most people experienced an horrific 2008 (I say "most people" as my clients made record profits - more on that shortly).

We've just had the biggest fall in financial markets since the Great Depression! The All Ordinaries had its worst calendar year on record plummeting 43 per cent, compared to the 32 per cent slump during the oil shock of 1974 and the 34 per cent fall in 1930 during the Great Depression. Why am I excited? I'm excited because a lot of my students had a record years in 2008 and 2009, generating incredible returns.

The purpose of this chapter is to give you the same key to financial freedom so that it doesn't matter if markets go up, down, or sideways, you will know the simple strategies that make great profits. By applying the principles that I'm gunna teach ya you can have TOTAL FINANCIAL FREEDOM FOR LIFE…

I teach a lot of different strategies, as diversification is the key to creating financial freedom, however, I'm gunna focus on one key strategy in this chapter that, thanks to the Internet, means some people spend less than 30 minutes per month "working" in order to live the life of their dreams.

This incredibly simple strategy can be implemented in both your instant gratification account (that's the account that you spend each month) and your superannuation account. This cashflow strategy can be implemented in self-managed superannuation accounts. Yeah, that's right…I'm gunna teach ya how to take control of your own financial future so those so-called experts out there no longer lose your money!

RENTING SHARES

The strategy I'm gunna teach ya can consistently return 10 per cent or more per month. YES, per month! You know what? That equates to 120 per cent per year.

Are you earning 120 per cent per year with your trading or other forms of investments? Is your super returning 120 per cent per year or is it performing like all of the other "NOT so super" funds?

Did you know that there were only five super funds in Australia that made a profit in the 2007/08 financial year? The top return was a reportedly pathetic 1.4 per cent. If you thought that was bad, imagine the results of 2008/09. I'm not even going there as I don't want to open any of your super wounds! Suffice to say, I'm sure you'll agree with me that NOW is the time to take back the control; after all, no one will take care of YOUR money better than YOU. No one has as big a vested interest in YOUR money than YOU.

Enough of the doom and gloom. I want ya to sit back, relax and let me put your mind at ease knowing that you'll soon have access to the secret cashflow formula of successful online trading. I'm gunna expose the secrets the so-called experts DON'T WANT YOU TO KNOW ABOUT. The secrets that can give you total financial freedom for life.

I also want to prove to you that you don't need a truckload of money to create your financial freedom. In the following pages I'll show you how to turn $5,000 into over ONE MILLION DOLLARS in five short years.

What I'm about to teach you is not a Get Rich Quick Scheme. It's exactly the opposite. It's a Get Rich Slow Scheme, although most people tell me that five years is pretty quick!

BONUS! FREE gifts at www.TGRProperty.com.au/Gifts

Cash is king mate; hence why my favourite cashflow strategy is online trading. Everything's EASY when you know how!

My motivation in sharing this powerful information is to sort out the "Gunna's" from the "Doer's". So many people over the years have told me that they want to change their lives and get out of the Rat Race but never do anything about it. I have devoted my life to helping people who really do want to help themselves.

My mission is SUCCESS. My team and I are 200 per cent dedicated to helping people become successful. All the information in the world is useless without action. Take the first step and immerse yourself in this knowledge; if you really are a "Doer", if you really are serious about achieving financial success, then let's make it happen.

RENTING SHARES

Renting shares is the online strategy that I'm gunna focus on here. It is one of the most consistently profitable strategies that I've ever come across and it's so, so simple to do. Of course, there's a few basic fundamental rules that you're gunna have to learn first but I'll tell ya right now upfront, you'll be so glad you put in the time to study this as its potential is mind blowing!

The best way to start learning about renting out shares is to think of real estate. If you owned real estate, would you rent it out or would you leave it vacant? No doubt you said that you'd rent it out, right? Why on earth would you leave it vacant? Why would you want to miss out on that rental income each month?

So what about shares? If you own some, are you renting them out? If not, why not? Think of the income that you are missing

RENTING SHARES

out on each month! Imagine if you could earn five per cent per month from renting out shares. That would equate to a whopping 60 per cent per annum, without compounding. A little later I'm gunna expose a little known secret that will enable you to double it. That's right, I'll expose a technique that can earn 10 per cent per month or an incredible 120 per cent per year. Mate, this is found money! This is money that could, no should, be added to your trading account each month.

Imagine the difference after a few years. Why don't you grab a calculator and do your maths (or for my American friends, "math") and see what kind of difference this could make on your long-term investments.

Imagine the difference it could make to your superannuation fund (Aussie retirement fund) or your IRA (Yankee retirement fund) or your RRSP (Knuck retirement fund).

Imagine the difference it could make to you right now. If you're retired, what could the possibility of an extra five per cent make to your quality of life? If you are still working, could an extra five per cent per month help towards a mortgage payment?

Yeah I know, now that I've mentioned 10 per cent per month, you're not interested in five per cent. Hang in there with me, you've gotta learn how to make five first and then I'll teach ya how to double it, OK?

The concept of renting shares is to earn a monthly income from selling someone the right to buy your shares from you. The strategy is known as "Writing Covered Calls", which is an option trading strategy.

Before we get into writing covered calls, there are a few option basics that you need to understand first.

OPTION BASICS

I must admit, this is the boring stuff and it might seem a little daunting at first, but hang in there with me because when you get through this next few pages, it will certainly be worth it as I'll then be teaching you how to make incredible profits. Like anything, there is always a bit of study to do so roll up your sleeves and let's get through this. Just a few minutes of pain could give you total financial freedom for life.

There are only two options:

1. Calls
2. Puts

If you BUY calls, you are buying the rights to buy shares. If you SELL (write) calls, you are selling someone else the rights to buy shares.

Yes, there are two things you can do with calls:

1. You can buy the rights to buy shares; or,
2. You can sell someone else the rights to buy shares.

[I won't be discussing **puts** in this chapter as the strategy that I'm teaching you relates to **calls** only.]

One option contract controls 100 US shares. Therefore, if you buy one call, you are buying the rights to buy 100 shares. In Australia, one option contract controls 1,000 shares. I prefer to do this strategy with US shares for two reasons:

RENTING SHARES

1. In the US, you only have to buy 100 shares so it is a lot less capital intensive. You see, if the shares were trading at $25, in Australia you'd have to outlay $25,000 while in the US, you'd only have to outlay $2,500.

2. US options pay a lot higher premium than Australian options. In other words, you have the opportunity to make a lot more money.

So that's a no-brainer, eh! Outlay less money with the opportunity to make more money…

If you sell (write) calls, you are selling someone else the rights to buy 100 shares. Option contracts expire on the third Friday of the month in the US. In Australia, they expire on the Thursday before the last Friday of the month. Again, we're gunna focus on doing this on US stocks so all we need to know is that options expire on the third Friday of the month.

Therefore, if you buy a September call, you are buying the rights to buy 100 shares by the third Friday of September.

Now here's a trick question: When do February options expire? Well done, they expire on the third Friday of February. Too easy, eh!

Likewise, if you sell (write) a September call, you are selling someone else the rights to buy 100 shares by the third Friday of September.

You can choose which price you buy or sell (write) calls according to the following guidelines:

BONUS! FREE gifts at www.TGRProperty.com.au/Gifts

1. **Shares priced between $5 and $25:** You can buy or sell (write) calls in $2.50 increments. Therefore, you can buy or sell (write) $5 calls, $7.50 calls, $10 calls etc.

   For example, if a share was trading at $19, you can buy the rights to buy the shares at $2.50, $5, $7.50, $10, $12.50 and so on.

   Now stop wondering why you would do this. It'll all start making sense shortly. For now, we need to go through the rules then we'll put all of the rules together and start making some money. OK?

2. **Shares priced between $25 and $200**: You can buy or sell (write) calls in $5 increments. Therefore, you can buy or sell (write) $5 calls, $10 calls, $15 calls, $20 calls etc. For example, if a share was trading at $29, you can buy the rights to buy the shares at $25, $30, $35, $40 and so on.

3. **Shares priced $200 and more:** You can buy or sell (write) calls in $10 increments. Therefore, you can buy or sell (write) $10 calls, $20 calls, $30 calls, $40 calls and so on.

These are general guidelines; there are some cases that differ but most follow these guidelines.

STRIKE PRICE

The price that you choose to buy or sell (write) calls is known as the "Strike Price".

Now let's take a look at an example. Let's assume that you own 1,000 shares in Microflop that you bought for $23 and are now trading at $24. The September $25 calls are now going for $1.

RENTING SHARES

You could sell 10 calls and bring in $1,000 (one call controls 100 shares, so 10 calls control 1,000 shares, therefore, 1,000 shares x $1 = $1,000).

Why would someone pay you $1 per share for the rights to buy Microflop from you for $25 per share? Why wouldn't they simply buy them from you at the current market price of $24? They are hoping that Microflop goes up prior to the option expiring. If it went up to say, $28 per share, they could exercise their option and buy Microflop from you for $25.

Their net cost would have been $26 ($25 for the shares + $1 for the option) therefore, giving them a nice profit of $2 per share. Remember, they only paid $1 per share for the option so if they sold the stock immediately, they effectively made a $2 per share profit on a $1 per share investment or a pretty cool 200 per cent return on their investment!

So that's them, what about you? Why would you sell someone the rights to buy your shares from you at $25? Now this is where it gets really cool. The $1,000 they pay you gets transferred to your account immediately. So that's immediate profit to you no matter what happens to the shares.

If the shares go up (above $25) they would exercise their rights to buy your shares at $25 and you keep the $1,000.

If the shares go up (but not above $25) they WOULD NOT exercise their rights to buy your shares at $25. Their option would expire but you still keep their $1,000. You still own the shares so you could sell another option for the following month or simply sell your shares and do it on another stock.

BONUS! FREE gifts at www.TGRProperty.com.au/Gifts

If the shares go down, they WOULD NOT exercise their rights to buy your shares at $25. Their option would expire but you still keep their $1,000. You still own the shares so you could sell another option for the following month or simply sell your shares and do it on another stock. Their $1,000 has now reduced the loss that you would have made on your shares! That's pretty cool hey? It's like a form of insurance but you don't have to pay for the insurance, THEY PAY YOU!

So no matter what happens, if the shares go up, stay at the same price or go down, YOU get to keep their $1,000. Imagine doing this every month? Every month you'd be making $1,000 for doing what? For simply selling someone the rights to buy your shares.

How much time would you spend each month on your online trading business? Two-fifths of five-eighths of bugger all! Once you've implemented the trade, the cash is transferred to your account immediately and then off you go, enjoying your life. Seriously, can making money online be any easier than this?

Buy some shares and then sell someone the rights to buy them from you. Sounds crazy eh? So I guess you now know why the financial gurus don't like exposing their closely guarded little secrets. They want you to invest in their funds so they can charge you fees. Those days are now over, you are now starting to learn how to take control of your own financial future so you can look after your own money and not rely on someone else.

You excited yet? You should be! Let's now get into the actual mechanics of the strategy...

MECHANICS OF THE STRATEGY

1. **Write:** means to sell
2. **Covered:** means that you own the shares.

RENTING SHARES

Therefore, to write a covered call simply means to sell a call option against the shares that you already own. Yes, you need to own shares to do this. If you don't own shares, what do you do? That's right, buy some...

Here's another example. Let's assume that you own 1,000 shares which you bought for $8 and they're now trading at $9. The September $10 calls are going for $1.15. You could sell 10 calls and bring in an extra $1,150 (1,000 shares x $1.15). Why could you sell 10 calls? That's right, one option contract controls 100 shares so if you own 1,000 shares, you could write 10 contracts. Simple maths, eh!

You are selling someone the rights to buy your shares from you by the third Friday of September for $10 and they have paid you $1.15 for the right.

The real exciting benefit with this strategy is that you get to keep the $1,150 whether your shares go up, stay the same price or even if they go down!

If the shares are higher than $10 at expiration (third Friday of September), then it is highly likely that they will be bought from you at $10. If so, that adds an additional $1,000 profit to the trade (because your shares had to have gone up from $9 to $10). Remember, they are currently trading at $9 so if they are over $10 at expiration, that means that you have made an additional $1 per share.

When you have your shares taken from you, it is known as being "Called Out".

Now let's compare a couple of different scenarios:

BONUS! FREE gifts at www.TGRProperty.com.au/Gifts

AUSSIE ROB

1. Buy the shares and sell the shares

> Buy 1,000 shares for $23 and then sell them for $25
> **Outlay:** $23,000
> **Profit:** $2,000
> **Return on Investment (ROI):** 8.7%
> (Cash In: $2,000 divided by Cash Out: $23,000 x 100)

Now you can double that return if you take advantage of our brokers by buying your shares on "Margin".

Margin is a very simple strategy that I am so surprised that most people don't know about. You can ask your broker to pay half of your initial purchase. For example, if your shares were trading at $23, you could get your broker to fund 50 per cent of your purchase so you would only have to pay $11.50 per share. Pretty cool, eh? So there's a little tip that nearly doubled your return!

Now of course your broker won't lend you 50 per cent of your share purchase for free. He'll probably charge you around eight or nine per cent per annum.

Let's do the maths again but this time with buying your shares on margin:

> Buy 1,000 shares for $23 (but only outlay $11.50) and then sell them for $25
> **Outlay:** $11,500
> **Profit**: $2,000
> **ROI**: 17%
> (Cash In: $2,000 divided by Cash Out: $11,500 x 100)

BONUS! FREE gifts at www.TGRProperty.com.au/Gifts

RENTING SHARES

Of course you'll have to deduct the eight to nine per cent per annum from your profit to cover your broker's margin interest. If you are only in the trade for a month, you'd only have to pay him one month's interest. So, I'm sorry, but your return would only be about 16 per cent instead of 17 per cent - but I'm sure you could live with that!

Oh, and of course your broker has to eat so he'll charge you commission for buying the shares and commission to write the call. Commissions vary from broker to broker so I won't be factoring in commission with any of these examples. Just remember that you'll have to adjust the returns a tad to cover commission.

2. Write a covered call and get called out

> Buy 1,000 shares for $23
> **Outlay:** $23,000
> Sell $25 calls for $1.15 (brings in $1,150 cash into your account)
> Get called out for $25 ("called out" means getting your shares bought from you)
> **Profit:** $3,150 ($1,150 for selling the calls and $2,000 profit on the shares)
> **ROI:** 13% (Cash In: $3,150 divided by Cash Out: $23,000 x 100)
> **ROI if on margin:** 27% (Cash In: $3,150 divided by Cash Out: $11,500 x 100)

You would only do this if you really wanted to sell the shares at $25. If you didn't, you could sell the next strike price out ($27.50) which would bring in less premium (amount for writing the call) but you would have a better chance of keeping the shares.

BONUS! FREE gifts at www.TGRProperty.com.au/Gifts

So as you can see, you've just made an extra five to 10 per cent by writing a covered call and getting called out at $25 instead of simply selling the stock at $25! If you do that every month, that means a difference of between 60 and 120 per cent per annum. I'm sure you'll agree that this extra cash would be better in your account, right?

TIPS FOR NOT GETTING CALLED OUT

1. If you want to keep the shares and not get called out, you should always sell the call at a strike price that you don't think the stock will get to prior to expiration.

2. If it looks as though the shares are going to be higher than the call's strike price, buy back the calls and then sell the next higher strike price. For example, buy back the $25 calls and sell the $27.50 calls.

3. If the share price goes higher than the call's strike price, don't panic, sit tight and wait until most of the "Time Value" has gone from the premium and then buy it back. You would then be just buying "Intrinsic Value" (I teach all about time value and intrinsic value in the bonus section at the end for those who want to really master this cashflow strategy).

BUY WRITE

A "Buy Write" is just like writing a covered call except you don't already own the shares. So with a buy write, you buy the shares and sell the calls in the same transaction.

Let's use the previous example with Microflop but this time, given that you don't already own them, you buy 1,000 shares at $24 and, in the same transaction, you sell 10 September $25 calls for $1.15.

RENTING SHARES

Now let's compare a buy write to just buying shares:

1. Buy the shares and sell the shares

> Buy 1,000 shares for $24 and then sell them for $25
> **Profit:** $1,000
> **ROI:** 4.1% (Cash In: $1,000 divided by Cash Out: $24,000 x 100)
> **ROI if on margin:** 8.2% (Cash In: $1,000 divided by Cash Out: $12,000 x 100)

2. Buy a buy write and get called out

> Buy 1,000 shares for $24 and simultaneously sell $25 calls for $1.15 (brings in $1,150 cash into your account)
> Get called out for $25
> **Profit:** $2,150 ($1,150 for selling the calls and $1,000 profit on the stock)
> **ROI:** 8.9% (Cash In: $2,150 divided by Cash Out: $24,000 x 100)
> **ROI if on margin:** 17.9%
> (Cash In: $2,150 divided by Cash Out: $12,000 x 100)

Now let's dig a bit deeper…

SELLER OF "TIME"

Writing covered calls is simply selling "time". You are selling someone the right to buy your shares from you at a certain price by a certain time. They are buying time from you; time they hope will be enough for the stock to go above the strike price.

BONUS! FREE gifts at www.TGRProperty.com.au/Gifts

HOW MUCH TIME?

I prefer to write the current month or next month's calls. In other words, I sell four to eight weeks of time. Selling further out in time can give you a larger upfront premium but I have found that selling calls each month will generally make you more money than selling calls further out in time. By going further out in time, you'll generally get less per month. Covered calls are all about getting regular monthly income so I like to fine-tune it to get the biggest bang for my buck!

WHICH SHARES SHOULD YOU WRITE COVERED CALLS ON?

Finding shares that pay high yields was difficult in the past but now it's a breeze. I have developed a software program called High Yield Covered Call Scanner that finds great candidates.

It's important in any profession to have the right tools because they can make a profound difference to your profitability.

My High Yield Covered Call Scanner has filters that will only display shares that return greater than five per cent per month. If you buy the shares on margin, that effectively means that your five per cent per month doubles to an incredible 10 per cent per month!

So now there is no reason why you shouldn't have the opportunity to earn over 100 per cent per annum. And YES, you can do this in a self-managed superannuation fund too. Imagine how quickly your retirement fund could increase by applying this simple but extremely potent strategy. Everything's easy when you know how!

RENTING SHARES

SHARE PRICE RANGE

I have found that shares priced between $5 and $30 produce the best returns. Remember, one option contract controls 100 shares, therefore, to write one covered call on a $100 stock would require an investment of $10,000 ($100 x 100).

I would much rather put the same money into a $20 share and write five covered calls ($20 x 100 x 5 = $10,000). Writing one covered call on a $5 stock only requires an investment of $500 ($5 x 100). Actually, that is not correct! Why? Well, one of the great things about writing covered calls is that the premium that is paid to you is deposited into your account IMMEDIATELY. Therefore, if you were paid say, $1 per share to write a covered call on a $20 stock, you would effectively be only paying $19 per share as the $1 per share call premium would be paid into your account immediately!

How cool is that? Now check this out...

If you bought the $20 stock on margin, you'd only be paying $10 per share and you'd IMMEDIATELY bring in $1 per share for writing the covered call. You're now effectively only outlaying $9 per share! DOUBLE COOL!

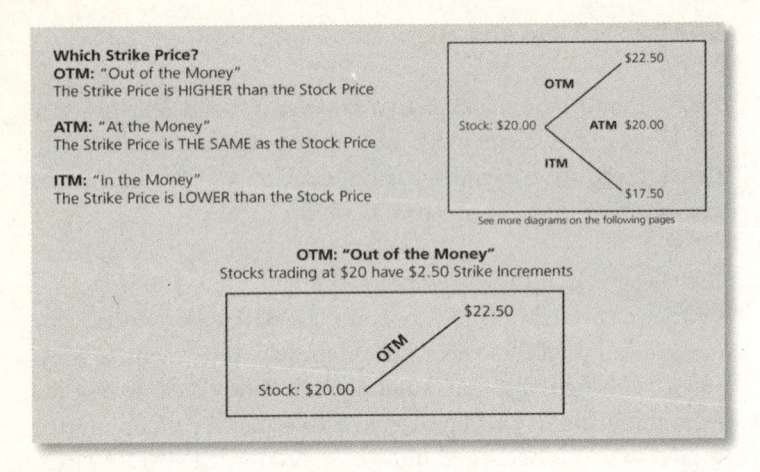

Which Strike Price?
OTM: "Out of the Money"
The Strike Price is HIGHER than the Stock Price

ATM: "At the Money"
The Strike Price is THE SAME as the Stock Price

ITM: "In the Money"
The Strike Price is LOWER than the Stock Price

```
                        $22.50
                 OTM
Stock: $20.00    ATM   $20.00
                 ITM
                        $17.50
```
See more diagrams on the following pages

OTM: "Out of the Money"
Stocks trading at $20 have $2.50 Strike Increments

```
                       $22.50
              OTM
Stock: $20.00
```

In this example, the shares are trading at $20 and you are selling someone the rights to buy your shares for $22.50. Let's assume that the option premium is $1 per share.

There are three different scenarios that can happen at expiration:

1. **If the shares are trading above $22.50 at expiration,** the shares will be bought from you at $22.50, giving you a $3.50 profit ($2.50 for the increase in the share price and $1 for the option premium).

2. **If the shares are trading below $22.50 but above $20 at expiration,** the option owner would not exercise their rights to buy the shares from you at $22.50 because they could buy them cheaper from the market. Therefore, you keep the option premium and the shares, giving you the opportunity to write another call on your shares for the next month's expiration. In this scenario, you would make a profit on the shares going up PLUS you keep the option premium. Let's say the shares went up to $21; you would make a $2 profit ($1 for the increase in the share price and $1 for the option premium).

3. **If the shares are now trading below $20 at expiration,** the option owner would not exercise their rights to buy the shares from you at $22.50 because they could buy them cheaper from the market. Therefore, you keep the option premium and the shares, giving you the opportunity to write another call on your shares for the next month's expiration. In this scenario, you could make a loss on the shares but some of the loss would be offset by the option premium.

Breakeven (Share Price – Option Premium): Your breakeven on this trade would be $19 ($20 - $1) so you could even be profitable on shares that go down a bit, so long as they don't go below the breakeven.

You get to have your cake and eat it too!

Writing "Out-of-the-Money" (OTM) covered calls enables you to capitalise on the increase in share value AND you get to collect the option premium. (I'll explain out-of-the-money, at-the-money and in-the-money concepts in detail in the bonus section.)

INSURANCE

Writing covered calls is a form of insurance as the option premium is your protection. Your shares have to fall greater than the amount of the option premium that you are paid before you start losing money.

What is so cool about this insurance is that you get paid to take the policy! How is that? Well, you get paid the option premium, don't you?

BONUS! FREE gifts at www.TGRProperty.com.au/Gifts

REPAIR STRATEGY

The only danger of writing covered calls is if your shares fall below the breakeven. Therefore, a simple repair strategy is:

> Buy back the call if the share price drops to the strike price and then sell the shares.

If you do this at the sold strike price you will still be profitable in the trade. I explain how this works in great detail in my home study course. Unfortunately I don't have the space in this chapter to cover every detail.

I love this strategy. If the trade goes against you a bit, you still make money!

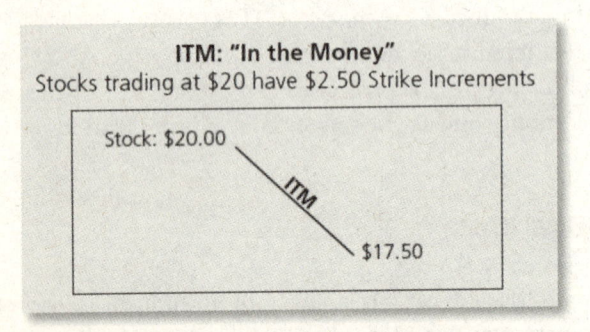

ITM: "In the Money"
Stocks trading at $20 have $2.50 Strike Increments

Stock: $20.00
ITM
$17.50

In this example, the shares are trading at $20 and you are selling someone the rights to buy your shares from you for $17.50.

Writing "In-the-Money" (ITM) is my favorite, which really puzzles people at first. They initially think, "Why on earth would you ever sell someone the rights to buy your shares from you for less than you paid for them?"

RENTING SHARES

To me, writing covered calls is all about the PREMIUM! I don't care about the capital gains (growth of the shares), I just want the option premium. I just want the CASH. Good, consistent monthly CASHFLOW.

Let's assume that the option premium is $3.50 per share ($2.50 because the strike price is $2.50 below the share price and an additional $1 as per the previous example).

There are three different scenarios that can happen at expiration:

1. **If the shares go up,** the option owner would exercise their rights to buy the shares from you at $17.50, giving you a $2.50 loss on the shares; however, you brought in $3.50 for the option premium, which results in a $1 per share profit. That equates to a five per cent return on investment ($1 profit on a $20 investment). Remember, that return is PER MONTH! A five per cent per month return equates to 60 per cent per annum, without compounding.

2. **If the shares go down a bit** but not below $17.50 at expiration, the option owner would again exercise their rights to buy the shares from you at $17.50 (your profit would again be the $1 per share from the option premium). Imagine the shares dropping 10 per cent to $18. The option owner would exercise their rights to buy the shares from you at $17.50, giving you a five per cent return for the month on shares that have just dropped 10 per cent. How cool is that?

3. **If the shares go down below the strike price** of $17.50 at expiration, the option owner would not exercise their rights to buy the shares from you at $17.50 because they could buy them cheaper from the market. Therefore, you

BONUS! FREE gifts at www.TGRProperty.com.au/Gifts

keep the option premium and the shares, giving you the opportunity to write more calls on your shares for the next month's expiration. In this scenario, you could make a loss on the shares but some or all of the loss would be offset by the option premium.

Breakeven (Share Price – Option Premium): Your breakeven on this trade would be $16.50 ($20 - $3.50) so you could therefore be profitable on shares that go down quite a lot, so long as they don't go below the breakeven.

Did you get that? You can still make a profit on shares that go down. Now that's powerful as you have so much protection with this strategy and you have so much opportunity for profit.

If the shares go up YOU MAKE MONEY!
If the shares stay at the same price YOU MAKE MONEY!
If the shares go down a bit YOU STILL MAKE MONEY!
If the shares go down a lot part of your loss is offset by the option premium!

Like I mentioned before, this is like taking out insurance without having to pay a premium. In actual fact, you get PAID to take out the insurance!

Writing ITM covered calls is such a great strategy as you can make a great profit with a very high level of protection.

WHY WRITE COVERED CALLS?

1. They enable you to generate two income streams:

    - Monthly rental of your shares - Generates monthly cashflow, month after month after month; and

RENTING SHARES

- Capital gain on your shares - If they go up and you write OTM calls.

2. They're relatively safe; that's why the Government allows you to do this in your retirement fund.

3. They create discipline. Most traders do not have a plan. They have no idea when they are going to sell their shares or at what price. Writing covered calls enforces a plan as you determine when to sell (expiration date) and at what price (strike price).

THE DOWNSIDE OF WRITING COVERED CALLS

Hmmm, that's a tough one…They cap the upside potential of the shares. In other words, you could miss out on some extra potential profit.

I'd much rather run a scan using my Lifestyle Option Scanner, write an ITM covered call and make five per cent, 10 per cent or higher for the month, get called out, and then do it again next month. After all, who out there is making 60 per cent, 120 per cent or more per year?

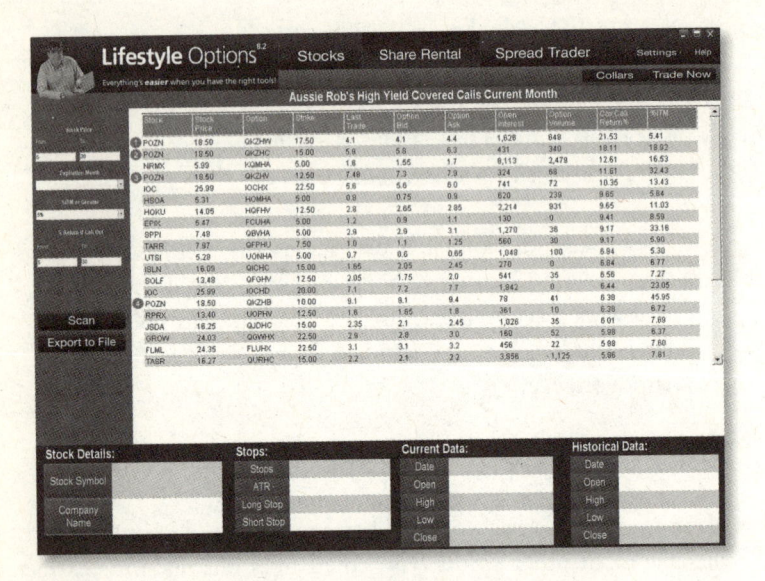

Above is a screenshot of my powerful Share Renting Scanner. You'll see 4 POZN Covered Call Candidates.

Here is what the figures mean:

1. POZN is trading at $18.50. By selling someone the rights to buy it from you at $17.50, you would want POZN to stay above $17.50 at expiration (third Friday of the month). The shares would then be bought from you at $17.50, making you an incredible 21 per cent return for the month.

2. The second POZN candidate is an even safer trade, as you would then be selling someone the rights to buy POZN from you at $15. The objective of this trade is for POZN to stay above $15 at expiration (third Friday of the month). The shares would then be bought from you, leaving you a pretty cool 18 per cent return for the month.

RENTING SHARES

3. The third POZN candidate is safer again as you would then be selling someone the rights to buy POZN from you at $12.50. The objective of this trade is for POZN to stay above $12.50 at expiration (third Friday of the month). The shares would then be bought from you, leaving you with an 11 per cent return for the month.

As you can see with these three examples, you could be profitable writing covered calls if the POZN shares went up, stayed at the same price and amazingly, you could still make money if they went down a tad!

Actually, take a look at the fourth POZN candidate. POZN could drop $8.50 - or an incredible 45 per cent - and you'd still make six per cent for the month.

Now of course you know that if you did each of these trades on margin, your return would double! So that means, with the fourth POZN example, POZN could drop $8.50 - or an incredible 45 per cent - and you'd still make 12 per cent for the month. That's a massive 144 per cent per annum!

Do you get it?

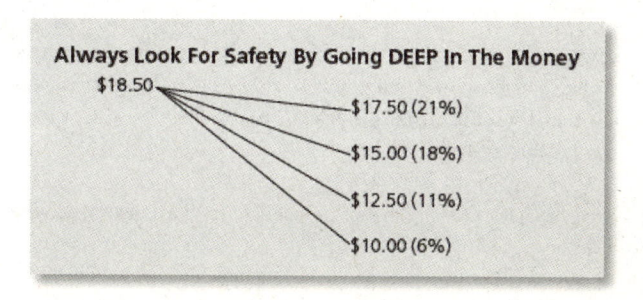

Always Look For Safety By Going DEEP In The Money

$18.50
- $17.50 (21%)
- $15.00 (18%)
- $12.50 (11%)
- $10.00 (6%)

BONUS! FREE gifts at www.TGRProperty.com.au/Gifts

I'm sure you'll agree that writing covered calls is a great way to create regular monthly income and on top of that, they're a lot safer than just buying the shares. I'm also sure you'll agree that one of the best Internet businesses out there is online trading!

TRACKING YOUR RESULTS

Now don't go jumping live into the market tomorrow. I suggest you read this chapter again - and then once more - to make sure you totally understand the strategy. I then suggest that you start paper trading, practice trading.

Do you think you'll make mistakes when you first start? Of course you will. And which would you prefer to lose, pretend money or your hard-earned cash? You should always paper trade a new strategy until you are 500 per cent confident that you know what you are doing and are comfortable with the strategy itself.

WHY DO YOU KEEP BREAKING THE RULES?

Here's a copy of a message that I sent to my clients that I'm sure you'll benefit from too.

> Lemme start by saying that I am not directing this at anyone personally, although, when you read this you could quite possibly think that I am directing this at you. If you feel that way, then ya better pay attention!
>
> Why is it that you keep breaking the rules? You know that when you do, you generally lose. So why do you keep doing it?

RENTING SHARES

Oops, I forgot about earnings!
Oops, I forgot about news!
Oops, I forgot to look at support and resistance!
Oops, I forgot to complete my trade sheet!
Oops, I forgot about all the rules!

What you should be saying is, "Oops, I must confess that I'm a greedy little bugger. I know that by earning 10 per cent per month with following the rules, I will be in the top five per cent of traders in the world but for some crazy reason, doubling my account each year is not good enough."

Time out for a minute: If you're new to trading you're probably wondering, "Why on earth would anyone ever break the rules when they know that if they just stick to them, they could earn a pretty cool 10 per cent per month or a whopping 120 per cent per annum?"

When some people start earning great, consistent income, greed sets in. If I just tweak it this way or if I just do that, I can earn more...

Come on now, let's be realistic here. You hold the key to financial freedom; the key that can elevate you to the top five per cent of traders in the world, the key that can provide both you and your family financial freedom for life. WHY WOULD YOU JEOPARDISE THAT?

I am bringing this to your attention so you can learn from other people's mistakes. Ya gotta learn to stick to the rules! The sooner you do, the sooner you will be financially free for life!

BONUS! FREE gifts at www.TGRProperty.com.au/Gifts

AUSSIE ROB

OK, back to the message: Aah well, I only lost $200, that's okay. Is it? Think about it. If you earn $20 per hour net in your J-O-B (Just-Over-Broke), your tiny $200 loss equates to 10 hours' work. Yeah, that means you have to work another 10 hours to help your boss get rich and you get nothing out of it because you're just covering the costs of your trading loss!

That could mean working a Sunday instead of enjoying the day with your family and friends. That could mean…? Well think about it, what ramifications could it have to you and your family's life?

That could result in you eventually giving up by proclaiming, "This doesn't work" when you should be proclaiming, "This does work, I don't work. I just don't have the discipline to follow the rules." Hmmm, having to work an extra day a week to make up for my lack of discipline shines a different light on it, eh!

So why do YOU keep breaking the rules?

The rules are so simple; you know what they are and you know how important they are. If you don't know what the rules are, then what da heck are ya do'n trading? Get edumacated first!

Just a little discipline prior to placing a trade is all it takes. Create a trading plan containing all the rules then follow the plan. You've heard it before, "Plan the trade and trade the plan". No rocket science here folks, just commonsense.

Bottom Line: If you don't have the discipline to plan the trade and trade the plan then you shouldn't be in this business. Put your money to work elsewhere as all you'll be doing is giving it to the market.

They say "education is power". I say, "BS, it's acting on the education that's power"!

BONUS! FREE gifts at www.TGRProperty.com.au/Gifts

FIVE YEARS TO FINANCIAL FREEDOM

There's a lot of wisdom in the old saying, "Rome wasn't built in a day." That same wisdom is applicable to our trading. We don't have to conquer the world immediately. Taking baby steps is what trading is all about.

Let's put it another way. Do you know how to eat an elephant? One bite at a time!

Conquering trading is like eating an elephant. Initially, it can look quite daunting but when you break it down to tiny chunks of information and study bit by bit, it is very simple.

Trading has been around for a long time and I dare say, the markets are gunna be around for a lot longer so you don't need to go 200 kilometers per hour (or mph for my American friends).

Unfortunately, some people jump into the markets without being edumacated first. They feel that they can jump in boots 'n all with just a snippet of information. Wow, how dangerous is that? Like lambs to the slaughter!

I liken the journey that you are now undertaking to the journey of a university student. You're now back at school; the exciting trading school.

Now consider this…

Spend three months studying and paper trading (practice trading) then start with only $5,000 trading capital. At the end of your fifth year you would have accumulated **over one million dollars** if you earn 10 per cent per month. You know how to achieve 10 per cent per month. It's easy if you have the right tools. At the end of five years (the same amount of time a doctor spends at medical school), you would be earning a doctor's yearly income, monthly!

Month	1st Year	2nd Year	3rd Year	4th Year	5th Year
January	Study	12,969	40,701	127,738	400,898
February	Study	14,266	44,772	140,512	440,987
March	Study	15,692	49,249	154,563	485,086
April	5,500	17,261	54,174	170,020	533,595
May	6,050	18,987	59,591	187,022	586,954
June	6,655	20,886	65,550	205,724	645,650
July	7,321	22,975	72,105	226,296	710,215
August	8,053	25,272	79,315	248,926	781,236
September	8,858	27,800	87,247	273,818	859,360
October	9,744	30,580	95,972	301,200	945,296
November	10,718	33,637	105,569	331,320	1,039,825
December	11,790	37,001	116,126	364,452	1,143,808

Where will YOU be in five short years?
Are YOU ready to take the next step?

BONUS SECTION FOR THE SERIOUS...

You know what? You've got me excited because you wanna dig a bit deeper, right? Ya see, I've added this section at the end to go a bit deeper into the stuff from the beginning. Clear as mud?

The danger with teaching options is that by going too deep at the beginning, some people feel there is too much to learn and give up. So I deliberately glossed over the beginning so I could fast-track to the "meat". The meat is the info that makes the money...

Yeah I know, we live in a world of instant gratification where we want everything now, right now. At the beginning I heard ya scream'n, "Show me the money!" So with the danger of you not reading any further and missing out on this incredible opportunity, I showed you the money pretty quickly.

Now that I've got ya hooked - well ya must be or ya wouldn't still be reading, right? - I can take you back to the beginning to delve a bit deeper into the essentials of what options are all about and the nuances of why, what, how and when.

Some of this you have already learnt but I'm including it again to show you how far you really have come in such a short period of time and to "lock in" the fundamental information that you've gotta know before you can take the next step in your new online trading Internet business.

Here's a basic summary of options:

BONUS! FREE gifts at www.TGRProperty.com.au/Gifts

AUSSIE ROB

I don't know why people make options sound so complicated because they are so simple. Ya see, there are only two options:

1. Calls ↑

2. Puts ↓

Calls increase in value when a stock goes up; conversely, puts decrease in value when a stock goes down.

The best way to remember the difference between calls and puts is to try and remember back to your dating days at high school. I had my eye on a hot little chick and finally got the courage to pick UP the phone to CALL her out on a date.

And guess what she said? Aah, thanks for the confidence…You were right, she said no, so I PUT the phone back down.

So the best way to remember the difference between CALLS and PUTS is to think about how lousy my love life was in high school…

OK, let's get serious now. Why and when would you use calls and puts? Well, if you thought a stock was gunna go up, you would buy a call. Why? Because a call costs a heck of a lot less than the stock. Buying calls is a way to capitalise on the capital gains of a stock by only putting a tiny amount of money on the table.

For example, if a stock was trading at say, $20, you could buy a $20 call for say, $1. You are paying $1 per share for the rights to buy the stock at $20.

RENTING SHARES

If you didn't buy calls and simply bought the stock for $20 and it went up to $25, you would have made $5 on a $20 investment, or in other words, 25 per cent.

Now here comes the real exciting part....

If you bought the $20 call option for $1 and the stock went up to $25, you have the right to exercise your option and buy the stock at $20. Alternatively, the call would now be worth $5, so if you were only interested in making the money and not actually buying the stock, you would simply sell the call for $5 and not exercise your rights to buy the stock.

Buying a call for $1 and then selling it for $5 gives you a whopping 500 per cent return compared with only 25 per cent if you just bought the stock for $20 and then sold it for $25. Pretty cool, eh?

Do you now know why I ask, "Why on earth would anyone ever buy stocks?" Why on earth would you ever pay $20 for a stock when you could pay only $1 to have the rights to buy the stock? Interesting, eh?

And on top of that, what about the risk? Well, how far can a $20 stock fall? That's right, it could go to zero. Therefore, your maximum risk would be $20. Now on the flip side, if you bought an option for $1, the maximum you could ever lose is the $1 premium that you paid. You see, you're actually paying $1 per share for the "right to buy" the stock.

It goes without saying, if the stock goes up, you would exercise your rights to buy the stock so you can capitalise on the capital gains, or just sell the option for a profit, while conversely, if the stock went down, you would never exercise your rights to buy it.

BONUS! FREE gifts at www.TGRProperty.com.au/Gifts

For example, if the $20 stock went down to say $15, you'd never exercise your rights to buy it for $20 when the market value is only $15.

What an amazing difference in risk:

1. If you bought the stock for $20 and it went down to $15, you'd lose $5 per share.

2. If you bought the option for $1, you would let it expire worthless. You'd only lose $1 per share.

Hmmm, a $5 loss or only a $1 loss? Tough decision, eh? Ya with me? When you buy calls you want the stock to go up!

So what about puts? Simple, they're exactly opposite to calls so when a stock goes down in value, a put goes up. However, I won't be going into puts a lot in this chapter as it is dedicated to making money out of calls.

Now when you **buy** an **option**, it gives you the right but not the obligation to buy a **certain stock** at a **certain price** by a **certain time**.

Let's break it down into tiny chunks to see what that really means:

BUY: To "buy" means that you have the "right to buy" the stock. As a trader, when you buy stuff, you want the price to go up so if you thought a particular stock was going to go up, instead of buying the stock, you could buy an option to buy the stock. In this case, you would buy a call option.

RENTING SHARES

OPTION: An "option" means that it is your choice. You choose whether you exercise your option and buy the stock or alternatively, you choose not to exercise your option and simply let it expire worthless. You can also sell your option at any time prior to it expiring.

CERTAIN STOCK: You can trade options on a lot of different things. You can trade options on commodities like gold, oil and wheat etc. You can trade options on Forex, the Foreign Currency Exchange, where you trade two currencies against each other like the Aussie Dollar versus the US Dollar. You can even trade options on real estate. But what I am focusing on here is trading stock options so the "certain stock" is the actual stock that you are interested in buying.

Take Microflop as an example. Instead of buying Microflop shares, you could simple buy a call option to give you the rights to buy Microflop. It is important to know from the outset that not every stock is optionable. More on this later…

CERTAIN PRICE: The "certain price" is the price that you have the option to buy the stock at. If, for example, Microflop was trading at say, $20, you could buy the rights to buy Microflop at $20. The "certain price" is also known as the "strike price".

CERTAIN TIME: The "certain time" is known as the "expiration date". It is the time that you have to decide whether you exercise your option to buy the stock or not. Like I mentioned before, if the stock went up, you'd exercise your rights to buy the stock or you'd simply sell your option for a profit. If the stock went down, you wouldn't exercise your rights to buy the stock. You'd simply sell your option prior to it expiring if it had any value left or you'd let it expire worthless.

BONUS! FREE gifts at www.TGRProperty.com.au/Gifts

AUSSIE ROB

I prefer to trade US options and not Aussie options, as the US market is massive compared with the tiny Aussie market. What I teach in this chapter can be applied to the Aussie market however, there are some fundamentally different rules which I will bring to your attention at the right time.

The Aussie rules are going to be totally irrelevant in the end as I know that when you've finished reading you'll want to trade the action-packed US market!

US options have far, far greater premiums than Aussie options. Hypothetically speaking, if you could earn a 50 cent premium on an Aussie option or $1 on a US option, which would you prefer? Yeah, I thought so, you're just like me. You wanna earn the biggest bang for ya buck! Now back to the "certain time"…

An option gives you the right to buy a certain stock at a certain price by a certain time.

So we've determined the certain stock that we'd like the rights to buy is Microflop. We've also determined the certain price that we'd like the rights to buy it at, being $20. So now we have to determine the certain time that we'd like to make our decision whether to buy it or not.

US options expire on the third Friday of the month while Aussie options expire on the Thursday before the last Friday of the month.

So what you're saying is that Aussie options expire on the last Thursday of the month? No, not at all. What happens if the last day of the month is a Thursday? That would make the "Thursday before the last Friday" the second last Thursday of the month! Hmmm, Aussies get most things right but we really screwed up

BONUS! FREE gifts at www.TGRProperty.com.au/Gifts

RENTING SHARES

on this one! The good news is we don't have to worry about it because you'll soon be convinced to trade the US market instead of the Aussie market.

So when do US options expire? The third Friday of the month. TOO EASY!

Aussie Expiration Date	**US Expiration Date**
Last Thursday before the last Friday of the month	Third Friday of the month

For example, if we wanted the rights to buy Microflop for $20 by the third Friday of September, we'd nominate September's expiration. If we wanted more time, we could simply nominate another month further out in time. It doesn't matter which month we choose, they all expire on the third Friday of the month.

The further out in time you go, the more expensive the option is. Why is that the case? Well think about it. The person who owns the stock and sells you the rights to buy it from them cannot sell it in the open market as you effectively have a caveat on their stock. In other words, they cannot sell it to anyone else but you. They cannot sell it in the open market until your option expires.

So, with that in mind, the further out in time you go, the more the person who owns the stock would want for you putting a hold on their stock. This is no different to real estate.

Let's assume that someone wanted an option to buy your home and they were willing to pay you a premium for that option.

BONUS! FREE gifts at www.TGRProperty.com.au/Gifts

Which would you want more for, an option to buy your home in a month or an option to buy your home in six months' time? Don't forget, they are only buying an option to buy your home, not an actual unconditional contract AND they have locked in the price. They have the rights but not the obligation to buy your home AND you are not allowed to sell your home to anyone else within that time.

Let's assume they wanted the rights to buy your home for $500,000 and you agreed on a six-month option. A lot of things could happen in six months. For one, the price of your home could go up from $500,000 to, say, $550,000. As the option seller, you have locked in your price so you can't ask more for your home in a couple of months as your "option contract" stipulated that the other party had the rights to buy your home for $500,000.

What else could happen? Gee, you might even get a better offer within the next six months, however, you cannot sell it to anyone else as you have sold those rights to the option buyer.

Can you now see that the further out in time you go, the more expensive the option will be? Commonsense, right?

I assume you understand by now why a person would buy an option? That's right, to pay a small amount of money to lock in the price at a future date, then only exercise their option and buy the stock or your home etc. if the price went up.

But why on earth would someone ever sell an option against their stock or their home? How'd I know you were gunna ask that? Be patient, I'm coming to that shortly. Now back to time again…

RENTING SHARES

Time is the lifeblood of an option. As each day goes by, it loses value until it expires worthless. In other words, it's a depreciating asset.

OK, there are a few more basic fundamentals that ya need to know:

CONTRACT VALUE: One option contract controls 100 shares of stock.

In other words, if you'd like the rights to buy 100 shares of Microflop, you'd buy one call option. If you'd like the rights to buy 1,000 shares, you'd simply buy 10 contracts.

Aussie Contract Size	**US Contract Size**
1,000 shares of stock	100 shares of stock

As you can see, you have far more flexibility trading US options as one contract controls only 100 shares of stock. For example, if an Aussie stock was trading at $20, the total contract value would be $20,000 (1,000 x $20) so if you exercised your rights to buy the stock, you would have to purchase $20,000 of shares. If an American stock was trading at $20, the total contract value would only be $2,000 (100 x $20) so if you exercised your rights to buy the stock, you would only have to purchase $2,000 of shares.

This is a biggie especially when it comes to cashflow. You need far less money to trade the US market than the Aussie market.

STRIKE PRICES: You remember what the strike price is? That's right, it's the price that you have the rights to buy the option at. Now you can't just choose any old price that you want to buy the stock at. To keep liquidity in the market there are three set strike prices:

BONUS! FREE gifts at www.TGRProperty.com.au/Gifts

AUSSIE ROB

1. **Shares priced up to $25** have $2.50 strike increments. Therefore, you can write $5 calls, $7.50 calls, $10 calls etc.

2. **Shares priced between $25 and $200** have $5 strike increments. Therefore, you can write $25 calls, $30 calls, $35 calls etc.

3. **Shares priced from $200 and more** have $10 strike increments. Therefore, you can write $200 calls, $210 calls, $220 calls etc.

These are general guidelines; some cases differ but most follow these guidelines. There is one abnormality that I must make you aware of. At the time of writing, there were 20 or so stocks that had $1 strike increments.

Imagine if there were no set strike increments. Imagine if there was a $19.99 strike and a $19.98 strike and a $19.97 strike. There would be way too many choices and not enough liquidity to create a decent market. By reducing the number of strike increments, people have fewer choices, therefore, creating more liquidity.

And what about Aussie options? Well strangely enough, they have $0.50 increments. This one just doesn't cut it with me. There are too many choices in such a tiny market. What do you think the liquidity would be like? Yeah, pretty lousy!

Aussie Strike Prices	US Strike Prices	
	Stock Price	**Increment**
All: $0.50	$5 - $25	$2.50
	$25 - $200	$5
	$200+	$10

BONUS! FREE gifts at www.TGRProperty.com.au/Gifts

IN-THE-MONEY (ITM) / AT-THE-MONEY-(ATM) / OUT-OF-THE-MONEY (OTM)

Speaking of strike prices… there are three distinct relationships between the strike price and the stock price.

1. IN-THE-MONEY (ITM)
2. AT-THE-MONEY (ATM)
3. OUT-OF-THE-MONEY (OTM)

Again, I am focusing on calls in this book so what I'm gunna explain now only pertains to calls. Puts are exactly the same, except opposite!

Let's start with the last one first. An option is OUT-OF-THE-MONEY when the strike is above the stock price. Great, but what does that mean? Well think about it. If a friend called you on the phone crying, "I'm out of money", what would he or she really be saying? They've got kids? Probably, but if it was to do with trading, it would mean that they have lost money.

Applying that to options, if the strike was above the stock price then you'd have the rights to buy the stock for more than what it is worth in the market. For example, if a stock was trading at $20, the next strike out-of-the-money would be $22.50. Would you exercise your rights to buy a $20 stock for $22.50? No. If you did, you'd definitely be out of money, right?

Believe it or not, there are strategies that utilise out-of-the-money options. I teach them at my hands-on training workshops. The ones that I teach have made me a truckload of money. Like most opportunities in life, thinking outside the square can produce the greatest results.

BONUS! FREE gifts at www.TGRProperty.com.au/Gifts

If a stock was trading at $20, two strikes out-of-the-money would be $25. And what would three strikes be? Well done, $30, as we just moved up into a higher strike increment bracket. Remember, greater than $25 means $5 increments.

The second option is AT-THE-MONEY, which simply means that the strike is at the same price as the stock. For example, if a stock was trading at $20, the at-the-money strike would be $20. You have the rights to buy the stock at $20.

And what about two strikes at-the-money? There ain't no such thing. At-the-money is at-the-money so there can only be one at-the-money strike!

Now that leaves one left, my favorite, IN-THE-MONEY...

Why is it my favorite? Well, if your friend calls screaming, "I'm in the money", they'd really be saying that they've made some money, right?

Applying that to our $20 stock, one strike in-the-money would be $17.50. Imagine having the opportunity to buy a $20 stock for only $17.50. You'd have to be in the money, wouldn't you?

So what would two strikes be? Great job, $15. And three? Yup, you got it, $12.50.

So what would you rather be? IN MONEY or OUT OF MONEY? That's a no-brainer, right?

This will all come together and make total sense shortly when we apply these basic fundamentals to our actual trading strategies.

RENTING SHARES

CALL OPTIONS

OUT OF THE MONEY CALL OPTION — $22.50

AT THE MONEY CALL OPTION — $20.00

IN THE MONEY CALL OPTION — $17.50

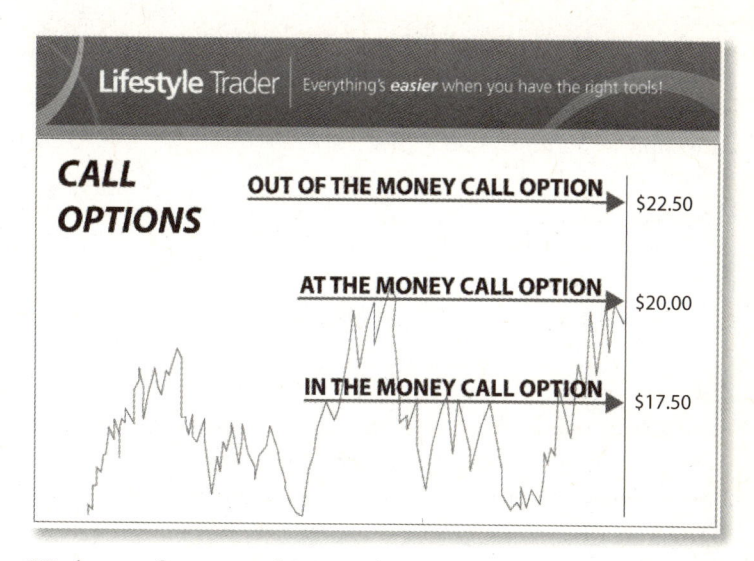

Lifestyle Trader | Everything's easier when you have the right tools!

We have a few more things to learn and then I'm gunna refer back to in/out/at-the-money so you can see its relevance and the importance of knowing which is which. Some strategies require trading out-of-the money whilst others require trading in-the-money and some require trading at-the-money too!

The next fundamental you need to understand is what the actual option premium is made up of.

Once we've nailed this next bit, we then get to the crux of options – and one step closer to achieving financial freedom for life!

OPTION PREMIUM

The option premium is the cost of the option; the option buyer pays the premium and the option writer receives the premium. I'll get more into paying and receiving the premium shortly.

BONUS! FREE gifts at www.TGRProperty.com.au/Gifts

It's really important to understand what the premium is made up of. It actually consists of two totally different components that, when understood correctly, can make a ginormous difference to your option trading.

The two components are:

1. Intrinsic Value
2. Time Value

Intrinsic value: I like calling intrinsic value "real value" as the intrinsic value IS the real value of the option. Here's why. Intrinsic value is the difference between the option strike price and the stock price. So for example, if you bought a $17.50 call option on a $20 stock, you have the rights to buy that $20 stock for only $17.50. The $17.50 call would therefore have $2.50 of intrinsic value. Yup, that's right, there is $2.50 of "real value" in that option. In other words, if you had the opportunity to buy a $20 stock for only $17.50, you'd be buying it at a $2.50 discount so there would be $2.50 of "real value" in that deal. Got it?

Time value: Time value is the difference between the option premium and the intrinsic value. For example, if the option premium is $3.50 and the intrinsic value is $2.50, the time value is $1 ($3.50 - $2.50). "Time" is what options are all about. It is their lifeblood. When you buy a call, you are buying the rights to buy the stock at a pre-determined price by a certain time. In other words, you are buying time to see if the stock goes up. As expiration is approaching, you'd be getting ready to make a decision on whether to exercise your rights to buy the stock.

If the stock was-in-the-money at expiration, you'd either exercise your rights to buy the stock or you'd sell the call.

RENTING SHARES

If the stock was out-of-the-money at expiration, you wouldn't exercise your rights to buy the stock, you'd simply let it expire worthless.

You see, the call would be worthless at expiration if it was out-of-the-money as there would be no intrinsic value and because that expiration is upon us, there would be no time value left either.

As you've probably gathered by now, out-of-the-money options are 100 per cent time value. There is no real value in them. You are simply buying time - time for the stock to go up. That is why out-of-the-money options are always cheaper than in-the-money options.

The final piece of the ITM/ATM/OTM puzzle is the further out-of-the-money you go, the cheaper the option is. Why is that the case? Well, the option has to be in-the-money to have any value at expiration, as there is no time left. If there is no time left, the only value left in the option is the intrinsic value. If the option is out-of-the-money at expiration, it will be worthless.

Therefore, the further out-of-the-money you go, the lower the probability of the option being in-the-money at expiration.

TIME DECAY

The chart over the page is the crux to trading options. To me, it is the be all and end all. When you grasp how time decay affects an option, the light bulb will go off, sparking a new way of thinking.

On face value, people feel that as time goes by, an option will gradually expire worthless in an even daily amount. For example, if the time value of an option was $5 and there were 50 days

BONUS! FREE gifts at www.TGRProperty.com.au/Gifts

AUSSIE ROB

left until expiration, basic economics would say that the option would depreciate, or decay, at the rate of 10 cents per day.

Nothing could be further from the truth. And understanding the truth shines a totally different light on trading!

Take a look at the chart below. See how the chart is a curve instead of a straight line from top left to bottom right? An option loses one third of its value in the first two thirds of its life and two thirds of its value in the last third of its life.

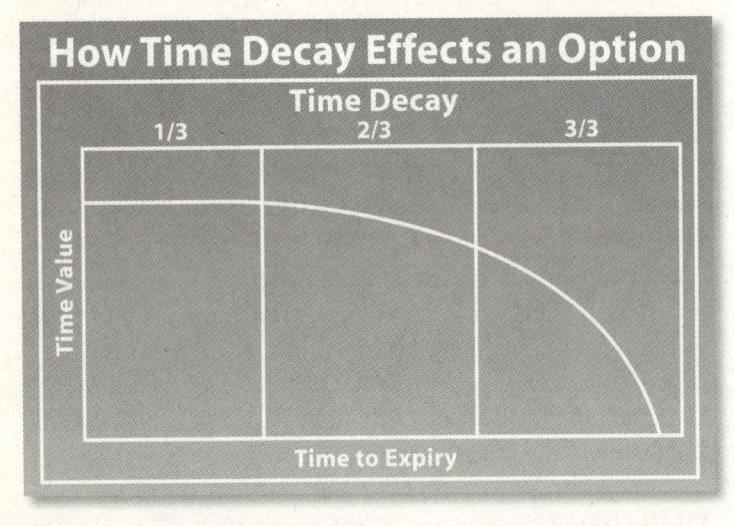

How Time Decay Effects an Option

Wow, this is an absolutely amazing phenomenon that can give you a real edge with your trading!

Aussie Rob's two time decay golden rules:

1. **Buy:** Three to four months out in time
2. **Write:** Current month

RENTING SHARES

How did I come up with those two golden rules and what do they mean? Well, remember a few pages back I said: "The option premium is the cost of the option; the option buyer pays the premium and the option writer receives the premium…"

Let's put that into perspective with our trading to see how we can benefit from my two golden rules as either the "buyer" or the "writer". When you nail this, the money will flow…

WHAT CAN YOU DO WITH OPTIONS?

You can "buy" options and you can "write" options. Let's look at both of these options (excuse the pun) in detail to determine why you should or shouldn't buy or write (again, we will only be focusing on calls).

1. **Buying calls:** When you buy calls, you are paying the option writer a premium for the rights to buy the stock at a pre-determined price by the expiration date.

Imagine Microflop trading at say $20, and the $20 call was going for $1. Why on earth would someone pay $1 per share for the rights to buy Microflop for $20? Well, they are hoping that Microflop goes up prior to the option expiring. If it went up to say, $23 per share, they could exercise their option and buy Microflop for $23.

Their net cost would have been $21 per share ($20 for the shares + $1 for the option) therefore, giving them a nice profit of $2 per share. Remember, they only paid $1 per share for the option so if they sold the stock immediately, they effectively made a $2 per share profit on a $1 per share investment or a pretty cool 200 per cent return on their investment!

BONUS! FREE gifts at www.TGRProperty.com.au/Gifts

Alternatively, if they didn't want to keep the stock, they could simply sell the call for $3 and make the same $2 profit!

The call has to be worth $3. Why? Well, what is the option premium made up of? That's right, intrinsic value and time value. So, if the strike was $20 and the stock was trading at $23, how much intrinsic value would be in the option? Why, $3 of course!

And how much time value would be left in the option? Well, if it's now at the expiration date, there would be no time value left. Therefore, the option premium would be $3.

You with me on this? If you are, you are definitely on your way to becoming financially free for life!

HOW DOES TIME DECAY EFFECT AN OPTION BUYER?

Now this is where it gets even more interesting. If you had bought Microflop $20 calls for $1, the strike was at-the-money. As you know, at-the-money options are 100 per cent time value as there is no intrinsic value in them so you need to really pay attention to time decay.

As every day goes by, your option is depreciating due to time. Time is your number one enemy as it is constantly working against you.

Imagine buying an option for $1 and there are only 10 days left until expiration. Your option is gunna depreciate 10 cents per day. Now remember, the objective of buying options is for the strike to be in-the-money at expiration or the option will expire worthless. So, in this example, the stock would have to go up more than 10 cents per day just to breakeven.

RENTING SHARES

So what was my golden rule for BUYING options? Buy three to four months out in time.

Why? Well, take a look back at the time decay chart and you'll see that the option will depreciate a lot less three to four months out in time than say in the last month of its life.

What if the time decay rate was only two cents per day three to four months out compared with 10 cents in the last two weeks? Doesn't it make more sense to actually pay more for the option upfront to reduce the time decay effect? If you planned to be in the trade for only a few days or a week or so, then you would get a majority of the extra money you paid for time back as it would not have depreciated much over that time.

Ya learning something here? Good! If ya gunna buy options, buy three to four months out in time!

2. **Writing calls:** When you write calls, the option buyer pays you a premium for the rights to buy your stock at a pre-determined price by the expiration date.

Imagine Microflop trading at say $20, and the $20 call was going for $1. Why on earth would you sell someone the rights for $1 per share to buy Microflop from you for $20? There are two reasons:

1. **Cashflow:** The $1 per share that you receive for writing the call is cash in your back pocket. It's money for jam. No matter what happens to your stock, whether it goes up, stays at the same price or even if it goes down, the $1 is yours to keep. Now, not every stock pays $1 per share, however, my potent option scanner finds the ones that pay AT LEAST $1 per share.

BONUS! FREE gifts at www.TGRProperty.com.au/Gifts

2. **Protection:** If you paid $20 for a stock and then you were paid $1 for the rights to buy it from you, what would your net outlay be? That's right, $19. So that means you have $1 of protection in case the stock goes down. That's pretty cool getting paid to take out insurance, eh!

HOW DOES TIME DECAY EFFECT AN OPTION WRITER?

If you had sold the $20 calls against your Microflop stock for $1, the strike was at-the-money. As you know, at-the-money options are 100 per cent time value as there is no intrinsic value. As the option writer, you don't need to pay attention to time decay as time is working in your favour.

As every day goes by, the option that you wrote is depreciating due to time. Time is your best friend as it is constantly working for you.

Imagine writing an option for $1 and there are only 10 days left until expiration. Your written option is gunna depreciate 10 cents per day. That means that you are effectively earning 10 cents per day for doing what? For selling someone the rights to buy your stock from you at the same price that you just paid for it. Again, this is money for jam. Money for do'n diddly squat!

So what was my golden rule for WRITING options? Write current month.

Why? Well, take a look back at the time decay chart and you'll see that the option will depreciate a lot more in the last month of its life than say three to four months out in time.

RENTING SHARES

What if the time decay rate was only two cents per day three to four months out compared with 10 cents in the last two weeks? Doesn't it make more sense to receive less for the option upfront to increase the time decay effect? If you planned to be in the trade for a few months, couldn't you simply write the current month option now and then do it again next month, and again the following month?

So, can you see why my golden rule for writing options is to write current month? This little gem has just added double digit profits to your trading account! No, don't thank me, buy me a beer when you see me next. Better still, I think this one's worth a good bottle of red!

WHICH IS BETTER, BUYING OR WRITING?

1. Brokers estimate that 80 per cent of options expire worthless (bad for the option BUYER, great for the option WRITER).

2. Time works against the option BUYER but for the option WRITER.

3. BUYING options gives you a one in three chance of making money.

    - If the stock goes up, you **make** money.
    - If the stock stays the same, you **lose** money.
    - If the stock goes down, you **lose** money.

4. WRITING options gives you a possible three out of three chance of making money.

    - If the stock goes up, you **make** money.
    - If the stock stays the same, you **make** money.

BONUS! FREE gifts at www.TGRProperty.com.au/Gifts

- If the stock goes down a bit, you still **make** money.

Let's clarify that:

1. If the stock goes up, the option buyer will exercise their rights and buy your stock from you. You have missed out on any capital growth on the stock but **you still make the buck per share!**

2. If the stock stays the same, the option buyer wouldn't exercise their rights and buy your stock but **you still keep the buck per share!** AND you keep the stock so you can do it again next month!

3. If the stock goes down a bit (less than $1), the option buyer wouldn't exercise their rights and buy your stock but **you still keep the buck per share!** AND you keep the stock so you can do it again next month!

Trading is all about probabilities. You want to stack as many of those little "probables" in your favour. This chapter has helped to do just that and I look forward to teaching you more.

This book contains three free tickets to see me at Stuart Zadel's Think and Grow Rich® events so do whatever it takes to book in. Do it NOW while it's fresh in your mind.

In closing, I sincerely hope that I've made a positive impact on your life. I hope that I have been able to help you open your mind to the tremendous opportunities that exist in trading global markets online and I really hope that you're a person who takes action. All the knowledge in the world is useless unless it's followed by action. It's the number one quality that successful people have – they get off their butts and make things happen!

See you at a Think and Grow Rich® event real soon. Let's make this happen!

FREE BONUS GIFT

Aussie Rob has generously offered a FREE BONUS GIFT valued at $29

FREE eBook - "Death of the Managed Fund" by Aussie Rob and Scott Goold. Learn why exchange traded funds are taking over from managed funds and how to profit from them.

Visit the website below to receive this free gift
www.TGRProperty.com.au/Gifts

Chapter 7

MINIMISE TAX
MAXIMISE PROTECTION

"We make the taxman work as hard for you as you do."

ADRIAN HILL

ADRIAN HILL

Adrian Hill is one of only a few accountants talking the talk and walking the walk on the wealth-creation trail. A CPA accountant with 20 years' experience, he is constantly surprised by the amount of hard-earned money that people don't claim back from the tax office.

Adrian's wealth-creation journey began in 2000 when he started reading books and attending seminars on subjects including rental properties as well as share and option trading. He bought his first rental property in 2001 and has continued to buy property every year since then. He has traded shares and options over the years and in 2008 undertook a couple of subdivisions.

Adrian's mission is to "minimise tax and maximise asset protection". He also strongly believes "the taxman should work as hard as you do". It has been his experience that if you don't have a rental property or believe in asset protection, then you don't know the magic that can be achieved. Through learning tricks of the trade, you can legally use the tax laws to your advantage.

He is extremely passionate about properties, taxation reduction strategies and protecting your hard-earned assets. He loves to educate and will gladly spend hours assisting anyone who is willing to take steps towards financial freedom.

In 2004 he founded Superior Tax Solutions Pty Ltd to do just that, and so far has attracted 100 per cent of clients through referrals. Adrian's team is currently assisting more than 250 like-minded client groups to make the taxman work up a sweat!

RENTING SHARES

So I guess I could summarise this last couple of pages by saying, "Get rid of the story, just make it happen!"

My personal story is a lot deeper than what I've written here; you're just gunna have to wait till I publish my autobiography one day. No doubt you have a "story" too. We all do. We can all say, "But you were lucky, you had (such and such)" or "But it won't work for me because…" All I can say about that is "BS"!

We all have stories. Get rid of them. Get over it and make a decision to make an impact with your life.

What I'm gunna be introducing you to here in this book has worked for thousands of people around the world so there is absolutely no reason why it can't work for you too. Actually, there is a reason why it may not work for you. It won't work for you if you don't want to make it work.

You see, I've discovered that there are two types of people:

1. Those who look for all of the reasons why something WON'T WORK; and

2. Those who look for all of the reasons why something WILL WORK!

Which one are you?

I'm gunna finish this intro with a little success secret…

> *The difference between success and failure is minimal. The starting point is the most crucial, and that is simply getting off ya butt and doing SOMETHING.*

BONUS! FREE gifts at www.TGRProperty.com.au/Gifts

WHY TRADE ONLINE?

I'm so excited to be contributing to this book as the world's financial markets continue to be unpredictable. You may be wondering what financial markets have to do with the Internet. Well, my objective in this chapter is to open your mind to the incredible cashflow and investment opportunities that are right in front of you with online trading.

So why consider online trading as a business? Well think about this...

Question: How many employees do you need for an online trading business?

Answer: NONE

Question: How much money do you need to spend on advertising, Google AdWords, pay-per-click campaigns etc. for your online trading business?

Answer: NONE

Question: How much rent do you have to pay for your online trading business?

Answer: NONE

Question: How much inventory would you have to hold for your online trading business?

Answer: NONE

MINIMISE TAX MAXIMISE PROTECTION

HOW TO GET WHAT YOU'RE ENTITLED TO AND PROTECT WHAT YOU ALREADY HAVE

My story is a financial one but it begins in a very personal way. I met my beautiful wife Anita during the first subject of our six-and-a-half year degree at Monash University. We quickly fell in love and got married, then produced two wonderful girls who are the light of our lives.

Having a family of four at such a young age gave us some very sharp lessons in the difficulties of life. We struggled to save for our first home and, even with the help of our Nan who let us move in with her and live as cheaply as possible, it was a definite struggle. It was during this period that we learned the first of many key lessons that have helped us go from that precarious financial position to become millionaires: the only way to get ahead is to have a budget. Yes, I know many people consider the dreaded "b" word to be a dirty one but it taught us to respect money and to make sure we always know where it goes and what it is used for. In short, it put us in control of our own finances.

Our first home was a three-bedroom place in Cheltenham, 20 kilometres out of Melbourne. In hindsight, it would have been the perfect first rental property but at that stage we weren't yet able to recognise the fact. That first house was bought very much under the old school of thought, which basically states you have to work like a dog until you can afford to buy a house, then spend the rest of your life working to pay off the mortgage.

BONUS! FREE gifts at www.TGRProperty.com.au/Gifts

We always felt there ought to be more to life than that but it took us a long time to find the correct path. We would spend long hours walking the dog, talking and – both being accountants – crunching the numbers but we still couldn't understand why anybody would bother to own a rental property. The rent never covers the mortgage repayments, so what's the point of owning something that continually loses money?

Then we discovered two little words that changed everything: capital growth. In fact, they're so important I'm going write them again in big capital letters:

CAPITAL GROWTH.

The basic principle behind this is that the property continues to grow in value while the loan always stays the same. It gives rise to another excellent word, equity, which pretty much means getting money for nothing. I can't think of anybody who would say no to that.

Of course, harnessing this principle relies on continued capital growth and having a stable or increasing income, plus you will need to build in contingencies to ride out the short-term market fluctuations.

Obviously one of the dominant forces behind capital growth is the scarcity of land. It's a commodity that everybody in the world wants and needs, yet it's the one thing they're not making any more of and never will again. The amount of land in the world today, being shared between six billion people, is exactly how much 10 billion people or more will have to share in fifty years' time. In fact, if the experts are right about global warming and rising sea levels there could be even less.

MINIMISE TAX, MAXIMISE PROTECTION

Therefore, it's a good bet that any property you own will increase in value. The rate of the increase constantly varies as the market moves back and forth, up and down, but there are two things you should always keep in mind:

- historically it's been shown that over a period of time property will grow at two to three per cent above inflation;
- any fall-off in prices, which does happen from time to time, can affect all property values but more so those in the middle to high-priced property markets.

You can see, then, that owning rental property gives you a double bonus: income from rent in the short term and capital growth over the long term.

Of course, our path to financial freedom was not a straight one. Because we were feeling our own way through the dark and there was nobody out there to hand us the information we needed in a neat package, like this book is giving it to you, we had a few false starts that taught us some very valuable lessons. One of those came in the early 1990s when I was working in Collingwood. We decided to move to Park Orchards and bought some land there for $125,000 that we planned to build on. After six months, though, we realised we couldn't yet afford to build our dream home so we sold it for $200,000. In that situation our inexperience cost us twice over, as the property was re-sold again six months later for $300,000 when the Eastern Freeway opened.

There are two valuable lessons to be found in that experience. The first – and I cannot possible stress this enough – is that land will always go up in value. The second, though, is that land is also very expensive to hold onto if you're not planning to build a rental property in the near future. I'll get to the reasons for

BONUS! FREE gifts at www.TGRProperty.com.au/Gifts

that in a short while but first I want to introduce you to one of the key principles that allowed us to go from being penniless university students to millionaires. It is simply this:

Money is a tool.

That's all. Again, it seems like a laughably simple concept, almost a trite statement really, but accepting it as a fact requires a fundamental shift in your thinking and a complete re-evaluation of your relationship to your finances. You need to see money as a means to an end, not an end in itself. Your ultimate goal is not to accumulate as much money as you can in your bank account before you die, it's to use the money that has passed through your hands in your lifetime to give you the best possible quality of life. Think of your life as a journey you are taking, a long distance car trip for instance, and money is simply the fuel that keeps you moving in much the same way as the food you consume gets you through each day. You need to be dispassionate about allocating appropriate amounts of money to your living expenses, home loan repayments, entertainment and so forth, always setting aside as much as possible for investing.

There are many different types of investing, with rental properties being the one we've dealt with most and gained the most profit from. The strategy we used worked for us because we were almost 100 per cent focused on building a business at the same time. Having read this far into the book, you would be aware of at least five other strategies to turbo-charge your wealth-creation from property.

However, there's one investment that needs to be your very first port of call on the journey to financial independence. Before you invest a cent in property, or anywhere else for that matter, you need to invest in yourself. By simply reading this book you've

MINIMISE TAX, MAXIMISE PROTECTION

made an excellent start, trying as you are to benefit from the experience of those who have already made the journey you're trying to begin. Now I'll let you in on a little secret – that's exactly the same way that we started. Our practical education began back in 2000 when we started reading books just like the one you hold in your hands right now. As well as that we attended a number of seminars where we learned things they never taught us during our degrees or afterwards; we have spent close to $50,000 on self-education. It's certainly a lot of money but it's important not to dwell on that fact. The trick is to write the money off as a cost of business and think of it as an investment in yourself, which is easy for us to do as that money we initially spent has created a high enough return to make us millionaires.

It's amazing, really, to think of how much time Anita and I both spent in accounting firms without ever learning how to become financially free. You'd think it would be the first perk of a life spent juggling numbers for other people but none of our colleagues was asking the right questions and none of our superiors seemed to have the answers anyhow.

Of course, that lack of assistance turned out to be beneficial in one way, as it left us to learn everything the hard way. We passed through the school of hard knocks and picked up the skills we now have by actually doing things rather than simply observing or reading about them. For instance, nobody ever told us one of the most important equations for those undertaking a wealth-creation journey; we had to figure it out for ourselves.

BONUS! FREE gifts at www.TGRProperty.com.au/Gifts

It goes like this:

$$\text{Asset} + \text{time} = \text{wealth}$$

Or, to put it another way:

$$\text{Property} + \text{time} = \text{wealth}$$

WHY RENTAL PROPERTIES?

We settled on rental properties as our wealth-creation vehicle for a number of reasons including:

- the benefits of capital growth and equity;
- good debt versus bad debt (we wanted assets that appreciate and/or earn income, not those that depreciate and/or lose income);
- the tendency for rents to double every decade;
- the fact that 30 per cent of Australians currently rent with more likely to do so in the future;
- a high income is generally not needed to buy an income property; and
- value can be added easily by renovating.

But by far the best reason of all is that the tenant and the tax man – that's right, the tax man – help you pay for the rental property. Let's look at how.

HOW TO GET HELP OWNING YOUR RENTAL PROPERTY

If you keep the property in excellent condition you will get the maximum amount of rent from your tenant, which can be put towards paying down your mortgage. The taxman's part, though, is a little more complicated and can be a lot more profitable to your bottom line.

MINIMISE TAX, MAXIMISE PROTECTION

There are two things I should mention before proceeding: you should avoid buying vacant land, unless you intend to immediately build a rental property on it, develop it or add value in some other way, because unless your property is producing an income you won't get the many excellent tax benefits I'm going to spell out for you. Also, you should keep in mind that owning two smaller rental properties is better than owning one big one.

If you have a solid understanding of tax law or, even better, have a good accountant who knows it backwards, you can claim many tax deductions that will significantly increase your wealth and hasten your journey towards financial freedom. The key words there, of course, are "good accountant". You might think it's reasonable to assume that all accountants would know what I'm about to tell you but unfortunately that is not the case. The education received by accountants, both at university and throughout their on-site training, is patchy at best so you have to be extremely careful about choosing one that can not only talk the talk but also walk the walk.

It was this realisation that actually lead us to create our business, Superior Tax Solutions Pty Ltd, because we recognised a massive gap in the market that simply wasn't being filled by the majority of accountants who were out there.

It's not just an accountant that you need as you begin your journey to financial freedom, either. You need to build an entire team to support you along the way and help you reach your goals, each member of which will play a crucial role. Team members should include:

- accountant
- mortgage broker / financier
- property manager

- insurance broker
- solicitor
- quantity surveyor.

TAX DEDUCTIONS - GENERALLY

As accountants, there are lots of tricks we can share with you to help buy-and-hold your property, particularly in regard to maximising your tax deductions and asset protection. To start at the very beginning, an item is tax deductible if it is an expense incurred (that is, paid) while you were earning income. If you're not sure if an expense is tax deductible simply keep the tax invoice and seek your accountant's advice when your tax return is being prepared. The accountant should be on your side and will try to claim as much as possible to allow you to minimise your tax each year. It's their job to be proactive in this area and it's your right to claim everything you're entitled to.

RENTAL PROPERTY TAX ISSUES IN GENERAL

Rental income is, as you would expect, the income you receive in rent from your tenant each financial year.

HINT FOR TAX RETURN

If you do not receive your rent for June 2008 until 1 July, that rent is not income in the 2008 tax year but will be included in the 2009 tax year.

YOUR SHARE OF RENTAL INCOME AND EXPENSES

Your share of rental income and expenses is divided up according to who legally owns the property. For instance, property can be owned as:

- joint tenants, who each hold an equal interest in the property;

MINIMISE TAX, MAXIMISE PROTECTION

- tenants in common, who may hold unequal interests in the property. One could have an 80 per cent interest and the other 20 per cent.

> **HINT FOR TAX RETURN**
> Your rental income and expenses must be allocated to each according to their legal interest in the property, no matter what agreements they make between themselves.

RENTAL EXPENSES

You can claim a deduction for certain expenses you pay during the period your property is being rented or is available for rent.

There are three types of rental expenses:

1. Expenses that cannot be claimed as deductions;
2. Immediate deductions, which can be claimed in the financial year that you pay them;
3. Deductions expensed over a number of financial years.

1. Deductions that cannot be claimed

PURCHASE AND SALE COSTS

You cannot claim a deduction for the costs of purchasing or selling your rental property. However, they may form part of the cost base of the property for Capital Gains Tax (CGT) purposes. Below is an example that shows the kind of expenses you can claim as part of the cost base:

Purchase details:
Date of signing contract: 19 July
Date of settlement: 19 September

BONUS! FREE gifts at www.TGRProperty.com.au/Gifts

Purchase price	$300,000
Stamp Duty	$15,000
Legal costs	$1,000
Travel to purchase property	$2,000
Building inspection	$500
Pest inspection	$500
Buyer's agent fees	$6,000
Total Purchase Costs	**$325,000**

This means that when the above property is sold, $325,000 will be included in the cost base from which the amount of any capital gain or capital loss will be figured out.

HINT FOR TAX RETURN
The signing date of the contract is the triggering point for Capital Gains Tax purposes, while the settlement date is the triggering point for depreciation to start. Your total purchase costs, when you sell the property, may be reduced by depreciation and building write-off claimed.

---

2. Immediate deductions

Immediate deductions are those that can be claimed in the same financial year as they have been paid. Examples include:

- advertising for tenants
- bank fees
- body corporate fees and charges *
- cleaning
- council rates
- electricity and gas

MINIMISE TAX, MAXIMISE PROTECTION

- gardening and lawn mowing
- gifts to tenants and/or property managers
- in-house audio/video service charges
- insurance (including building, contents and public liability)
- interest on loans *
- Land Tax
- lease document expenses (including preparation, registration and stamp duty)
- legal expenses * (excluding acquisition costs and borrowing costs)
- mortgage discharge expenses *
- pest (annual check)
- property agent's fees and commission
- quantity surveyor's fees
- repairs and maintenance *
- security patrol fees
- servicing costs – for example, servicing a water heater
- stationery and postage
- telephone calls and line rental
- travel and car expenses for rent collection, property inspection and maintenance*
- water rates and charges.

Items marked with an asterisk (*) are discussed in detail overleaf.

HINT FOR TAX RETURN
You can only claim these expenses if you pay for them and are not reimbursed by the tenant.

BONUS! FREE gifts at www.TGRProperty.com.au/Gifts

BODY CORPORATE FEES AND CHARGES

Body corporate fees apply when you own an apartment, unit or any dwelling that has common property. The body corporate is responsible for the upkeep of the common property – such as lawns, driveways and lifts – as well as sometimes for the maintenance of external walls. It will usually issue a quarterly invoice to cover the costs of the above. These contributions are, in the majority of cases, covering a "general purpose sinking fund" and are fully claimable when paid.

A general purpose sinking fund is one that's established to cover a variety of unspecified expenses (some of which may be capital expenses) that are paid by the body corporate in maintaining the common property. This generally involves things like painting the common property and repairing or replacing fixtures and fittings. These are immediately deductible.

What is not immediately deductible, however, is if the body corporate requires you to make payments to a "special purpose fund" to pay for particular capital expenditure. A special purpose fund is set up to cover a specified, generally significant, expense that is not covered by ongoing contributions to a general purpose sinking fund. Most special purpose funds are established to cover the cost of capital improvement to the common property.

> **HINT FOR TAX RETURN**
> These special purpose contributions generally will be claimable at the rate of 2.50 per cent per annum.

INTEREST ON LOANS

If you take out a loan to purchase a rental property, you can claim the interest charged on that loan as a deduction. The important

MINIMISE TAX, MAXIMISE PROTECTION

thing to be aware of here is that the deductibility of the interest depends entirely on what the money was used for. Incidentally, what property is secured against the loan is irrelevant when figuring out the deductibility of the interest.

While the property is being rented, or is available for rent, you may also claim interest charged on loans taken out for the following purposes:

- to purchase depreciating assets
- for repairs
- for renovations.

> **HINT FOR TAX RETURN**
> You have to keep your personal loans entirely separate from the loans you intend to be tax deductible. To give an example, if you buy a property for a total cost of $325,000 (which included a contract price of $300,000) the bank would normally give you an 80 per cent loan, secured against that property, of $240,000. You need to finance the remaining $85,000 from elsewhere. If you take out a loan for that amount, then make sure that no money for personal purposes is ever withdrawn or deposited into it, you can claim the interest on both loans against any rent received from the property.

Similarly, if you take out a loan to purchase land on which to build a rental property or to finance renovations to a property you intend to rent out, the interest on the loan will be deductible from the time you take the loan out. However, if your intention changes – if, for example, you decide to move into the property yourself or you no longer intend to use it to produce rent or other income – you cannot claim the interest after your intention changes.

BONUS! FREE gifts at www.TGRProperty.com.au/Gifts

> **HINT FOR TAX RETURN**
> Interest is not the only expense you can claim in the period between buying the land and building a rental property on it. You can also claim other holding costs such as water rates, land tax, lawn mowing, council rates and insurance.

Where personal and property loans are combined
The first thing I have to say about combining personal and property loans is that you shouldn't do it. Your accounting will be much simpler if you are able to keep the two entirely separate. For instance, if you take out a loan to buy a rental property and a private car you have to divide the interest on the loan into deductible and non-deductible parts depending on how much each item cost.

If you have a loan account that has a fluctuating balance due to a variety of deposits and withdrawals, and it is used for both private and rental property purposes, you must keep accurate records so you can calculate the interest that applies to the rental property portion of the loan. In other words, you need to figure out how much interest you paid as part of earning income through rent (which is deductible) and how much you paid as part of the personal loan (which is not).

> **HINT FOR TAX RETURN**
> You can see now why I always suggest keeping your deductible debt totally separate from your non-deductible debt. It is time consuming and costly for you or your accountant to determine the correct amount of interest claimable. It's an area where the tax office often finds errors and therefore it is crucial to get it right.

MINIMISE TAX, MAXIMISE PROTECTION

Example: Apportionment of interest

You decide to use your bank account to take out a loan of $355,000 from which $325,000 is used to buy a rental property and $30,000 is used to buy a private car. To determine the claim using a loan interest rate of 6.75% per annum, and assuming that the property is rented from 1 July:

Interest for year one = $355,000 X 6.75% = $23,963

Apportionment of interest payment related to rental property:

Total interest expense	X	rental property loan / total borrowings	=	Deductible interest
$23,963	X	$325,000 / $355,000	=	$21,938

Where you purchase a new home to live in and keep your old one to rent out

Some rental property owners borrow money to buy a new home and then rent out their previous home. If there is an outstanding loan on the old home and that property is used to produce income, the interest outstanding on the loan – or at least part of it – will be deductible.

However, an interest deduction cannot be claimed on the loan used to buy the new home because it is not used to produce income. This is the case regardless of whether the loan for the new home is secured against the former home.

Example – Old house rented

You bought your home five years ago for $275,000 (including all costs). The loan was $250,000 at the time of purchase but is now down to $100,000. The house is now worth $500,000.

BONUS! FREE gifts at www.TGRProperty.com.au/Gifts

You buy a new home for $450,000 (including all costs), using two loans to complete the purchase. One is for $360,000, secured against the new home, and the other is for $90,000, secured against the old home. You move into the new property and rent out your old home.

The only interest claimable is that from the $100,000 loan, which is being used for the purpose of creating income.

> **HINT FOR TAX RETURN**
> If I was purchasing a home in the future I would always utilise an offset account loan type, which is explained in greater detail a little further.

THE MAIN TYPES OF LOAN PRODUCTS UTILISED BY RENTAL PROPERTY INVESTORS

Line of Credit (LOC)/Redraws

A line of credit is a loan, similar to a credit card, which can be drawn up to a pre-determined maximum limit. Interest is only charged on the drawn balance and not on the available (undrawn) balance. For the interest to be deductible, you have to make sure there is a clear distinction between the business and personal uses of the loan.

For example, you might set up a $100,000 LOC, secured against your private home. If you use this to help you buy a rental property, the interest will be deductible against the rent received from your property. Your aunt passes away, leaving you $20,000 that you deposit into the LOC, dropping the balance to $80,000. You then dip back into the loan, taking $20,000 out to buy a boat for your personal use and bringing the balance back up to $100,000.

MINIMISE TAX, MAXIMISE PROTECTION

By doing this you've effectively created two loans, one of $80,000 that is tax deductible against the income received from your property and one of $20,000 that is not. You've turned $20,000 of deductible debt into non-deductible debt, which isn't good and demonstrates how careful you need to be when moving money around.

Making it even more difficult is the fact the tax office won't let you allocate repayments solely against the boat loan. If you choose to pay $1,000 into the above LOC it would be deemed to be reducing the boat loan by $200 ($1,000 x 20 per cent) and the rental property loan by $800 ($1,000 x 80 per cent).

Line of Credit (LOC) versus offset account

There is another way you could have proceeded with the previous example, one that would have been far more advantageous.

When you receive the $20,000 from your aunt's estate, instead of depositing it into the $100,000 LOC you could put it into a separate account held by the same bank. The bank can then "offset" the interest charged to you on the $100,000 loan against the interest they would pay you on the $20,000 deposit being held in the offset account.

Instead of paying the interest on $100,000 and receiving interest on $20,000, you will only have to pay the interest on $80,000. To put it another way, the $20,000 in your offset account gets subtracted from the $100,000 in your LOC before any interest in calculated.

You can then buy the $20,000 boat from the offset account, leaving the original $100,000 loan fully intact.

BONUS! FREE gifts at www.TGRProperty.com.au/Gifts

I favour offset accounts because they keep your interest deduction options as open as possible, particularly when you're going to pay a loan down by depositing money into it.

You should even set up an offset account on your private home loan, so you can maximise the interest deductions if you ever decide to rent it out in the future. Even if you don't think you will ever rent it out, you're keeping your options open and that's always a good thing.

LEGAL EXPENSES
Some legal expenses incurred in producing your rental income are deductible, such as the cost of evicting a non-paying tenant.

Most legal expenses, however, are of a capital nature and are therefore not deductible. These include the costs of purchasing or selling your property and defending your title to the property. It's not all bad news, though. Non-deductible legal expenses may form part of the cost base of your property for Capital Gains Tax purposes.

Example: Deductible legal expenses
In August 2008 your tenants moved out owing four weeks' rent. You retained the bond money and took the tenants to court to terminate the lease and recover the balance of the rent. The legal expenses are fully deductible because they were incurred while seeking to recover assessable rental income and you wished to continue earning income from the property.

MINIMISE TAX, MAXIMISE PROTECTION

> **HINT FOR TAX RETURN**
> You must include the retained bond money and the recovered rent as assessable income in the financial year received.

MORTGAGE DISCHARGE EXPENSES

These are the costs involved in discharging a mortgage other than through payments of principal and interest. Mortgage discharge expenses may include penalty interest payments, early termination fees or deferred establishment fees. They're claimable in the year they are paid.

REPAIRS AND MAINTENANCE

Repairs can generally be categorised into two types:

1. Repairs that are immediately claimable
2. Repairs that are depreciable.

Immediately claimable repairs

These repairs must directly relate to wear and tear or other damage that occurred as a result of you renting out the property.

They generally involve the replacement or renewal of a worn-out or broken part, such as guttering torn down during a storm or part of a fence that was damaged by a falling tree branch.

A repair simply restores the item to its original state prior to it needing to be fixed.

Some of the repairs you can claim deductions for include replacing broken windows, maintaining plumbing and repairing electrical appliances.

BONUS! FREE gifts at www.TGRProperty.com.au/Gifts

> **HINT FOR TAX RETURN**
> You need to consider how long you have been renting out the property before a repair is deemed to be from the wear and tear associated with the use of the tenant.

Depreciable repairs
The following expenses are depreciable at the rate of 2.50 per cent per annum:

- the replacement of an entire structure or unit of property, such as a complete fence or set of kitchen cupboards;
- improvements, renovations, extensions and alterations;
- initial repairs, which means fixing defects and repairing damage that existed in the property on the date you acquired it.

Example: Improvements
You've been renting a property out for a number of years when a section of the timber fence – not the entire fence but only part of it – comes apart and needs replacing. If you replace the timber fence with a Colorbond fence it is deemed to be an improvement rather than a repair.

Example: Initial repairs
You need to make some repairs to your newly acquired rental property before the first tenants move in. You pay an interior decorator to repaint dirty walls, replace broken light fittings and repair doors on two bedrooms. You also discover white ants in some of the floorboards, which requires white ant treatment and replacement of some of the boards.

It is considered that these expenses were incurred to make the property suitable for rental and did not arise from your use of the property to generate rental income.

MINIMISE TAX, MAXIMISE PROTECTION

GENERAL GUIDE TO CLAIMING REPAIRS
Repairs to a rental property will generally be claimable if:

- the property continues to be rented on an ongoing basis; or
- the property remains available for rent but there is a short period when the property is unoccupied, such as when unseasonable weather causes cancellations of bookings or advertising is unsuccessful in attracting tenants.

If you no longer rent the property, the cost of repairs may still be deductible provided:

- the need for the repairs is related to the period in which the property was used by you to produce income; and
- the property was producing income during the financial year in which you paid for the repairs.

Example: Repairs when the property is no longer rented out

August 2009 – Your tenants move out.

September 2009 – You discover the stove doesn't work, kitchen tiles are cracked and the toilet window is broken. You also discover a hole in a bedroom wall that had been covered with a poster.

October 2009 – You pay for this damage to be repaired.

Despite the fact that the property is no longer being rented out, you can still claim the repairs to the property. This is because the repairs relate to the period when the property was being rented and the repairs were completed before the end of the financial year in which the property ceased to be rented out.

BONUS! FREE gifts at www.TGRProperty.com.au/Gifts

> **HINT FOR TAX RETURN**
> You need to have some rental income in the same financial year that you claim the repairs. This applies even if you use the property as your home after the tenants move out.

TRAVEL EXPENSES

You can travel to inspect, maintain your property or collect the rent and you may be able to claim the costs of doing so.

Potential claimable travel expenses:

- airfares (retain boarding pass and ticket)
- taxi, bus and train fares
- accommodation
- phone calls
- meals
- parking costs and bridge tolls
- car hire and petrol
- cents per kilometre usage of your own car.

Example: Cents per kilometre usage of your own car

Although your local rental property is managed by a property agent, you decide to inspect the property three months after the tenants move in. During the income year you also make a number of visits to the property to carry out minor repairs. You travel 162 kilometres during the course of these visits. At the rate of 69 cents per kilometre for your 2.6 litre car, you can claim the following deduction:

Distance travelled	x	rate per km	=	deductible amount
162 kms	x	69 cents per km	=	$111.78

BONUS! FREE gifts at www.TGRProperty.com.au/Gifts

MINIMISE TAX, MAXIMISE PROTECTION

On your way to cricket each Saturday, you also drive past the property to "keep an eye on things". These trips are not deductible in any way because inspecting the property is incidental to the primary purpose of enjoying the cricket.

Apportionment of travel expenses

You are allowed a full claim where the sole purpose of the trip relates to the rental property. However, in other circumstances you may not be able to claim a deduction or you may be entitled to only a partial deduction.

If you fly to inspect your rental property, stay overnight and return home on the following day, all of the airfare and accommodation expenses can be claimed as long as the sole purpose of your trip is to inspect the property.

Where travel related to your rental property is combined with a holiday or other private activities, you may need to apportion the expenses.

If this is the case you need to take into account the reasons for your trip. If the main purpose of your trip is to have a holiday and the inspection of the property is incidental to that main purpose, you cannot claim a deduction for the cost of the travel. However, you may be able to claim local expenses directly related to the property inspection and a proportion of accommodation expenses.

Example: Apportionment of travel expenses

You own a rental property in Cairns on the north coast of Queensland. You spend $1,000 on airfares and $1,500 on accommodation when you travel from your home in Melbourne, mainly for the purpose of holidaying but also to inspect the property. You also spend $50 on taxi fares for the return trip from

BONUS! FREE gifts at www.TGRProperty.com.au/Gifts

the hotel to the rental property. One day of your 10-day holiday (10 per cent) is spent on matters relating to the rental property and nine days (90 per cent) swimming and sightseeing.

No deduction can be claimed for any part of the $1,000 airfares but $50 can be claimed for the taxi fare.

Given that 10 per cent of the holiday is spent attending to the rental property, a deduction for 10 per cent of the accommodation expenses ($150 in this case) would be considered reasonable. The total in travel expenses you can claim is therefore $200 ($50 taxi fare plus $150 accommodation).

PRE-PAID EXPENSES

If you pre-pay a rental property expense – such as interest – that covers a period of 12 months or less and the period ends on or before 30 June, you can claim an immediate deduction.

Example: Pre-paid expenses

In June 2009 you pay interest in advance of $16,000 on a loan for your rental property, which represents the interest you would pay in an entire year. Because you pay it in June 2009, and because it relates to a period of no more than 12 months, you can claim the interest in the 2009 financial year.

MINIMISE TAX, MAXIMISE PROTECTION

> **HINT FOR TAX RETURN**
>
> The interest has to actually be paid to the bank before 30 June to be claimed in that year. That means you will need to allow an appropriate amount of time for you to contact your lender, have your lender agree to this, send out the paperwork for the pre-payment and for the payment to be made.
>
> Pre-payments can be made and claimed for rental properties owned by:
>
> 1. An individual
> 2. Individuals jointly or as tenants in common.
>
> Pre-payments cannot be made and claimed for rental properties owned by:
>
> 1. Trusts
> 2. Companies
> 3. Super funds.

3. Deductions over a number of financial years

We've already spoken about deductions that cannot be claimed and those that can be claimed immediately. Now it's time to move on to those deductions you can claim over a period of time.

BONUS! FREE gifts at www.TGRProperty.com.au/Gifts

There are three types of rental expenses that fall into this category:

1. Borrowing expenses
2. Amounts for decline in value of depreciating assets
3. Capital works deductions (building write-off).

Each of these categories is discussed in detail below.

BORROWING EXPENSES

If the total deductible borrowing expenses are $100 or less, they are fully deductible in the income year they are incurred. However, if your total borrowing expenses are more than $100, the deduction is either spread over five years or the term of the loan – whichever is less.

These are some of the expenses directly incurred in taking out a loan for the property:

- loan establishment fees
- title search fees
- mortgage broker fees
- Stamp Duty charged on the mortgage
- valuation fees
- mortgage insurance.

HINT FOR TAX RETURN

If you repay the loan early and in less than five years, you can claim a deduction for the balance of the borrowing expenses in the year of repayment.

If you obtained the loan part way through the income year, the deduction for the first year will be apportioned according to the number of days in the year that you had the loan.

BONUS! FREE gifts at www.TGRProperty.com.au/Gifts

MINIMISE TAX, MAXIMISE PROTECTION

Example: Borrowing expenses

To buy a rental property for $300,000 you secure a 25-year loan of $316,000. You pay a total of $3,670 in various expenses, including establishment fees and stamp duty. Because these expenses are greater than $100 they must be spread out over five years or until the end of the loan, according to whichever comes first.

If you obtain the loan on 17 July 2009, you would work out the borrowing expense deduction for the first year as follows:

PRE-PAID BORROWING EXPENSES

Mortgage Stamp Duty	1,264
Registration fee	70
Establishment fee	700
Settlement fee	200
Mortgage insurance	1,436
	3,670

	Days in year	Claim	Balance
30 June 2010	350	703	2,967
30 June 2011	365	733	2,234
30 June 2012	365	733	1,501
30 June 2013	365	733	768
30 June 2014	366	735	33
30 June 2015	16	33	-
	1,827	3,670	

BONUS! FREE gifts at www.TGRProperty.com.au/Gifts

> **HINT FOR TAX RETURN**
>
> If you refinance the above property on 30 June 2011, the remaining borrowing costs yet to be claimed – in this case $2,234 – can be written off in full when the refinance happens.
>
> A new calculation (similar to the one above over five years) will also need to be done for the new loan that is going to pay out the old loan.

DEDUCTION FOR DEPRECIATING ASSETS

This is one of the most attractive benefits from a tax deduction point of view, particularly as it's one of those that is often overlooked even by professionals.

Depreciation is a tax deduction that you get each year, without having to spend a cent. It's built into the purchase price of the property.

Depreciation is meant to reflect the fact that the assets are worth less as time goes by, simply because of the "wear and tear" associated with having tenants use them.

Even if a property is 15-20 years old when you buy it there can still be some fantastic depreciation benefits available to you as the purchaser. It depends on how much you pay for the property and what plant and equipment are in it at the time of purchase.

MINIMISE TAX, MAXIMISE PROTECTION

Items of interest would include:

- stove
- oven
- hot plates
- hot water service
- curtains
- light fittings
- blinds
- ducted heating
- dishwasher
- ducted cooling
- stand alone heating unit
- stand alone air-conditioning unit
- security system
- carpet.

A quantity surveyor is the best option to determine your depreciation entitlements. The difference between a good quantity surveyor and an average one can have a substantial impact on the depreciation and building write-off that is claimable. This applies to both the level of detail provided in the report as well as the dollar value you can get out of a genuine professional.

Trust me, you will want to get a decent quantity surveyor. Valuers, real estate agents, accountants and solicitors generally won't have the skills and experience to get you everything you're entitled to.

A quantity surveyor's fees are also tax deductible in the year they are paid for.

BONUS! FREE gifts at www.TGRProperty.com.au/Gifts

Personal experience

I can speak from my own personal experience and say that quantity surveyors truly are a gift from the tax office.

We had recently bought our first rental property and were sitting outside one sunny afternoon reading *Australian Property Investor* magazine when we came across an article about quantity surveyors. We were stunned. Could the tax office really be that generous? We were both accountants; why had we never heard of this?

We researched the topic and, sure enough, discovered one of the most wonderful little tools available. At the time we were both working for a family company that owned 40 service stations throughout Victoria, so we kept researching and discovered that it applied to commercial property as well as residential. Some time later we were able to give our employers an extra one million dollars in their pockets after tax.

It made us realise there aren't many accountants out there who know everything that will help you with your rental properties. That's when Superior Tax Solutions Pty Ltd was created.

HINT FOR TAX RETURN

The tax deductions available through depreciation and building write-off can significantly reduce the holding costs of the property. This is one reason why Superior Tax Solutions Pty Ltd amends, on average, 80 per cent of our new clients' tax returns.

Amended tax returns are now restricted in the majority of cases to two years, which is why it's imperative that your accountant is looking after your interests.

MINIMISE TAX, MAXIMISE PROTECTION

Example: The difference a good quantity surveyor can make
One of my clients commissioned an average quantity surveyor who was relatively cheap. They got the following results:

- property purchased for $150,000 in January 1997
- has three bedrooms and a study, as well as ducted heating, dishwasher, carpet, curtains, stove, oven, range hood, etc.
- built in 1987 and still had all original fixtures and fittings
- total depreciation calculated by quantity surveyor: **$13,639**
- total building write-off calculated by quantity surveyor: **$45,354** ($1,814 per annum).

I, on the other hand, spent a little extra money and commissioned a good quantity surveyor to achieve the following results:

- property purchased for $210,000 in June 2001
- has three bedrooms and a study, as well as ducted heating, dishwasher, security system, carpet, curtains, stove, oven, range hood, etc.
- built in 1987 and still had all original fixtures and fittings
- total depreciation calculated by quantity surveyor: **$53,615**
- total building write-off calculated by quantity surveyor: **$12,873** ($1,126 per annum).

Given that approximately 60 per cent of depreciation is claimed back in the first five years, the above example means the following:

Average quantity surveyor – Claims over five years:

$13,639 x 60 per cent	=	$8,183
$1,814 x 5	=	$9,070
Total Claims		**$17,253**

BONUS! FREE gifts at www.TGRProperty.com.au/Gifts

Good quantity surveyor – Claims over five years:

$53,615 x 60 per cent	=	$32,169
$1,126 x 5	=	$5,630

Total Claims — **$37,799**

Difference in claims over five years = **$20,546**
Tax savings foregone at 31.50 per cent = **$6,472**
(Cashflow lost by average surveyor)

This clearly highlights the importance of a good quantity surveyor but, even more than that, it shows the cost of not using a quantity surveyor at all.

How do you work out your depreciation deduction?
There are two methods of calculating depreciation:

1. Diminishing value method
2. Prime cost method.

The **diminishing value method** assumes that the decline in value each year is a constant proportion of the remaining value, thereby producing a progressively smaller decline over time.

For depreciating assets bought after 10 May 2006, you generally use the following formula to work out the decline using the diminishing value method:

$$\text{base value (asset's cost)} \times \frac{\text{days held}}{365} \times \frac{200\%}{\text{asset's effective life}}$$

MINIMISE TAX, MAXIMISE PROTECTION

Example:
You buy a dishwasher for $1,000 on 1 August 2009. Assuming its operational life expectancy is 10 years, it has a depreciation rate of 20 per cent under the diminishing value method.

Year 1
$1,000   x   334/365   x   20%   = $183 ($1,000 – $183 = $817)

Year 2
$817   x   365/365   x   20%   = $163 ($817 - $163 = $654)

Year 3
$654   x   365/365   x   20%   = $131 ($654 - $131 = $523)

The **prime cost method**, on the other hand, assumes the value of a depreciating asset decreases uniformly over its effective life. The formula for working out decline in value using the prime cost method is:

$$\text{asset's cost} \times \frac{\text{days held}}{365} \times \frac{100\%}{\text{asset's effective life}}$$

Example:
You buy a dishwasher for $1,000 on 1 August 2009. Assuming its operational life expectancy is 10 years, it has a depreciation rate of 10 per cent under the prime cost method.

Year 1
$1,000   x   334/365   x   10%   = $92 ($1,000 – $92 = $908)

Year 2
$1,000   x   365/365   x   10%   = $100 ($908 - $100 = $808)

Year 3
$1,000   x   365/365   x   10%   = $100 ($808 - $100 = $708)

BONUS! FREE gifts at www.TGRProperty.com.au/Gifts

> **HINT FOR TAX RETURN**
> Due to the fact that rental properties usually cost more to hold in the first few years, we recommend using the diminishing value method as this will maximise your depreciation claim each year and increase your tax refund.

Effective life
Generally, the effective life of a depreciating asset is how long it can be used for a taxable purpose.

Immediate deduction for certain non-business depreciating assets costing $300 or less
You can get an immediate deduction for the cost of an asset if its purchase price was under $300. This deduction is available if the asset meets all the following tests:

- it cost $300 or less
- you use it mainly for the purpose of obtaining rental income
- it is not one of a number of identical, or substantially identical, assets that together cost more than $300 (example below).

Example: Immediate deduction
You buy a blind for your rental property at a cost of $70. You can claim an immediate deduction as the blind is used to obtain rental income.

Example: No immediate deduction
You buy four blinds costing $90 each for your rental property. You cannot claim an immediate deduction for any of these because they are identical, or substantially identical, and the combined cost is more than $300.

MINIMISE TAX, MAXIMISE PROTECTION

> **HINT FOR TAX RETURN**
> In the previous example, you should have bought three of the blinds in one year and one in the next year. Then you could have fully claimed them in the respective financial years they were bought and paid for.

Low-value pooling
A low-value pool is a simplified method of depreciating any assets that cost less than $1,000 per item. These assets are allocated to the pool each year and stay there once they've been added. The pool shows one cumulative dollar value for all the assets inside it, along with one depreciation amount for the entire pool.

This compares to the traditional method of showing a depreciation schedule with individual assets listed separately, each with its own depreciation calculation per year.

For the income year you initially purchase an asset, you work out its depreciation at a rate of 18.75 per cent. For the following years the deduction uses a diminishing value rate of 37.5 per cent.

Example: Depreciation claim – low-value pool
On 1 August 2007 you bought a blind for $400 and two air-conditioners for $900 each on 30 June 2008.

ADRIAN HILL

2008 financial year depreciation claim:

$400	x	18.75%	=	$75
$900	x	18.75%	=	$169
$900	x	18.75%	=	$169
Total Depreciation Claimed			=	**$413**

Low-value pool totals are:

Total items bought during year	$2,200
Less: Depreciation claim per above	($413)
Closing Value Of Pool	**$1,787**

2009 financial year depreciation claim:

Opening Value Of Pool			=	$1,787
$1,787	x	37.50%	=	$670
Total Depreciation Claimed			=	**$670**

Low-value pool totals are:

Opening Value Of Pool	$1,787
Total Items Bought During Year	$0
Less: Depreciation Claim Per Above	($670)
Closing Value Of Pool	**$1,117**

HINT FOR TAX RETURN

It does not matter if an asset costing under $1,000 is bought at the start or end of the financial year because the depreciation claim will be the same. A good accountant will be vigilant in moving applicable depreciation items to the low-value pool to maximise your depreciation claims each year.

BONUS! FREE gifts at www.TGRProperty.com.au/Gifts

MINIMISE TAX, MAXIMISE PROTECTION

CAPITAL WORKS DEDUCTIONS (BUILDING WRITE-OFF)

You can claim building (construction) expenditure over 25 or 40 years.

Examples of building expenditure include:

- plumbing
- electrical
- roofing
- slab
- carpentry
- bricklaying
- architect's and engineer's fees
- frame
- a building or an extension, such as adding a room, garage, patio or pergola
- alterations, such as removing or adding an internal wall
- structural improvements to the property, such as adding a gazebo, carport, sealed driveway, retaining wall or fence.

Examples of building expenditure not included:

- the cost of the land on which the rental property is built
- expenditure on clearing the land prior to construction
- expenditure on landscaping.

HINT FOR TAX RETURN

No claim is available until the construction is complete and you can only claim deductions for the period during the year(s) that the property is rented or is available for rent.

The claim percentage available is determined by figuring out when construction was first started. That means, from the date the foundations were laid.

BONUS! FREE gifts at www.TGRProperty.com.au/Gifts

Summary of building write-off claim percentage

Date construction started	Percentage rate of claim each year
17 July 1985 – 15 September 1987	4 per cent
After 15 September 1987	2.50 per cent

Estimating construction costs

Where a new owner is unable to precisely determine the construction costs of a building, an estimate from an appropriately qualified person may be used. As discussed earlier, this person would ideally be a quantity surveyor.

A WORKSHEET EXAMPLE TO HELP YOU CLAIM EVERYTHING YOU'RE ENTITLED TO FOR YOUR PROPERTY

You are now in a position to put together all the information you need for your tax return, as well as to determine how much you have made from your rental property in a year and how much you've paid to hold onto it.

Income	$
Rental income	14,500
Bond money refunded in lieu of rent	800
Gross rent	**15,300**
Expenses	
Advertising for tenants	98
Bank charges	100
Body corporate fees and charges	600
Borrowing expenses **	359
Cleaning	200

MINIMISE TAX, MAXIMISE PROTECTION

Council rates	800
Depreciation claim **	3,896
Gardening/lawn mowing	450
Gifts to tenant/agent	400
Gas and electricity	200
Insurance	695
Interest on loan(s)	12,475
Land Tax	300
Legal expenses	250
Pest control	150
Property agent fees/commission	1,200
Quantity surveyors fees	660
Repairs and maintenance	1,500
Building write-off claim **	3,745
Stationery, telephone and postage	80
Travel expenses	536
Water charges	250
Sundry expenses	195
Total expenses	**29,139**
Net rental loss ($29,139 − $15,300)	**13,839**

** These items should be worked out each year by your accountant

Note: All the above expenses are inclusive of GST as no GST claims can be made on residential rental properties.

SELLING YOUR RENTAL PROPERTY - CAPITAL GAINS TAX (CGT)

Our strategy has always been to buy-and-hold rental properties. However, no rule is without its exceptions and on two occasions it was the right decision to sell properties.

BONUS! FREE gifts at www.TGRProperty.com.au/Gifts

ADRIAN HILL

As a result we needed to work out how much money we would make on the sale (known as a capital gain) or what loss, if any, was incurred (known as a capital loss). This applied to us because we had purchased our property after 19 September 1985. If you bought your house before this date you would be exempt from Capital Gains Tax in the majority of cases.

Capital gain basically means that you receive more money from the sale of your rental property than the total you paid for it. A capital loss, on the other hand, means that the base cost of the property exceeds the amount you ultimately receive for it.

If you are a co-owner of an investment property, your capital gain or loss will be figured out in accordance with the percentage of your ownership interest in the property.

Here is our most recent capital gain calculation as an example:

Purchase details:
Date of signing contract: 19 July 2005
Date of settlement: 19 September 2005

Purchase price	$300,000
Stamp Duty	$15,000
Legal costs	$1,000
Travel to purchase property	$2,000
Building inspection	$500
Pest inspection	$500
Buyer's agent fees	$6,000
Total Purchase Costs	**$325,000**

MINIMISE TAX, MAXIMISE PROTECTION

Sale details:
Date of signing contract: 19 June 2008
Date of settlement: 19 August 2008

Sales price	$500,000
Sales commission	$(15,000)
Advertising	$(3,000)
Legal costs	$(1,000)

Total Net Sales Proceeds   **$481,000**

Net capital gain is:

Net sales proceeds		$481,000
Less:		
Total purchase price	$325,000	
Less: depreciation and building write-off claimed *	$(23,000)	$302,000
Net capital gain		$179,000

As we owned the property jointly between ourselves, the net capital gain was reduced by a 50 per cent discount from $179,000 to $89,500. We each declared Capital Gain Income of $44,750 in our respective personal tax returns.

*   Building write-off and depreciation claimed during the ownership period is $23,000

BONUS! FREE gifts at www.TGRProperty.com.au/Gifts

HINT FOR TAX RETURN ONE

Depending on who owns the property – if, for instance, it's owned by an individual(s) or a trust – the net capital gain can be reduced by a 50 per cent discount. To get the discount the property needs to be owned for more than one year from purchase contract date to sales contract date.

If a company owns the property it is not entitled to the 50 per cent discount.

HINT FOR TAX RETURN TWO

Most accountants don't believe in the benefit of claiming the depreciation and building write-off, as they are both added back at the time of sale as shown above.

However, we believe that as long as the property is held, from purchase contract to sales contract, for at least one year, you will always be in front by claiming your entitlement. To demonstrate using facts from the previous example:

Depreciation and building write-off claimed for the period of ownership	$23,000
Depreciation and building write-off added back at sale	$23,000
Less: 50 per cent discount available at sale	($11,500)
Actual amount added back at sale	$11,500

Therefore, you are $11,500 better off by claiming your depreciation and building write-off.

MINIMISE TAX, MAXIMISE PROTECTION

HOW TO DEFER YOUR CAPITAL GAINS TAX

Using the previous example, because the sales contract was signed in June 2008 the capital gain needs to be declared as income in the 2008 tax year. This is despite the fact that the sale did not settle until August 2008.

It would have been better to move (defer) the capital gain into the next tax year. As the capital gain is taken from the date both parties sign the contract and not settlement, it would be great to lock the purchaser in to the deal but defer the gain until next year.

You need to contact a solicitor who understands this type of transaction. You enter a simultaneous put and call option contract that works as follows:

- you give the buyer a put option to sell your property to the purchaser, which is not exercisable before 1 July and expires by the end of August;
- the buyer takes a call option to be able to purchase the property from you after 1 July but they must exercise the option by the end of August;
- the normal sale of property contract is attached to the option agreements;
- you now have the right to sell your property after 1 July and the purchaser has the option to buy the property after 1 July;
- when either party exercises their option after 1 July, the contracts are officially signed and dated by each party;
- therefore, the contract date now falls after 1 July and into the next tax year.

BONUS! FREE gifts at www.TGRProperty.com.au/Gifts

KEEPING RECORDS - CAPITAL GAINS TAX

You must keep records relating to your ownership of the property, including all the costs of acquiring and disposing of it, for five years after the date it is sold.

You must keep records that include:

- the date you acquired the asset
- the date you disposed of the asset
- the date you received anything in exchange for the asset
- the parties involved
- any amount that would form part of the cost base of the asset
- whether you have claimed an income tax deduction for an item of expenditure.

KEEPING RECORDS - GENERALLY

You should always keep records of both income and expenses relating to your rental property, for at least five years after you lodge your tax return.

Records of rental expenses must include:

- name of the supplier
- amount of the expense
- nature of the goods or services
- date the expense was incurred
- date of the document.

If a document does not show the payment date you can use independent evidence, such as a bank statement, to show the date the expense was incurred.

MINIMISE TAX, MAXIMISE PROTECTION

WHAT NEEDS TO BE CONSIDERED WHEN DECIDING WHO SHOULD PURCHASE THE PROPERTY?

When you and your partner are buying a property there are a number of things you need to take into account before deciding who, legally, will make the purchase. Some of the things you should consider include:

- when the high income earner will retire or become the low income earner;
- when any children will reach the age of 18;
- how long it will take the property to become positive;
- ages and expected incomes of any potential beneficiaries;
- how long you intend to hold the property (it will usually be for the long term due to the high costs involved in buying and selling properties). This will also guide you as to when any capital gain may arise on the sale of the property.

We will discuss the various property ownership options taking into consideration two major factors:

1. Tax issues, especially if the property runs at a loss (negatively-geared);
2. Asset protection issues, which comes into effect if the tenant or anybody else sues you.

Quite often you need to forego asset protection to get tax effectiveness and vice versa. Ultimately, it comes down to the compromise you're most comfortable with. There is no right or wrong answer. The individual situation of each person and family needs to be taken into account when making these types of decisions. Each must be considered on a case by case basis.

INDIVIDUAL OWNERSHIP

Every day we see people buying properties in their own names, either because they didn't know they could do it differently or because they are purely focused on the short-term tax benefits.

If you purchase a property in your name you are definitely going to receive a tax benefit in the first few years. However, the rent will eventually start to rise and your interest payments may drop, which may lead to the situation where the rental property becomes positive. If the property was purchased in the high income earner's name, the tax will need to be paid by them each year.

Also, if the property is sold for a profit more tax will need to be paid by the high income earner.

1. Tax issues

Any losses from a rental property can be offset against any other income earned by the individual. The tax refund will be the loss, in dollars, multiplied by the individual's marginal tax rate percentage.

However, any capital gains from the sale of a rental property after receiving the potential 50 per cent capital gains tax discount will be paid by the individual(s) at their applicable marginal tax rate percentage.

Here is a list of tax rates for the 2008/2009 tax year:

- $0 - $6,000   nil
- $6,001 - $34,000   15% for each $1 over $6,000
- $34,001 - $80,000 $4,200 plus 30% for each $1 over $34,000
- $80,001 - $180,000 $18,000 plus 40% for each $1 over $80,000
- $180,001 and over $58,000 plus 45% for each $1 over $180,000

Please note that Medicare levy of 1.50 per cent needs to be added to each of the above tax rates listed.

MINIMISE TAX, MAXIMISE PROTECTION

Here, then, is an example showing the refund you can get from negative-gearing:

- **Rent received for year** $15,000

- **Less : Cash expenses**
  Bank fees $300
  Body corporate fees $1,200
  Council rates $1,100
  Insurance $700
  Interest paid $16,000
  Property agent's commission $1,200
  Repairs $1,000
  Water rates $400
  Total cash expenses   ($ 21,900)
  CASH SHORTFALL   **($6,900)**

- **Less : Non-cash expenses**
  Decline in value (depreciation) $3,700
  Capital works deduction $3,300
  Borrowing costs amortised $500
  Total non-cash expenses   ($7,500)
  TOTAL RENTAL PROPERTY LOSS   **($14,400)**

Cash shortfall each year (from above)   **$6,900**

Less: Tax refund

Marginal tax rate	Tax refund	After cash	Tax shortfall
16.50% ($14,400 x 16.50%) =	$2,376	$6,900 - $2,376 =	$4,524
31.50% ($14,400 x 31.50%) =	$4,536	$6,900 - $4,536 =	$2,364
41.50% ($14,400 x 41.50%) =	$5,976	$6,900 - $5,976 =	$924
46.50% ($14,400 x 46.50%) =	$6,696	$6,900 - $6,696 =	$204

BONUS! FREE gifts at www.TGRProperty.com.au/Gifts

Instead of receiving a large tax refund at the end of the financial year, you can apply to vary the tax instalments that your employer deducts before paying your salary each pay period. This is done by lodging a s.1515 variation form with the Australian Taxation Office.

The benefit of doing this can be seen in the above example. The cash shortfall was $6,900 each year. The tax refund at 31.50 per cent (which is the bracket that the majority of people fall into) is $4,536. The cash shortfall for the year after tax is $2,364.

By applying to vary your tax instalments from your salary, you are effectively getting that tax refund each pay period instead of in one lump sum after you lodge your tax return. This will help fund the costs of holding the property, which is what makes it an option I prefer.

Some may choose to receive the lump sum refund at the end of the year, as a means of forced savings. That is, if they receive a small amount each pay period the money may be easily wasted whereas a lump sum will be better utilised.

If you are planning to lodge an s.1515 variation with the tax office, it will only take effect each year from 1 July to 30 June. A new one will need to be prepared for each new financial year.

You need to allow at least 28 days for the form to be processed by the tax office. It can be lodged electronically via the Internet.

2. **Asset protection issues**

    A high proportion of taxpayers fall into the 31.50 per cent tax bracket – that is, with taxable incomes ranging between $34,000 and $80,000 – for the 2009 tax year.

MINIMISE TAX, MAXIMISE PROTECTION

From the above example, it would cost them $2,364 per year after tax refund ($46 per week) or $6,900 per year ignoring the tax refund ($133 per week).

The difference between the two is the tax refund of $4,536 or $87 per week. This is effectively the price of asset protection, which means holding the property in a trust instead of holding the property personally.

There is no asset protection at all. The tenant or anybody else who sues you can attack any assets that are in your name or your share of what is held in joint names.

To minimise your exposure you need to ensure you have a mortgage as high as possible on every one of your personal assets and your share of jointly owned assets. This ensures that your personal net worth is as low as possible, preferably set at zero.

COMPANY OWNERSHIP

A company is a separate legal entity and exists independently of the directors and shareholders (owners). The most common type is a Pty Ltd company.

The company is divided into ownership portions, each of which is called a share. Having shares gives you ownership rights, meaning that part of the company belongs to you. Directors control and are responsible for the company but are not necessarily the shareholders.

Provided that the annual reporting and tax obligations are met, a company can continue forever. It can own assets and borrow money, as well as sue and be sued.

Assets owned by the company can be attacked by litigants, as can the director(s) of the company. Usually the director(s) can hide behind the "corporate veil" and be protected from being sued by the company. However, the tax office does have the power to go behind the company and personally sue the directors where the company owes the tax office any money. A director can also be personally liable if the company continues to trade whilst insolvent (meaning the company cannot pay debts when they are due).

Administration of companies includes:

- keeping the statutory registers up to date (this is where all directors' and shareholders' minutes are signed and filed);
- checking the annual information/statement provided by ASIC, which oversees the conduct of all companies, and paying the annual filing fee to ASIC;
- preparation of annual financials and tax return.

1. **Tax issues**

    Any losses are trapped inside the company and can be offset against any other income earned by the company in its own right. You should be aware, though, that there are strict rules you need to stick to in order for losses to be carried forward in a company.

    Any profits in a company are taxed at the flat rate of 30 per cent and there is no income splitting that is readily available to companies. Please note that you can personally earn up to $80,000 and pay tax at the maximum marginal rate of 31.50 per cent, compared to the company's flat rate of 30 per cent for the 2009 tax year.

MINIMISE TAX, MAXIMISE PROTECTION

Companies do not qualify for the 50 per cent Capital Gains Tax discount and will therefore pay 30 per cent tax on the full profit. Purchasing long-term buy-and-hold assets, such as rental properties, in a company is not a great idea.

The only way to get profits out of a company is via dividends given to shareholders after tax has already been paid. This may lead to tax being personally paid by the shareholder(s) on the dividend being received. Here's an example:

Profit for year	$10,000
Tax payable at 30 per cent	$3,000
Profit after tax	$7,000

Note: A fully franked dividend of $7,000 can be paid to shareholders (including an imputation credit of $3,000).

Your taxable income	$60,000
Tax refund	$3,500

You now receive a $7,000 fully franked dividend with an imputation credit of $3,000.

Taxable income now	$70,000 ($60,000 + ($7,000 + $3,000))
Tax payable on dividend	$3,150 ($10,000 x 31.50%)
Less: imputation credit	$3,000
Additional tax on dividend	$150
Tax refund after dividend	$3,350 ($3,500 - $150)

BONUS! FREE gifts at www.TGRProperty.com.au/Gifts

2. Asset protection issues

As a shareholder, you are entitled to receive dividends from the company.

The shares held by you in the company are also deemed to be part of your assets if you are sued by a tenant or anyone else who personally sues you. Your shares have a value that depends on what assets are held in the company itself. For example, if the company owns a rental property that has a market value today of $500,000 but also has a mortgage of $300,000 against it, then the property has a net worth of $200,000. If the tenant sues the company the net worth of $200,000 is at risk.

If you're the sole shareholder and someone personally sues you, your shares are worth $200,000 in the example outlined above. These shares become part of your personal assets and are at risk of being lost to the suing party.

Therefore, the asset protection provided by companies depends on whom or what owns the share(s) of the company.

Your accountant can easily help you establish a company, taking the stress and hassles out of the process. You will need to set up the company, sign all the appropriate documents and create a bank account in the name of the company.

TRUST OWNERSHIP

A trust lasts for 80 years, during which time the trustee holds the trust property for the beneficiaries.

The trustee, usually a company, is the legal owner of the property and anyone who receives a distribution(s) from the

MINIMISE TAX, MAXIMISE PROTECTION

trust is a beneficiary. The beneficiaries cannot be held liable for the actions of the trust.

The trust owns the assets and, because there are no shareholders (unlike a company), there is no actual owner of the trust. The trust is a separate legal entity that can sue and be sued.

Trusts are used mainly to protect assets, though tax minimisation is also possible. This is done because, in the event of legal action, it is the trustee of the trust that is sued.

If the trust is sued, the trustee company has the right to be indemnified out of the assets of the trust. For example:

- the trust is sued for $1,000,000 by the tenant of the property that the trust owns;
- the trust owns one rental property which is worth $900,000;
- there is a mortgage on the property of $400,000;
- thus, the trust has net assets of $500,000 ($900,000 - $400,000);
- the trustee company can access the net assets of the trust – $500,000 – first to settle the tenant's $1,000,000 law suit;
- this leaves a shortfall of $500,000.

Because of the shortfall, the lawsuit will go up to the trustee company and attack its assets to satisfy the remaining $500,000 of the lawsuit. However, the trustee company's only asset will be its issued shares (which could be anything from $12 - $120). Thus the remainder of the lawsuit will fail.

At that stage the appointor (discussed overleaf) will sack the current trustee company and appoint a new one. Thus a new trustee takes control of the assets of the trust.

BONUS! FREE gifts at www.TGRProperty.com.au/Gifts

Elements of a trust

- **Settlor** – Most trusts have a settlor who establishes the trust through a gift of property, often little more than $10. This person cannot benefit from the trust at all and is often the accountant.

- **Trustee** – Is the legal representative of the trust and has to administer the trust in accordance with the terms of the trust deed. Makes decisions about the trust, such as what to invest in and who to distribute to. Trustees can be individuals or a company, though we would strongly advise against an individual taking on the role. If a tenant sues and the assets of the trust aren't enough to cover the lawsuit, the individual trustee's personal assets are potentially at risk. This is why a corporate trustee should always be used.

- **Powers of trustee** – These are dependant on the trust deed. The trust can often buy assets, borrow, set up bank accounts and carry out other similar tasks.

- **Liability of trustee** – The trustee is personally liable for the debts which they incur on behalf of the trust. The trustee does have the right to be indemnified out of the trust's assets, as discussed above.

- **Trust deed** – This governs the trustee, listing the powers and rights of the trustee, beneficiaries and others. The deed may be varied by a deed of variation.

- **Appointor** – Holds the power of the trust, with the ability to hire or fire the trustee. You have to carefully consider who has this role.

MINIMISE TAX, MAXIMISE PROTECTION

- **Beneficiaries** – These are usually named in the trust deed. The trustee has the discretion to choose who to distribute the profits of the trust to (provided it is a discretionary trust).

Administration of trusts with a trustee company includes:

- keeping the statutory registers up to date of the company (this is where all directors' and shareholders' minutes are signed and filed, etc);
- checking the annual information/statement provided by ASIC for the company and paying the annual filing fee to ASIC, which oversees the conduct of all companies;
- preparation of annual financials and tax return for the trust and beneficiaries.

Your accountant can easily help you establish a trustee company and trust.

Set-up issues

Please note that you will need to set up both the trustee company and trust, sign all the appropriate documents, create a bank account in the name of the trust and get the trust deed stamped (if required) at the State Revenue Office in the state in which your trust was established. This will all need to occur before you can sign a contract to purchase a property in the name of the trust.

The bank account will need to be established as follows: "ABC Pty Ltd as Trustee for ABC Trust."

The name on the property purchase contract will also be: "ABC Pty Ltd as Trustee for ABC Trust".

Once again, the loan from the bank for the property purchase would also be to: "ABC Pty Ltd as Trustee for ABC Trust"

(note: "As Trustee for" can also be shortened to "ATF".)

BONUS! FREE gifts at www.TGRProperty.com.au/Gifts

One thing you mustn't overlook is the updating of your wills once the trust and trustee company have been established. A company has directors and shareholders, while a trust has an appointor, all of whom are usually yourself and/or your family members. Your will needs to cater for the transfer of such positions upon the death of yourself or your spouse.

UNIT TRUST

This is a trust in which all beneficiaries have, by virtue of their holdings of units in the trust, a fixed entitlement to the income and capital of the trust. It's similar to companies issuing shares to shareholders, except units are issued to unitholders.

1. **Tax issues**

   Any losses are trapped inside the unit trust. They can be offset against any other income earned by the unit trust in its own right.

   Any profits in a unit trust are distributed to the unitholder in direct proportion to their unitholding percentage, as no income splitting is readily available. You can personally earn up to $80,000 and pay tax at the maximum marginal rate of 31.50 per cent. For example, if there are 120 units issued and you own 60 of them, you will receive 50 per cent of the profits from the unit trust. You will therefore pay tax on the distribution at the appropriate marginal tax rate percentage, as discussed earlier.

   Unit trusts do qualify for the 50 per cent Capital Gains Tax discount.

   Sometimes with trusts like these the borrowing is kept outside the trust.

MINIMISE TAX, MAXIMISE PROTECTION

To give you an example:

Profit for year	$10,000
Your taxable income	$60,000
Tax refund	$3,500

You now receive a $10,000 distribution from the unit trust, as sole unitholder.

Taxable income now	$70,000 ($60,000 + $10,000)
Tax payable on distribution	$3,150 ($10,000 x 31.50%)
Additional tax on distribution	$3,150
Tax refund after distribution	$350 ($3,500 original refund - $3,150)

If, on the other hand, you have borrowed to buy your units it would look like this:

You, the sole unitholder have borrowed to buy your units. The loan will therefore be in your name.

Interest paid during the year for this loan $15,000.

Taxable income (original)	$60,000 (as above)
Plus: Distribution received	$10,000
Less: Loan interest paid	$15,000

BONUS! FREE gifts at www.TGRProperty.com.au/Gifts

Adjusted taxable income	$55,000 ($60,000 + $10,000 - $15,000)
Your taxable income now decreases by	$5,000 ($60,000 - $55,000)
Additional tax refund	$1,575 ($5,000 decrease x 31.50%)
Tax refund after distribution and interest	$5,075 ($3,500 original refund + $1,575)

2. Asset protection issues

As a unitholder, you are entitled to receive distributions from the unit trust.

The units held by you in the unit trust are also deemed to be part of your assets if you are sued by a tenant or anyone else who personally sues you.

Your units also have a value on them depending on what assets are held in the unit trust itself. For instance, if the unit trust owns a rental property that has a market value today of $500,000 and also has a mortgage of $300,000 against it then the property has a net worth of $200,000. If the tenant sues the unit trust this money is also at risk.

Also, if someone personally sues you then your units, worth $200,000, become part of your personal assets for the suing party and are at risk.

Therefore, the asset protection provided by unit trusts depends upon who or what owns the unit(s).

MINIMISE TAX, MAXIMISE PROTECTION

DISCRETIONARY TRUST

This is a trust in which no beneficiaries have any fixed rights to income and capital of the trust. The trust is held for the beneficiaries and distributed at the trustee's discretion.

Anyone who has a business or some other income source has a big advantage, as they can obtain tax effectiveness and asset protection too.

The trust provides the maximum flexibility when distributing income and capital gains made in any given tax year.

Therefore, it can be summarised as follows:

- you could be the director and shareholder of the company. This means you control the company but that you personally own nothing;

- the company is the trustee for the trust that owns everything. Therefore, as director of the trustee you control the trust;

- the trust distributes all profits to beneficiaries, who you nominate. That could be yourself, spouse, children, parents or anybody at all;

- to put it as simply as possible, you own nothing but control everything.

1. Tax issues

To begin with, discretionary trusts qualify for the 50 per cent Capital Gains Tax discount.

Any losses are trapped inside the discretionary trust and can be offset against any other income earned by the discretionary trust in its own right.

BONUS! FREE gifts at www.TGRProperty.com.au/Gifts

If another discretionary trust makes a profit for the year then – as long as both trust deeds allow – the trust with the profit can distribute to the trust with the loss to offset the loss and save tax on the profit.

For any profits left in the discretionary trust, which are not distributed to beneficiaries, the trust will pay tax at the top marginal rate – currently 46.50 per cent.

Any profits in a discretionary trust therefore need to be distributed each year to the beneficiaries. You should be aware that income splitting is readily available in discretionary trusts. You can personally earn up to $80,000 in a tax year and pay tax at the maximum marginal rate of 31.50 per cent, so you will pay tax on the distribution at your appropriate marginal tax rate percentage as discussed earlier.

Each year the trustee can choose who to distribute the profits of the trust to. Those who can be beneficiaries, depending on how the trust deed has been written, include:

- you
- your spouse
- your children
- your or your spouse's parents
- your or your spouse's grandparents
- your grandchildren
- brothers and sisters of you and your spouse
- nieces and nephews of you and your spouse
- other discretionary trusts that any of the above are beneficiaries of
- other companies that the above are directors or shareholders of.

MINIMISE TAX, MAXIMISE PROTECTION

Potentially distributing to a company (also known as a bucket company) will help cap the tax rate on the distributions from the trust at the company's tax rate.

You can also potentially distribute some of the trust's income to minors, if so allowed by the trust deed and its definition of beneficiaries. A minor is a child under the age of 18 at 30 June each tax year.

Below is a list of the maximum income that can be received by a minor each year without the need to pay any tax at all:

- Tax year ended 30 June 2008 $1,666
- Tax year ended 30 June 2009 $2,666
- Tax year ended 30 June 2010 $3,000
- Tax year ended 30 June 2011 $3,333
- Tax year ended 30 June 2012 $4,666

Utilising all the minors you're allowed to distribute to can save a significant amount of tax each year. Don't forget, though, to allow for any income they may earn already from bank interest or any dividends they may receive. You must take this into account to keep the minor under the relevant income threshold.

The trustee can also choose to distribute to those adult beneficiaries who are over 18 and who pay tax at a lower marginal rate than you or your spouse. Over many years these tax savings can add up to tens of thousands of dollars.

BONUS! FREE gifts at www.TGRProperty.com.au/Gifts

2. Asset protection issues

This trust offers the best form of asset protection available because none of the beneficiaries has a fixed right to any income or capital distribution paid by the trust. This means that creditors cannot force the trustee to distribute to them at all.

To go back to our early example, assume the discretionary trust owns a rental property that has a market value today of $500,000 and also has a mortgage of $300,000 against it. This leaves the property with a net worth of $200,000 that is at risk if the tenant sues.

If someone personally sues you then the assets of the discretionary trust are not at risk, for the reasons outlined above. Therefore, the assets of the discretionary trust worth $200,000 cannot become part of your personal assets for the suing party and are not at risk at all.

However, if you have several rental properties in the one trust and a tenant sues that trust, the total equity owned by all the properties is at risk in the law suit. One way around this is to buy each rental property in a separate trust, thus minimising the risk in each trust to only the property owned within it. This is the approach that we personally utilise.

HYBRID TRUST

Hybrid trusts have been popular due to the fact they offer potential tax benefits and asset protection. A hybrid trust deed has the elements of both a unit trust and a discretionary trust.

The taxpayer claims the interest deduction as a unit holder of a unit trust whilst it is negatively-geared. However, when the investment becomes positively-geared the trust then acts as a discretionary trust, allowing you to distribute the income to family members who are at a lower marginal rate.

In response to the increased use of hybrid trust arrangements, the ATO has significantly increased its interest in this area. The tax office will probably negate any benefits of this type of trust, which will not make them viable at all. Therefore, we're not going to cover this type of trust.

ISSUES TO CONTEMPLATE FOR FUTURE YEARS

Rental property ownership is a long-term strategy. Buying and holding is the common strategy for passive investors like the majority of us. Given that it costs around five to six per cent of the purchase price to buy and around three to four per cent of the sales price to sell, property needs to be held long-term to allow these costs to be absorbed by the property's growth in value.

Sometimes, though, a property will need to be sold if it was bought in error. The error could be that over an extended period of time it has not grown in value or that it's costing more to hold each year than you can afford to pay.

The good news is that when the economy struggles and the majority of the world is either in recession or close to it, there is no need to change your buy-and-hold strategy. Try not to read the papers or watch television, with their doom and gloom reports, and try to speak only to fellow investors rather than family or friends who are not in the market. The important thing is not to get caught up in the market bumps, interest rate adjustments and government changes along the way.

To quote a great man, *Think and Grow Rich* author Napoleon Hill, "You become what you think about" and "Every person is what they allow to occupy their mind".

History says that well-positioned property, bought for the long-term, is a great investment. Property will always appreciate in value over time.

OVERCOMING FEARS

There are a number of fears you will need to overcome during your journey to wealth, the chief among which is the fear of poverty. It's the most common fear among those of us who are rental property investors.

Common symptoms of the fear of poverty are:

- **Procrastination** – The habit of putting off to tomorrow what you can do today. This is a major cause of failure to achieve your goals. You may think about purchasing property but you find excuses and place obstacles in your own way so that nothing is ever done;

- **Over-caution** – Looking for the negative side of every situation leads to you thinking and talking about failure instead of concentrating on success;

- **Indecision** – Permitting others to do one's thinking and "sitting on the fence" means you become overwhelmed by other people's opinions and take no action.

CONSOLIDATION / REVIEW PERIOD

We're nearing the end of this chapter now, which makes it a good time to go over some of the things we've discussed in a way that will hopefully make the most important parts stick firmly in your mind.

MINIMISE TAX, MAXIMISE PROTECTION

First of all, it's always a good idea to have an available line of credit to take care of unexpected rental property expenses. However, you should never over-extend yourself with too high a level of debt. Constantly review the interest rates and fees you're paying and compare them to those offered by other financiers in the market. Consider refinancing to a lender with a lower interest rate, as long as the savings in interest rates are more than the cost of changing lenders. This applies to both your rental properties and private home.

Consider the purchase of a positive cashflow property to help defray the holding costs of your negatively-geared one(s). The trade-off with these properties is that the capital growth is often lower over the long-term.

We recommend that at the end of each year you reflect on what you have achieved during the past 12 months and whether you are closer to your goal of financial freedom. Also, plan your goals for the coming 12 months and five years. Be aware, though, that it's common to underestimate what can be achieved in five years and overestimate what can be achieved in 12 months.

Ensure that your credit cards are paid off in full each month and try to only put expenses on the credit card you can afford to pay in cash. Credit card interest rates are very high and can quickly bite into your cashflow.

Consider consolidating any other private debts or loans you have – such as car, boat, caravan or furniture loans – that have higher interest rates than your private home loan. This will also save cashflow.

BONUS! FREE gifts at www.TGRProperty.com.au/Gifts

OPPORTUNITIES TO PURCHASE PROPERTIES

The right time to purchase a rental property is always right now. If you take a long-term buy-and-hold approach then there's no such thing as the perfect time. It is time in the market that counts.

There are, however, some conditions for purchasing and holding rental properties that are especially favourable. These include:

- low interest rates
- residential rents increasing
- low rental vacancy rates.

THE BENEFITS OF HOLDING PROPERTY OVER TIME

Investors who have owned their properties for several years generally find their negatively-geared properties become positively-geared. For instance, we bought a rental property in Ringwood for $210,000 in 2001 that was paying a rental of $220 per week. This represents a gross rental yield of 5.44 per cent ($220 x 52 = $11,440 / $210,000).

In 2008 the property is paying a rental of $390 per week. This represents a gross rental yield of 9.65 per cent ($390 x 52 = $20,280 / $210,000). Our current interest rate payable on the loan for this property is 6.36 per cent per annum.

The property would therefore now be positively-geared.

CASHFLOW SUPPORT STRATEGIES

Consider the use of debt to help with funding the costs of holding rental properties each year. Each of the following four strategies can help you hold your rental properties when times are tough and cashflow is restricted. Feel free to use them but

MINIMISE TAX, MAXIMISE PROTECTION

keep in mind that each strategy involves increasing your level of debt to assist with the holding process. This will eat into future capital growth (equity) of the property(ies).

Example 1: Holding costs of rental property each year

- **Rent received for year** $15,000

- **Less : Cash expenses**
  Bank fees $300
  Body corporate fees $1,200
  Council rates $1,100
  Insurance $700
  Interest paid $16,000
  Property agent's commission $1,200
  Repairs $1,000
  Water rates $400
  Total cash expenses ($21,900)

  CASH SHORTFALL **($6,900)**

- The cash shortfall each year of $6,900 can be funded by a line of credit. The line of credit must not be mixed with private funds to maintain the loan's 100 per cent deductibility.

- The interest on the cumulative balance of this LOC would also be claimable. Here is an example, using 10 per cent interest per annum to keep the calculations as easy as possible:

Year	Shortfall	Claimable interest	LOC balance
1	$6,900	$690 ($6,900 x 10%)	$7,590
2	$6,900	$1,449 (($7,590 + $6,900) x 10%)	$15,939
3	$6,900	$2,284 (($15,939 + $6,900) x 10%)	$25,123

BONUS! FREE gifts at www.TGRProperty.com.au/Gifts

- This interest would be claimable against the property outlined above each financial year.

- According to the conclusion in PBR 69725 you are not required to fund the investment property cash shortfall with personal funds. This means you do not have to use your salary to pay the shortfall of holding costs each year.

- You can choose to use this personal money (that you do not need to utilise to fund holding the property) to pay down your non-deductible private home loan.

Example 2 : Claimable interest when building a rental property

The land costs you $240,000, including purchase expenses, while the building costs you an extra $200,000. The timeframe to complete construction is anticipated to be 12 months and it's expected that roughly $22,000 in interest will be paid during this time.

A line of credit for $462,000 can be established to fund the total cost of land and buildings ($440,000) as well as the $22,000 interest payable during the construction period.

As the intended use of the property is for rental purposes, and has been since the land was first purchased, any interest paid from that date is claimable.

Example 3: Cashflow mortgage product (PBR 69454)

Note: Before contemplating this type of finance please check that

MINIMISE TAX, MAXIMISE PROTECTION

the lender whose loan you are considering has a similar ruling on it. A PBR is a Private Binding Ruling and is only binding to those who applied for the ruling. It is not a public ruling and therefore cannot be relied on by the general public, though it does give the public a guide as to how the tax office is generally viewing the issues raised in the ruling.

You wish to take out a standard variable loan where part of the interest is capitalised, which is to say the interest is not actually paid but added to the balance of the loan. The loan is for $300,000 over a five-year period.

Year	Interest paid (Actually paid)	Interest capitalised (Added to loan)	Interest rate charged	Loan balance
1	**3.70%** $11,100	**4.25%** $12,750	**7.95%** $23,850	$312,750
2	**4.95%** $15,481	**3.00%** $9,383	**7.95%** $24,864	$322,133
3	**5.95%** $19,167	**2.00%** $6,443	**7.95%** $25,610	$328,576
4	**6.95%** $22,836	**1.00%** $3,286	**7.95%** $26,122	$331,862
5	**7.45%** $24,724	**0.00%** $0	**7.45%** $24,724	$331,862

The total amount borrowed will be used for income producing investments.

BONUS! FREE gifts at www.TGRProperty.com.au/Gifts

It is considered that the interest is incurred (paid) when it is charged to the loan account, even if it remains unpaid. As you can see above, in year one the interest of $23,850 is claimable for the property.

In year two you are entitled to an interest deduction of 7.95 per cent of the loan plus you are also entitled to a deduction for interest on the unpaid interest from year one. This means that in year two the interest of $24,864 is claimable for the property. Thus you are entitled to a deduction for the full amount of interest charged each year, even if part of the interest charged remains unpaid and is added to the loan balance (capitalised).

Please note that these types of products usually have high entry fees, most of which can be added to the loan balance up front, as well as high exit fees if you refinance the loan in the first few years. You are also usually restricted in that you can only pay down the loan principal in the first few years by a certain percentage of the original loan amount before penalties kick in.

Example 4: Rising debt scenario for retirement

Just imagine it is now 2011 and neither of us is able to work. How will our decision back in 2001, when we first commenced purchasing property, help us in retirement?

Let's see where we are now and where we may be in the future.

MINIMISE TAX, MAXIMISE PROTECTION

Year	Purchase price	Rent at start	Rent 2008	Value in 2008	Value in 2011 (est.)
JUN 2001	$205,000	$205	$390	$410,000	$450,000

Purchased two other properties in 2002 but sold them for a small profit.

AUG 2003	$258,000	$250	$350	$380,000	$500,000
NOV 2004	$256,850	$250	$340	$400,000	$515,000
SEP 2005	$196,240	$210	$335	$335,000	$400,000
SEP 2005	$276,290	$260	$360	$420,000	$555,000
NOV 2006	$296,993	$380	$400	$420,000	$595,000
TOTALS	**$1,489,373**	**$1,555**	**$2,175**	**$2,365,00**	**$3,015,000**

So in 2011 the debt hasn't changed, it is about $1.5 million, and the equity is roughly the same. Therefore the properties should have just about broken even and will cost us nothing to hold.

If we are unable to work and need to draw out the equity to live off, this will amount to $100,000 a year over ten years. That's a million dollars tax-free.

Even if interest is at 10 per cent, which is way over the top but will show you that it still works in a high interest environment, we'll have approximately $500,000 over the 10 years in capitalised interest.

That gives us a total of $1.5 million over 10 years.

Of course, by that stage the properties will have doubled again in value (even at a conservative estimate) and will be worth $6 million.

BONUS! FREE gifts at www.TGRProperty.com.au/Gifts

> **HINT FOR TAX RETURN**
> The interest on the money drawn out to live on is not tax deductible as it is private. A separate loan should be set up for the yearly drawings plus the interest.
>
> The interest on the original debt for the rental properties remains fully tax deductible.

Please note that despite drawing out money to live on, plus paying the appropriate interest on the money drawn, the equity we have after 10 years has still doubled.

Some people may not like the rising debt scenario but at least we have been able to manage, which is something we may not have been able to do without our property investments.

DISCLAIMER:

The information and comments in this section of the book are of a general nature only and do not constitute professional advice in any way.

You must seek your own independent professional advice relating to your particular circumstances, goals and risk profile before taking any action at all.

Every care has been taken to ensure the accuracy of the material contained in this book. Superior Tax Solutions Pty Ltd, its employees, presenters and representatives are not responsible or liable for any action taken by any person on the basis of information contained in this section of the book.

FREE BONUS GIFT

Adrian Hill has generously offered two FREE BONUS GIFTS valued at $354

FREE **Yearly Budget Template** to facilitate a review of all personal income and expenses, plus a FREE R**ental Property Purchasing Checklist.**

Visit the website below to receive these free gifts
www.TGRProperty.com.au/Gifts

THE NEXT STEP...

"To know and not to do, is to not know at all."
Bruce Lee

Let me first congratulate you on making it all the way through this book. I'm sure you'll agree it's been well worth your while and I also want you to know that you now know more about creating wealth through property than almost everyone else on the planet!

But like we said in the opening chapter, there is a big difference between what you know and what you do. It's only what you do that counts.

I invite you to recommit yourself to becoming one of our 1,000 new Prosperity Millionaires. The reward is worthy of your effort. If you haven't already, be sure to receive your gifts by going to www.TGRProperty.com.au/Gifts right this minute.

While you're there, make certain that you register for our next live workshop and remember, as ice hockey legend Wayne Gretzky says: "100% of the shots you don't take don't go in."

We'd love to hear your comments and triumphs from the book, and encourage you to get in touch via the website.

Napoleon Hill closed *Think and Grow Rich* by saying, "If we are related, we have, through these pages, met." In closing, may I borrow this thought, and say, "If we are related, through my seminars, we will meet soon." I look forward to it.

Stuart Zadel

BONUS! FREE gifts at www.TGRProperty.com.au/Gifts

DISCOVER THESE CLASSICS...

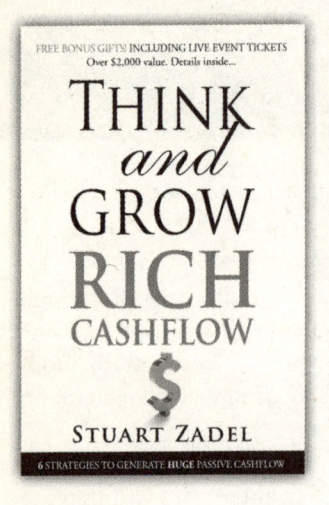

In *Think and Grow Rich® Cashflow*, Mind-Money Connection Expert, Stuart Zadel, brings together seven of his hand-picked team of cashflow entrepreneurs who will show you *exactly* how they generate huge passive cashflow and live the life of their dreams NOW.

If you're one of those millions who continues to work for a boss, this book will revolutionise the way you think about making a living.

In this book you'll discover:

- The little understood money mindset and how to get it
- Strategies for boosting your personal profile and doubling your income
- How to earn a six-figure salary from property renovations
- The new way to profit from the power of the connected global economy
- Creative ways to become a property entrepreneur using other people's money
- How to generate amazing cashflow when financial markets go up – or down!
- A model for getting what you want by helping others get what they want.

THESE BOOKS ARE AVAILABLE FROM BOOKSTORES ACROSS AUSTRALIA OR BY CALLING THE THINK AND GROW RICH® EVENTS OFFICE ON 1800 899 058.

DISCOVER THESE CLASSICS...

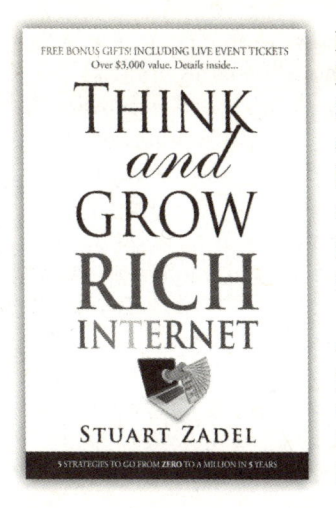

In *Think and Grow Rich® Internet*, Mind-Money Connection Expert, Stuart Zadel, brings together seven of his hand-picked team of Internet entrepreneurs who will show you how to profit from the power of the connected global economy.

A quarter of the earth's 6.7 billion people are now estimated to use the Internet. Quite simply, it is the biggest customer database in history!

In this book you'll discover:

- How to adjust your mindset to make more money than ever for less effort
- How to make money with no product, no website and no customer list
- Strategies for boosting your online personal profile and doubling your income
- The new way to reach - and sell to – billions of customers
- How to trade online from home and profit from share markets in any financial conditions
- One of the biggest-selling online products – and you don't even need a warehouse to store it!

THESE BOOKS ARE AVAILABLE FROM BOOKSTORES ACROSS AUSTRALIA OR BY CALLING THE THINK AND GROW RICH® EVENTS OFFICE ON 1800 899 058.

DISCOVER THESE CLASSICS...

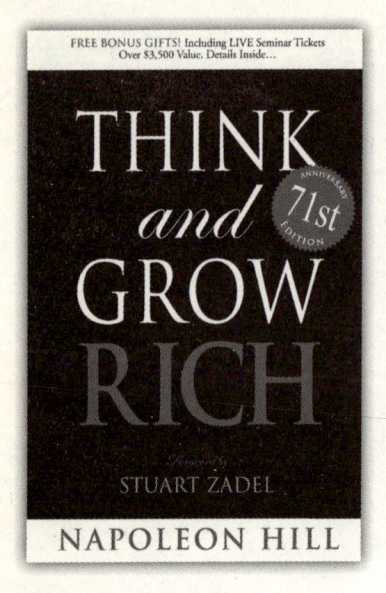

This all-time classic has sold more copies around the world and been responsible for the creation of more millionaires, than any other book in history. It's the result of 25 years of extensive research into the secret of 504 of the world's wealthiest people. Make no mistake; there is a secret to great wealth! The secret is so simple anyone can use it to become fabulously wealthy and successful in their chosen field. Are you ready to receive it?

In this book you'll discover:

- The secret used by all the world's ultra-wealthy people that when applied will work just as perfectly for you
- A practical, proven, step-by-step system for transforming your dreams into reality
- How to achieve balance, happiness and peace of mind in all you do
- How 28 very personal questions will reveal what's been standing between you and the riches you seek
- How to create your life to order by applying the 11 secrets of personal leadership.

THESE BOOKS ARE AVAILABLE FROM BOOKSTORES ACROSS AUSTRALIA OR BY CALLING THE THINK AND GROW RICH® EVENTS OFFICE ON 1800 899 058.

DISCOVER THESE CLASSICS...

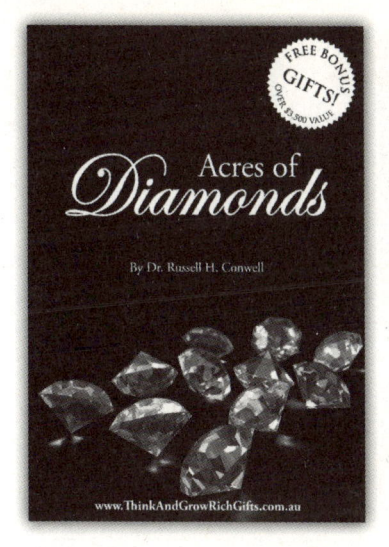

This all-time classic has had a profound effect on the lives of millions of people all over the world, and still does to this day. Dr Russell Conwell dedicated a good portion of his life to founding Temple University, in Philadelphia, by raising millions of dollars through this, his most famous speech. He delivered it more than 6,000 times all over the United States.

In this book you'll discover:

- The key to personal and business success
- Where to find your opportunity to get rich today
- How to get started with no capital
- What all great people have in common.

THESE BOOKS ARE AVAILABLE FROM BOOKSTORES ACROSS AUSTRALIA OR BY CALLING THE THINK AND GROW RICH® EVENTS OFFICE ON 1800 899 058.

DISCOVER THESE CLASSICS...

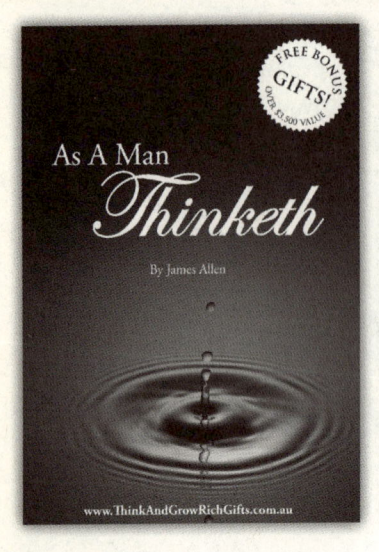

This all-time classic, penned in 1902, has inspired millions of people around the world and is partly responsible for the entire self-development movement. A must-have for any library, it has influenced many other writers including Earl Nightingale, Norman Vincent Peale, Louise Hay, Bob Proctor and Anthony Robbins.

In this book you'll discover:

- The law of cause and effect and how it applies to thought
- How your present thinking has shaped your current circumstances
- How your mind affects your health and your body
- Why we literally "become what we think about"
- How to find serenity, balance and peace of mind.

THESE BOOKS ARE AVAILABLE FROM BOOKSTORES ACROSS AUSTRALIA OR BY CALLING THE THINK AND GROW RICH® EVENTS OFFICE ON 1800 899 058.

DISCOVER THESE CLASSICS...

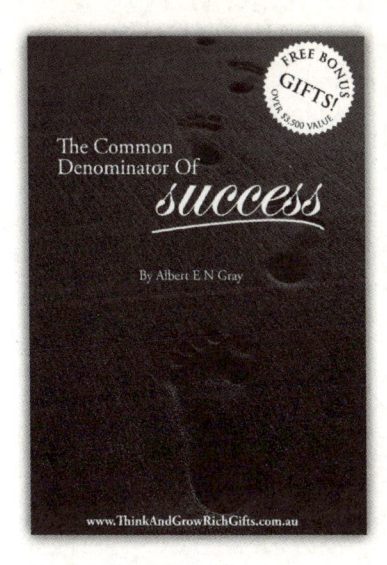

This all-time classic first appeared as a major address at the 1940 NALU (National Association of Life Underwriters) annual convention in Philadelphia. Its message is equally well suited to anyone in the sales profession, or anyone in any field of endeavour who seeks success in their professional, personal or spiritual lives.

In this book you'll discover:

- How to guarantee success in any endeavour
- Why "success" is achieved only by a minority of people
- The difference between logical goals and emotional goals
- How to find your purpose, identify it and surrender to it.

THESE BOOKS ARE AVAILABLE FROM BOOKSTORES ACROSS AUSTRALIA OR BY CALLING THE THINK AND GROW RICH® EVENTS OFFICE ON 1800 899 058.

HOW TO CLAIM YOUR FREE BONUS GIFTS*

As a "thank you" for purchasing this book, Stuart and the members of his Rich Property Entrepreneurs Mastermind Group would like to give you some valuable **free gifts…**

FREE GIFT # 1 ($1,491 value): **Stuart Zadel** offers you three (3) FREE tickets (worth $497 each) to **The Ultimate Think and Grow Rich® Property Entrepreneurs Conference.**

FREE GIFT # 2 ($59.90 value): **Stephen Tolle and Cherie Barber** offer you a FREE **How to do a Renovation Financial Feasibility Tips Sheet** plus a FREE **Trades Register Template** - Keep the contact details of all your tradies in one handy place for when you're in the thick of it on-site!

FREE GIFT # 3 ($495 value): **Sam Saggers** offers you a FREE **Property Analyser Report** - This valuable tool enables you to accurately analyse any property in relation to its income and expenses by producing a cashflow projection.

FREE GIFT # 4 ($147 value): **Carly Crutchfield** offers you a FREE Audio Download – **"Property Secrets of the Wealthy".**

FREE GIFT # 5 ($147 value): **Rick Otton** offers you a FREE Audio Download - **"Why You Can't Use Old Systems to Solve New Problems!"** Listen as Rick and his mentoring students challenge conventional wisdom in this closed-door training.

FREE GIFT # 6 ($29 value): **Aussie Rob** offers you a FREE eBook – **"Death of the Managed Fund"** by Aussie Rob and Scott Goold. Learn why exchange traded funds are taking over from managed funds and how to profit from them.

FREE GIFT #7 ($354 value): **Adrian Hill** offers you a FREE **Yearly Budget Template** to facilitate a review of all personal income and expenses, plus a FREE Rental Property **Purchasing Checklist.**

TOTAL VALUE OF YOUR BONUS GIFTS: $2,722.90

Visit the website below to receive these free gifts
www.TGRProperty.com.au/Gifts

* The FREE bonus gifts offered are current at the time of printing. We reserve the right to change, substitute or remove these gifts without notice.

NOTES

NOTES

NOTES

THINKANDGROWRICHSEMINARS

THIS TICKET ADMITS ONE TO ANY THINK AND GROW RICH® PROPERTY ENTREPRENEURS CONFERENCE. YOU MUST REGISTER ONLINE AT WWW.TGRPROPERTY.COM.AU PRIOR TO THE EVENT. REPLACEMENT TICKETS CAN BE SUPPLIED FROM THE THINK AND GROW RICH® OFFICE. CONDITIONS APPLY.
PLEASE CALL 1800 899 058 WITH ANY QUERIES ABOUT FUTURE EVENTS AND TO MAKE ADDITIONAL BOOKINGS.

By Receiving This Ticket You Have Just Been Given The Opportunity Of A Lifetime...
This ticket entitles you to join us for FREE at...

2 Days Valued at $497!

PAID

The Ultimate think & Grow Rich®

Property Entrepreneurs Conference

Promo Code:
PROPGIFT

Make sure you activate this ticket today at:
www.TGRProperty.com.au or Free Call **1800 899 058**

THINKANDGROWRICHSEMINARS

THIS TICKET ADMITS ONE TO ANY THINK AND GROW RICH® PROPERTY ENTREPRENEURS CONFERENCE. YOU MUST REGISTER ONLINE AT WWW.TGRPROPERTY.COM.AU PRIOR TO THE EVENT. REPLACEMENT TICKETS CAN BE SUPPLIED FROM THE THINK AND GROW RICH® OFFICE. CONDITIONS APPLY.
PLEASE CALL 1800 899 058 WITH ANY QUERIES ABOUT FUTURE EVENTS AND TO MAKE ADDITIONAL BOOKINGS.

By Receiving This Ticket You Have Just Been Given The Opportunity Of A Lifetime...
This ticket entitles you to join us for FREE at...

2 Days Valued at $497!

PAID

The Ultimate think & Grow Rich®

Property Entrepreneurs Conference

Promo Code:
PROPGIFT

Make sure you activate this ticket today at:
www.TGRProperty.com.au or Free Call 1800 899 058

THINKANDGROWRICHSEMINARS

THIS TICKET ADMITS ONE TO ANY THINK AND GROW RICH® PROPERTY ENTREPRENEURS CONFERENCE. YOU MUST REGISTER ONLINE AT WWW.TGRPROPERTY.COM.AU PRIOR TO THE EVENT. REPLACEMENT TICKETS CAN BE SUPPLIED FROM THE THINK AND GROW RICH® OFFICE. CONDITIONS APPLY.
PLEASE CALL 1800 899 058 WITH ANY QUERIES ABOUT FUTURE EVENTS AND TO MAKE ADDITIONAL BOOKINGS.

By Receiving This Ticket You Have Just Been Given The Opportunity Of A Lifetime...
This ticket entitles you to join us for FREE at...

2 Days Valued at $497!

PAID

The Ultimate think & Grow Rich®

Property Entrepreneurs Conference

Promo Code:
PROPGIFT

Make sure you activate this ticket today at:
www.TGRProperty.com.au or Free Call 1800 899 058